Restoring Layered Landscapes

Restoring Layered Landscapes

History, Ecology, and Culture

Edited by MARION HOURDEQUIN

AND

DAVID G. HAVLICK

OXFORD
UNIVERSITY PRESS

Oxford University Press is a department of the University of
Oxford. It furthers the University's objective of excellence in research,
scholarship, and education by publishing worldwide.

Oxford   New York
Auckland   Cape Town   Dar es Salaam   Hong Kong   Karachi
Kuala Lumpur   Madrid   Melbourne   Mexico City   Nairobi
New Delhi   Shanghai   Taipei   Toronto

With offices in
Argentina   Austria   Brazil   Chile   Czech Republic   France   Greece
Guatemala   Hungary   Italy   Japan   Poland   Portugal   Singapore
South Korea   Switzerland   Thailand   Turkey   Ukraine   Vietnam

Oxford is a registered trademark of Oxford University Press
in the UK and certain other countries.

Published in the United States of America by
Oxford University Press
198 Madison Avenue, New York, NY 10016

Library of Congress Cataloging-in-Publication Data
Restoring layered landscapes : history, ecology, and culture / edited by Marion Hourdequin
and David G. Havlick.
     pages cm
Includes bibliographical references and index.
ISBN 978–0–19–024031–8 (hardcover : alk. paper) — ISBN 978–0–19–024032–5 (pbk. : alk.
paper) 1. Restoration ecology. 2. Landscape ecology. 3. Historic preservation. 4. Historic
sites_Conservation and restoration. I. Hourdequin, Marion, editor. II. Havlick, David G.,
editor.
QH541.15.R45R558 2015
333.73'153—dc23
2015004268

9 8 7 6 5 4 3 2 1
Printed in the United States of America
on acid-free paper

For Adele and Tim

CONTENTS

Acknowledgments   ix

List of Contributors   xi

CHAPTER 1 Introduction: Ecological Restoration and Layered
Landscapes   1
Marion Hourdequin and David G. Havlick

PART I | Theoretical Perspectives on the Restoration
of Layered Landscapes

CHAPTER 2 Ecological Restoration, Continuity, and Change:
Negotiating History and Meaning in Layered
Landscapes   13
Marion Hourdequin

CHAPTER 3 The Different Faces of History in Postindustrial
Landscapes   34
Jozef Keulartz

CHAPTER 4 Nature and Our Sense of Loss   54
Alan Holland

CHAPTER 5 Layered Industrial Sites: Experimental Landscapes
and the Virtues of Ignorance   73
Matthias Gross

PART II | Approaching Layered Landscapes: Restoration in Context

CHAPTER 6   Restoring Wildness to the Scottish
             Highlands: A Landscape of Legacies   95
             Holly Deary

CHAPTER 7   Environmental versus Natural Heritage Stewardship:
             Nova Scotia's Annapolis River and the Canadian
             Heritage River System   112
             Jennifer Welchman

CHAPTER 8   "Get Lost in the Footnotes of History": The Restorative
             Afterlife of Rocky Flats, Colorado   133
             Peter Coates

CHAPTER 9   Restoration, History, and Values at Transitioning
             Military Sites in the United States   160
             David G. Havlick

PART III | Representation and Interpretation of Layered Landscapes

CHAPTER 10   Slavery, Freedom, and the Cultural Landscape:
             Restoration and Interpretation of Monocacy National
             Battlefield   183
             John H. Spiers

CHAPTER 11   Renaturalization and Industrial Heritage in America's
             Largest Superfund Site: The Case of the Warm Springs
             Ponds in Montana's Clark Fork Superfund Site   202
             Fredric L. Quivik

CHAPTER 12   Material Transformations: Urban Art and
             Environmental Justice   222
             Mrill Ingram

CHAPTER 13   Layered Landscapes, Conflicting Narratives, and
             Environmental Art: Dealing with Painful Memories and
             Embarrassing Histories of Place   239
             Martin Drenthen

CHAPTER 14   Conclusion: Layered Landscapes as Models for
             Restoration and Conservation   263
             David G. Havlick and Marion Hourdequin

             Index   267

ACKNOWLEDGMENTS

This book is the result of multiple collaborations, each of which played important roles in its final outcome. We are grateful to the National Science Foundation for a multiyear grant (award number 0957002) that provided essential support for the overarching project from which this book comes. Many of the contributions included here were first presented at a 2013 workshop, which was part of the NSF-supported work. A number of the ideas included in the book benefited from conversations and additional presentations offered during that workshop, and we thank the following participants for their ideas and insights: Andre Clewell, Justin Donhauser, Robert Earle, Erica Elliott, Rebecca Garvoille, William Jordan III, Jennifer Ohayon, and Allen Thompson.

Refuge officials from the US Fish and Wildlife Service (USFWS) provided important on-the-ground perspectives at the workshop as well. These public employees rarely receive adequate recognition for their fine work; we offer our sincere thanks to Steve Agius, Dionne Briggs, John Davis, Bruce Hastings, Libby Herland, Nancy Morrissey, Susan Rice, Joe Robb, and Graham Taylor. We are especially grateful to John Davis for providing multiple tours of the Rocky Mountain Arsenal National Refuge during the past five years, and to Bruce Hastings for his cooperation and support for more than ten years. Joe Robb, Libby Herland, and Graham Taylor also generously hosted us on multiple visits to refuges they manage. Many other USFWS employees, volunteers, Department of Defense officials and contractors, and representatives from citizen groups were generous with their time and knowledge during field work we conducted at refuges and former military sites. Though they are too many to list here, we very much appreciate their cooperation.

We are very grateful to the authors of the chapters included in the book. We expected in advance this would be a fine group to work with, and our experiences working through the process with them has only affirmed that.At Oxford University Press, Lucy Randall and Jamie Chu have been responsive, helpful, and supportive throughout the process. We appreciate their steady hands and sound guidance. We are also grateful for Ginny Faber's sharp copyediting, and the production efforts of Suvesh Subramanian, Project Manager at Newgen Knowledge Works.

We thank Eric Higgs and Allen Thompson for their constructive and very helpful reviews of the full manuscript.

We were fortunate to work with several talented student research assistants at various stages of this project. Our thanks go to Claire McCusker, Matthew John, Reginald Anderson, and Jon Harmon.

Finally, and always, we appreciate the unflagging support and encouragement of our families. They planted the seeds.

LIST OF CONTRIBUTORS

Peter Coates is Professor of American and Environmental History at the University of Bristol, UK. He specializes in nineteenth and twentieth-century American (US) history, especially environmental history. He has written books on a variety of subjects, including *Nature: Western Attitudes Since Ancient Times* (University of California Press, 1998/2005); *Salmon*, a "bio-biography" of the King of Fish (Reaktion, 2006); and *A Story of Six Rivers: History, Culture, and Ecology* (Reaktion, 2013). He is also co-editor of *Militarized Landscapes: From Gettysburg to Salisbury Plain* (Continuum, 2010), and has published articles in journals such as *Alaska History, Environmental History, Environment and History, Western Historical Quarterly, The Public Historian, Landscape Research, California History* and *Journal of American Studies*.

Holly Deary recently completed her PhD in Geography and Sustainable Development at the University of St. Andrews, Scotland. She graduated from the University of St. Andrews with a BSc (Hons) degree in Geography. Her current research interests lie in the areas of environmental management, nature conservation, and land use policy, and her doctoral work focused on wild land management in the Scottish Highlands and the emerging environmental ethic of "rewilding."

Martin Drenthen is Associate Professor of Philosophy at Radboud University Nijmegen (The Netherlands). He has published about the significance of Nietzsche's critique of morality for environmental ethics, the concept of wildness in moral debates on ecological restoration, ethics of place, and environmental hermeneutics. He is author of *Bordering Wildness: The Desire for Wilderness and the Meaning* *of Nietzsche's Critique of Morality for Environmental Ethics* [2003, in Dutch]. He co-edited *Ethics of Science Communication* (2005, in Dutch], *New Visions of Nature: Complexity and Authenticity* (Springer 2009), *Place: Philosophical Reflections on Connectedness with Nature and Landscape* [2011, in Dutch], *Interpreting Nature: The Emerging Field of Environmental Hermeneutics* (Fordham University Press, 2013), *Environmental Aesthetics: Crossing Divides and Breaking Ground* (Fordham University Press, 2014), and *Old World and New World Perspectives in Environmental Philosophy* (Springer 2014). His most recent research focuses on the relation between rewilding landscapes, cultures of place, and moral identity.

Matthias Gross is Professor of Environmental Sociology at Helmholtz Centre for Environmental Research—UFZ, Leipzig, and, by joint appointment, the University of Jena, Germany. His recent research focuses on alternative energy systems, risk and ignorance, ecological restoration and design, and experimental practices in science and society. He is a founding editor of the journal *Nature + Culture*. Publications include the books *Inventing Nature: Ecological Restoration by Public Experiments* (Lexington Books, 2003); *Ignorance and Surprise: Science, Society, and Ecological Design* (MIT Press, 2010); and his most recent monograph, *Renewable Energies* (with R. Mautz, 2015, Routledge).

David G. Havlick is Associate Professor of Geography and Environmental Studies at the University of Colorado in Colorado Springs. He is the author of *No Place Distant: Roads and Motorized Recreation on America's Public Lands* (Island Press, 2002), and publications in *Science, Ecological Restoration, Progress in Physical Geography, Conservation*, and *High Country News*. He is a co-founder of Wild Rockies Field Institute, and has degrees from Dartmouth College, the University of Montana, and the University of North Carolina at Chapel Hill.

Alan Holland is Emeritus Professor of Applied Philosophy, Department of Politics, Philosophy, and Religion, Lancaster University, UK. He was founding editor of the journal Environmental Values and is the author of *Environmental Values* (with John O'Neill and Andrew Light, Routledge, 2007). He also co-edited *Animal Biotechnology and Ethics* (with Andrew Johnson, Springer, 1997); and *Global Sustainable Development in the Twenty-First Century* (with Keekok Lee and Desmond McNeill, Edinburgh University Press, 2000). His published output focuses on philosophical questions raised by ecology, economics and the social sciences.

Marion Hourdequin is Associate Professor of Philosophy at Colorado College. She is the author of *Environmental Ethics: From Theory to Practice* (Bloomsbury, 2015), and has published articles in *Environmental Ethics, Environmental Values, Ethical Theory and Moral Practice, Philosophy East & West*, and other journals. Her current research focuses on the ethics of climate change and climate engineering, the philosophy of ecological restoration, and relational approaches to ethics. She holds degrees from Princeton University, the University of Montana, and Duke University.

Mrill Ingram's research focuses on human–nonhuman relations, science and environmental policy, and alternative agriculture. She has published specifically on microbial biopolitics in food safety, alternative farmer networks in the United States, and the making of US federal organic regulations. Dr. Ingram is the co-author of *The Power of Narrative in Environmental Networks* (with Raul Lejano and Helen Ingram, MIT Press, 2013). She is currently an environmental writer and curator with Upworthy, and was formerly Associate Project Director at the Farley Center for Peace, Justice and Sustainability, Madison, WI, and editor of the journal *Ecological Restoration*.

Jozef Keulartz is Emeritus Professor of Environmental Philosophy, Radboud University Nijmegen, Netherlands. Keulartz is an environmental philosopher with an emphasis on science, technology, and nature. He is author of *The Struggle for Nature: A Critique of Radical Ecology* (Routledge, 1998); and co-editor of *Pragmatist Ethics for a Technological Culture* (Kluwer, 2002); *New Visions of Nature: Complexity and Authenticity* (Springer, 2009); *Environmental Aesthetics: Crossing Divides and Breaking Ground* (Fordham University Press, 2014); and *Old World and New World Perspectives in Environmental Philosophy* (Springer, 2014). He has published in journals including *Science, Technology, and Human Values; Environmental Values; Environmental Ethics; Journal of Agricultural and Environmental Ethics; Nature and Culture; Landscape and Urban Planning*; and *Restoration Ecology*.

Fredric L. Quivik is Associate Professor of history in the Department of Social Sciences at Michigan Technological University in Houghton, Michigan. Before moving to Michigan Tech in January 2010, he worked for many years as an expert witness (expert historian) in Superfund and related environmental litigation, including the Clark Fork Superfund case, *U.S. v. ARCO*. He has also served as a consultant in the historic preservation field, specializing in cultural resources that have an engineering or industrial character. Much of his work in litigation and historic preservation has involved the history of mining in the American West. A graduate of St. Olaf College and the University of Minnesota's School of Architecture, he has a master's degree in historic preservation from Columbia University and a PhD in History and Sociology of Science from the University of Pennsylvania. He has published several articles on topics at the intersection of history of technology and environmental history, and he is the editor of *IA: The Journal of the Society for Industrial Archeology*.

John H. Spiers is an independent historian and former Visiting Assistant Professor of History at Boston College. His research focuses on how civic and social activists have shaped metropolitan development and environmental protection in the United States during the twentieth and early twenty-first centuries. His book, *Contesting Growth: Politics, Social Action, and the Environment in Metropolitan Washington*, will be published by the University of Pennsylvania Press in its series on Politics and Culture in Modern America. He has taught courses on US environmental history, American politics, and the history of modern colonialism.

Jennifer Welchman is Professor of Philosophy, Department of Philosophy, University of Alberta, Canada. Dr. Welchman's areas of specialization include ethics, the history of ethics, and applied ethics. She is the author of *Dewey's Ethical Thought* (Cornell University Press, 1995) and editor of *The Practice of Virtue: Classic and Contemporary Readings in Virtue Ethics* (Hackett, 2006). She has also published in journals including *Environmental Ethics, Philosophy and Geography, Journal of Social Philosophy*, and the *Canadian Journal of Philosophy*. She is currently working on a monograph, tentatively titled, *The Ethics of Environmental Stewardship: A Pragmatic Approach*.

Restoring Layered Landscapes

CHAPTER 1 | Introduction: Ecological Restoration and Layered Landscapes

MARION HOURDEQUIN AND DAVID G. HAVLICK

ALMOST EVERY LANDSCAPE IS a layered landscape. Through a combination of natural and cultural events, landscapes accumulate layers of history. These histories are inscribed physically—in soil horizons, bedrock layers, fossils, petrified wood, rotting stumps, and decaying bones—as well as in pot shards, arrowheads, ancient hearths, bullets, rusting factories, stone walls, abandoned mines, and plumes of contaminated groundwater. Our minds and our memories also harbor layers of meaning tied to landscapes. Physical landscapes evoke and intertwine with social and cultural meanings, and through the active management of landscapes urban, rural, and wild, we foreground some layers and background or bury others.

This book uses the concept of layered landscapes to explore contemporary issues in ecological restoration. The process of ecological restoration represents one effort to bring back particular landscape layers, to remove ecological damage and disturbance and rebuild ecological communities, returning them to a healthier state. For some time, scholars and practitioners of ecological restoration have struggled to come to terms with the role and significance of history in restoration. When ecological restoration coalesced as a distinct field and practice over the course of the twentieth century, restoration—particularly in North America—was understood as a way to return landscapes to their historical, predisturbance condition, or natural state. Roughly, restoration sought to bring landscapes back to something approaching their structure and functioning prior to human influence. As this book's chapters reveal, however, the idea of an ecosystem's "natural state" has been problematized in various ways, and restoration goals are being revised to take account of the natural dynamism in ecological systems, as well as to consider whether and how social, cultural, and political meanings might themselves be incorporated into restoration practice.

The concept of layered landscapes can assist with this reconceptualization of restoration goals. In recent years, many debates in restoration have been split between two camps, which we might call *historicists* and *futurists*. The historicists hold to the traditional goal of using a site's natural condition to set restoration targets; whereas futurists argue that in a world in which the human and natural are deeply intertwined and no longer separable, and climate change and large-scale landscape changes are altering the contexts in which restoration takes place, traditional restoration goals no longer make sense. Instead of looking to the past, we should strive to repair damaged landscapes to produce functional ecosystems that meet human goals. In response, historicists worry that futurist approaches leave restoration unmoored, and that without anchors to the past—to the natural systems that came before us—"restoration" will be driven by shallow human preferences or produce novel ecosystems that lack continuity with what came before.

There is truth on both sides of this debate, but neither side, we believe, provides an adequate lens for grappling with the complexities in layered landscapes, where human and natural histories intertwine over time. The approach developed in this book thus seeks to use paradigmatic examples of layered landscapes—the Scottish Highlands, a former mining region in Germany, postindustrial landscapes throughout Europe, a Virginia national battlefield memorializing the US Civil War, rivers in eastern Canada and the Netherlands, and former military sites turned wildlife refuges in the United States—to reveal the complexities and possibilities for restoration that takes the natural and cultural histories and the meanings of particular places seriously. The picture that emerges makes it clear that while we cannot typically restore all landscape layers simultaneously (nor would it make sense to try to do so), restoration need not be rigidly bound to the re-creation of a single, historical layer to the exclusion of all others.

There are many ways to restore layered landscapes. A key message of this book is that landscape layers carry distinct meanings and significance, and the process of restoration is not only a process of revitalizing ecological systems, but of considering which meanings to preserve and restore. Restoration of layered landscapes also needs to take into account the ways in which human and natural systems are interdependent and can be mutually supportive. In some cases, human uses create ecological systems that allow diverse animals and plants to thrive, and restorationists may seek to retain those human uses rather than extinguish them. It is often the case that ecologically oriented restoration goals—focused on ecological integrity, ecosystem functioning, and diverse plant and animal communities—can be integrated with social and cultural values to produce restored landscapes that preserve, revitalize, or problematize multiple landscape layers. Such approaches might rewild a domesticated landscape, for example, without removing all signs of domestication; or, in areas where human uses, such as farming or grazing, have produced flourishing socioecological systems, restoration might incorporate these practices. In other instances, we might choose a particular focal layer to restore ecologically—as managers have sought to bring back native short-grass prairie at the Rocky Mountain Arsenal National Wildlife Refuge in Colorado—yet supplement that restoration with elements signaling other layers: a tire swing, as Martin Drenthen suggests in chapter 13, to evoke memories of the primary schools that once stood on the site; or forms of landscape art that remind us of the site's military past.

These more flexible and creative forms of restoration provide rich opportunities to preserve and learn from complex meanings in layered landscapes, and they offer a new role for history in restoration. Whereas restoration has traditionally aimed to re-create the ecological conditions characteristic of a particular landscape layer (typically, the layer just prior to human disturbance), this volume opens up possibilities for a more pluralistic, multi-layered approach. This kind of approach can allow land managers to relax restrictive ideals of "authenticity" and to reconceptualize landscapes as complex and evolving socioecological systems that carry multiple forms of meaning, value, and significance. And there is a related, collateral benefit: these forms of landscape restoration can acknowledge past ecological damage without treating *all* prior human use as negative or problematic.

The chapters ahead explore the opportunities for the restoration of layered landscapes and consider how the role of history in ecological restoration might be broadened to allow for a variety of forms of "historical fidelity," or faithfulness to the past. Under the dominant twentieth-century paradigm, restoration aimed at historical fidelity through the faithful re-creation of natural or predisturbance landscapes, and restoration success was measured by the authenticity of the re-creation. Reinterpretations of authenticity and historical fidelity in layered landscapes provide new possibilities for restoration. However, opening up a wider range of options also may make choices more difficult and open to greater contestation.

Thus, restoring layered landscapes is not without its challenges. For example, there may be tensions between cultural and ecological goals, or difficulties in restoring one layer while preserving others. When ecological, social, and political values fail to align—as they frequently do—disagreements may arise over what and how to restore. For example, some scholars worry about the problem of "erasure" in restored and renaturalized military lands and suggest that visible traces of former layers be retained (see, for example, chap. 9 by Havlick and Drenthen's chap. 13 in this volume); whereas others suggest that traditional restoration goals should take priority and have fewer concerns about the loss of visible signs of a site's military past (see, for example, Coates, chap. 8, this volume). These are productive disagreements: they illuminate the distinct values at stake in the restoration of complex landscapes, and give us the opportunity to consider diverse perspectives on how to move forward. Our hope is that this book will succeed in making clearer what meanings, values, and ecological and social consequences are at stake in layered landscapes more broadly. There is no single prescription for restoration, which depends critically on context (Hourdequin and Havlick 2011), but the theoretical and practical perspectives offered here will, ideally, contribute to new framings of restoration that take its complex socioecological dimensions seriously. Our intent is not to prove that traditional restoration goals are necessarily mistaken or flawed, but rather to show how traditional ecological goals—such as restoring "undisturbed nature"—can be integrated with other values, and how the traditional goals of restoration are not always the only possible or reasonable ones to pursue.

The Structure of the Book

Restoring Layered Landscapes is organized into three main sections, followed by a brief concluding chapter. Part I offers theoretical perspectives on the restoration of layered landscapes, with particular attention to the role of history. Rather than focus exclusively on *ecological* histories, the contributors explore approaches to restoration that consider both human and natural histories, and their interrelationships, as we decide what and how to restore. Chapters 2 through 5 suggest that restoration need not reproduce the past, but that history can and should inform restoration in layered landscapes, which often carry important social, cultural, and ecological meanings. From this perspective, restoration can balance continuity and change, or meaning and loss, as various historical threads are rewoven into an evolving landscape. And as Matthias Gross emphasizes in chapter 5, restoration in complex, layered landscapes will inevitably require us to come to terms with our limited knowledge and to embrace an experimental approach in which we learn from both failure and success.

In chapter 2, Marion Hourdequin explains how the traditional goal of historical fidelity in restoration—with its focus on returning ecological systems to a natural, undisturbed state—has been challenged by (1) the insight that ecosystems are characteristically dynamic rather than drawn toward a single ideal state of balance; (2) significant, directional ecological changes due to global warming; and (3) the recognition that many landscapes historically thought to be "pristine" were in fact significantly influenced by humans. Although these perspectives undermine the unquestioning use of "undisturbed nature" as a restoration ideal, the chapter argues that history remains relevant to restoration. Using the example of Colorado's Rocky Flats National Wildlife Refuge, a former nuclear weapons production facility, Hourdequin describes the diverse meanings embedded in the site's history, and argues that conflicting narratives—though often difficult to reconcile—can be helpful in negotiating the management and restoration of layered landscapes.

Chapter 3 takes up the question of history from a different but related angle, using the work of Friedrich Nietzsche to explore "the different faces of history in postindustrial landscapes." Jozef Keulartz employs Nietzsche's tripartite distinction between *antiquarian history, monumental history*, and *critical history* to explore modes of restoration at former industrial sites. The antiquarian approach celebrates the past and the heritage it represents, yet risks a nostalgic attachment to history at the expense of the present and the future. Monumental history, in contrast, uses impressive examples of human achievement from the past to inspire and shape future aspirations. In this sense, it is more forward looking. However, the danger here is that we may fall "into a superficial pursuit of monumental effects," and this is a risk that critical history can mitigate. Keulartz argues that Germany's Landscape Park Duisburg Nord exemplifies a valuable integration of Nietzsche's three approaches to history, providing an important lesson for the restoration of postindustrial landscapes.

In chapter 4, Alan Holland explains how restoration might achieve a balance between meaning and loss. Holland argues that vulnerability to loss is "the price we pay for meanings," but that it is a price we "are glad to pay," as meanings play a critical role in our lives—through attachments to human and nonhuman others, to landscapes, and to the cultural and natural contexts we inhabit. Restoration offers a way of navigating and responding to loss, and in layered landscapes restoration is not only a way of recovering what has been lost, but of *attending* to loss and determining how best to go on. As Holland puts it, "Restoration . . . should be conceived not as an attempt to restore some lost value but as a response to certain sorts of threat to meaning." In layered landscapes, this response will take into account what came before, and the natural and cultural meanings embedded in that history.

Chapter 5, the final chapter in Part I, focuses less on the aims of restoration and more on the process. Matthias Gross suggests that we conceive of layered industrial sites as "experimental landscapes," where we explicitly acknowledge the importance of our own ignorance as restoration moves forward. In many industrial sites "nonknowledge" is prevalent: the forms and extent of residual contamination may be unknown, and the precise outcomes of remediation and restoration may be unpredictable. One approach to ignorance is to seek knowledge and certainty, or to try to tame uncertainty through risk assessment—and this requires that the probabilities of certain outcomes be known. Gross argues that this approach fails to fully appreciate the importance of the unknown or to acknowledge the unknown through an experimental approach to restoration and management of postindustrial lands. The experimental approach embraces the inevitability of surprise, and it allows us to confront and learn from our ignorance. The restoration of open-cast mining pits near Leipzig provides an example of how German managers successfully employed an experimental approach with "an openness to surprising results and a willingness to learn from failure." Given the inevitability of nonknowledge, experimental approaches may be crucial to effective restoration of layered, postindustrial lands.

Gross's chapter offers a nice segue to Part II, which focuses on layered landscape restoration in specific contexts. From the Scottish Highlands to Nova Scotia and from Virginia to Colorado, these chapters illustrate both unique and common challenges in restoring landscapes with complex histories. In chapter 6, Holly Deary highlights how restoration in the Scottish Highlands often invokes an imagined, idealized past, and she offers a more nuanced understanding of the complicated relationship between people and place in this region. In particular, Deary calls attention to the fact that the iconic, wild, and treeless landscapes of the Scottish Highlands were once heavily forested. What's more, these wild lands were widely settled prior to the Highland Clearances of the late eighteenth and early nineteenth centuries. Drawing on interviews with land managers from eighteen Highland estates, Deary explores managers' perspectives in relation to the concepts of authenticity and historical fidelity in ecological restoration. She finds that Highland managers recognize the storied and cultural dimensions of these landscapes and respond to the interplay of the natural and the cultural in their management strategies. Deary concludes that neither history nor authenticity are irrelevant in Highland restoration; but concepts such as "wild" and "civilized" might best be understood here as complexly interrelated rather than as dichotomous and mutually exclusive.

In chapter 7, Jennifer Welchman further explores the interrelationship of environmental stewardship and cultural heritage, this time in the context of Nova Scotia's Annapolis River. Welchman tells the story of a failed effort to achieve heritage recognition for a river, and how this failure emerged from Parks Canada's lack of clarity about environmental stewardship and its relation to cultural heritage stewardship. In this case, the Canadian parks agency had a particular conception of cultural heritage that was tied to a national identity based in wilderness exploration. Thus, only rivers that embodied *natural* characteristics associated with wilderness could qualify on *cultural* heritage grounds. Welchman argues that Parks Canada essentially collapsed cultural and natural heritage values, making it impossible for the Annapolis River advocates to establish cultural heritage value for the river in the absence of natural characteristics grounded in the agency's preferred vision of Canadian national identity. Ultimately, advocates for the river engaged in a successful environmental restoration effort that was unfettered by natural or cultural heritage concerns. Welchman suggests that environmental stewardship and heritage stewardship support different restoration and conservation goals, and that these goals may sometimes be difficult to reconcile.

In the next two chapters, Peter Coates (chap. 8) and David Havlick (chap. 9) take up a related topic: the relationship between environmental values, on the one hand, and values associated with a site's historical, cultural, and political meanings, on the other. Coates and Havlick offer two distinct perspectives on the renaturalization and restoration of layered landscapes at former military bases in the United States; Coates argues for the compatibility of ecological and cultural preservation goals, and Havlick identifies tensions (as well as points of connection) between wildlife-conservation goals and the aim of making visible the complex social, political, environmental, and military histories of these sites. Coates takes a historical approach, using Colorado's former Rocky Flats nuclear weapons plant (now the Rocky Flats National Wildlife Refuge) as his focal case, while Havlick presents results of empirical social science research at the Rocky Mountain Arsenal National Wildlife Refuge, a former chemical weapons manufacturing plant near Denver, and Assabet River National Wildlife Refuge in Massachusetts. Coates suggests that ecological restoration need not result in the problem of "historical erasure" that concerns some critics. Havlick suggests that erasure nevertheless remains a worry, and identifies some of the practical challenges and opportunities for integrating historical layers into renaturalized military sites.

Part III of the book focuses on the representation and interpretation of layered landscapes, developing the theme that layered landscapes carry important meanings and showing how restored sites themselves promote certain interpretations, though often unwittingly. These chapters recommend thoughtful and creative approaches to the representation and interpretation of restored sites. As noted above, restoration typically foregrounds some layers, while others are forgotten, erased, or relegated to the background.

In their chapters, John Spiers and Fred Quivik explore how restoration and interpretation can highlight or obscure various elements of a site's past in two specific contexts: Virginia's Monocacy National Battlefield and Warm Springs Ponds in Montana's Clark Fork River watershed, respectively. In chapter 10, Spiers shows how the significance of Monocacy National Battlefield extends beyond its identity as a Civil War memorial, encompassing the site's contemporary ecological value in a sea of suburban development as well as its agricultural heritage and its slave history. Spiers recommends an interpretation that expands the chronology of the site to begin prior to the Civil War and continue through the present, "[blending] natural and cultural histories together in a more dynamic and interconnected way."

In chapter 11, Quivik supports a similar approach, taking as his focus the postindustrial mining landscapes of the upper Clark Fork River in Montana. Quivik recommends an interpretive strategy that reveals the complexity of industrial ambitions and their consequences, and he suggests that the Warm Springs Ponds—constructed as settling ponds for mining waste over a century ago—exemplify this complexity. These ponds remain critical to mine remediation by removing heavy metals from Silver Bow Creek, which flows into the Clark Fork River, and they also serve as valuable wetland habitat for migratory birds and are a recreational resource for anglers and for hikers on nearby paths. Like Spiers, Quivik suggests that interpretation can provide a critical role, "[helping] the public appreciate the depth of time across which [Warm Springs Ponds] have been part of the human and natural story of the Deer Lodge Valley."

The final two chapters build on the suggestion that we broaden the interpretive strategies for layered landscapes, and here Mrill Ingram and Martin Drenthen explore the possibilities and potential for art to play a key role in restoration. In chapter 12, Ingram shows how restoration/art projects can contribute to urban restoration and environmental justice by addressing the environmental damage in places many would rather ignore or forget. The chapter describes a project in urban Chicago that "explores cultural heritage, but ... also embraces soil restoration, urban planning, phytoremediation research, and environmental justice." This effort, spearheaded by artist Frances Whitehead, focuses on the remediation of abandoned gas stations, and has as its aim the stabilization of contaminants, beautification of inner-city neighborhoods, and collaborative engagement with college students, scientists, and city agencies. Ingram argues that this melding of art and restoration offers a model in which restoration can be sensitive to social- and environmental-justice concerns from the outset, integrating local communities and institutions into the planning and processes of restoration, and selecting goals and strategies that benefit communities and are sensitive to local contexts.

In chapter 13, Martin Drenthen describes further possibilities for art and restoration in layered landscapes. Drenthen argues that we might see layered landscapes as palimpsests, or layered texts, requiring interpretation. Thoughtful restoration has the potential to enhance the legibility of various landscape layers and enable multifaceted interpretations. Art can assist in this effort and may play a valuable role in engaging painful and embarrassing histories at places such as the Rocky Mountain Arsenal National Wildlife Refuge. Drenthen offers an artistic work for the refuge—the piece "Nature Mocking Art"—to provoke a critical reading of the site's military history. This artwork is meant to prompt reflection on "the darker sides of our own past" and spur thoughtful consideration of the ongoing meaning of the Arsenal refuge. Rather than rest with a redemptive story of environmental cleanup and restoration, Drenthen asks us to grapple with the complexities of layered landscapes and their histories, and shows how art can contribute to this aim.

The chapters in this volume thus explore forms of restoration that take account of and make visible the multilayered character of many contemporary landscapes. As noted earlier, restoration needs to be responsive to context, and there is no simple formula appropriate for all layered landscapes. Nevertheless, we hope that the frameworks developed here can contribute to a more expansive understanding of the ways in which layered landscapes might be restored, while contributing to the development of restoration models appropriate for human-influenced landscapes more generally. We also hope that this book might offer a thoughtful middle way in the restoration debate between the futurist perspectives that see the past as irrelevant, and the strict historicist approaches, which may be too narrowly confined by traditional ideals of historical fidelity. Together, these chapters begin to develop a constructive reinterpretation of the traditional ideal of historical fidelity in restoration. The approach to restoration of layered landscapes developed here offers one way of accommodating dynamism and directional change in socioecological systems, while recognizing the past and its multifaceted significance.

Reference

Hourdequin, Marion, and David G. Havlick. 2011. "Ecological Restoration in Context: Ethics and the Naturalization of Former Military Lands." *Ethics, Policy and Environment* 14 (1): 69–89.

PART I | Theoretical Perspectives
on the Restoration
of Layered Landscapes

CHAPTER 2 | # Ecological Restoration, Continuity, and Change

*Negotiating History and Meaning
in Layered Landscapes*

MARION HOURDEQUIN

Introduction

As the reality of global climate change presses upon us, the role of history in mediating our relationship to the natural world seems ever more complex and contentious. For ecological restoration, the challenge is particularly acute, as restoration has always looked to the past in establishing goals and judging success. The very term *restoration* suggests going back, returning to a former state. Restorationists thus frequently use the techniques of historical ecology—tree-ring data, fire scars, and pollen analysis—to reconstruct past conditions at a given site and determine the historical forest structure, fire regimes, or plant and animal community composition. Historical fidelity, understood as faithful reconstruction of an ecosystem's undisturbed, natural state, has served as a guiding value in setting restoration goals.

The nature and degree of global environmental change calls traditional restoration goals into question, however. Whether due to natural disturbances, human development and changing landscape contexts, or climatic change, the relevance of historic reference conditions has been repeatedly challenged. More generally, restorationists continue to wrestle with the question of whether history is relevant *at all* in a rapidly changing world, and if so, why.

Although writers such as Eric Higgs (2003) have offered nuanced reasons to continue to take history into account, the debate too often centers on two opposing poles: one in which historical, predisturbance conditions remain the touchstone for restoration, and the other in which both history and nature are viewed as passé. By breaking down traditional binary categories, hybrid landscapes, such as former military sites, help to disrupt these polarities and open new possibilities for ecological restoration—and, in turn, for thinking through the relevance of the past in a changing world.

Taking the conversion of US military sites to wildlife refuges as a focal example, this chapter argues that these sites offer the potential to creatively explore the relationships between nature, culture, and history in ecological restoration. These sites have complex and often conflicting meanings for different constituencies, and restoration could provide a way to protect and restore wildlife while negotiating these conflicting meanings. What's more, the restoration and interpretation of these layered landscapes could help show how both natural and cultural histories remain relevant, even in the face of rapid environmental change.

What Role for History in a Changing World?

Not only in restoration but also in navigating our relationship with nature more generally, we now face a crucial question: What is the role and relevance of history in a rapidly changing world? For much of the twentieth century, the young field of ecology relied on notions of natural balance that implicitly supported the idea that "nature knows best."[1] The idea was that ecological systems, if undisturbed by humans, would reach a natural equilibrium, or balance, that would remain stable through time (cf. Cooper 2003). This balance-of-nature idea, in turn, grounded the use of historical baselines in ecology to identify the natural and favored conditions for a particular site, which then guided the development of restoration goals. The key value of historical fidelity in restoration embodies this perspective: good restoration is faithful to a site's historical, natural, predisturbance conditions. In North America, the pre-Columbian era has served as the classic baseline, and restoration in North America has traditionally aimed to regenerate ecological communities as they existed prior to European settlement.

In recent decades, the ideas of natural balance and pristine nature have been challenged from multiple disciplinary perspectives. Ecologists and environmental historians have documented the ways in which many North American landscapes—long conceptualized as pristine wildernesses prior to Europeans' arrival—were shaped by Native Americans for hundreds of years before the European colonists set foot on them (see, e.g., Cronon 1996; Denevan 1992; Williams 2000). Even more profoundly, the very idea of a "balance of nature" has been deeply problematized. The once-prevalent Clementsian idea that ecosystems develop in predictable stages until they reach a stable, climax state—just as individual organisms develop from birth to maturity—no longer holds sway. Instead, the "new ecology" emphasizes that ecosystems are dynamic and subject to repeated disturbances over time (Botkin 1990). These disturbances "reset" ecological systems and create a quilt-like pattern across the landscape, with patches in varying states of recovery and succession following disturbance. The new ecology also embraces contingency. Although successional patterns do exist, succession can take multiple trajectories. The straightforward conception of ecosystems as teleologically driven toward a single, stable end state no longer prevails.

Despite these challenges, the traditional idea of historical fidelity remains powerful in ecological restoration. Neither the new ecology nor even the revelation that what many took to be pristine landscapes were in fact strongly shaped by indigenous peoples fully dislodged the emphasis on returning ecosystems to their natural state. By replacing static reference states with the concept of *historical range of variability* and its almost synonymous counterpart, *natural range of variability* (and often naturalizing the influences of Native Americans; for discussion, see Duncan et al. 2010), it was possible to retain the concept of historical fidelity in a slightly revised form. This revised view of historical fidelity emphasized the restoration of natural patterns and processes—including disturbance—over time, rather than restoration of a snapshot of nature in an unchanging climax state.

Nevertheless, the shift to dynamic ecology created cracks in the armor of "nature knows best," and this view has sustained assault from many quarters. From an ecological perspective, it is not only with consistent patterns of disturbance that restorationists need to reckon. Ecosystems are now undergoing rapid directional changes, leading to "novel ecosystems" and "no-analog futures" (Williams and Jackson 2007; Hobbs, Higgs, and Harris 2009). Climate change and the globalized movement of animals and plants are generating new assemblages of species, calling into question the relevance of the past in restoration and prompting some to ask whether traditional conservation itself is merely a nostalgic enterprise (see, e.g., Kareiva, Marvier, and Lalasz 2012). Greater confidence in human ability to deconstruct and reconstruct ecosystems and to generate new, workable configurations of species (Palmer et al. 2004; Martínez and López-Barrera

2008) has produced deep doubts about whether nature really *does* know best (or for that matter, whether "nature" as free from human control, continues to exist). In the normative vacuum left behind, some are quick to endorse the perspective that *humans* know best. On this view, undisturbed nature has no normative priority: the natural or "given" world is raw material for us to shape at will.

A view of the world as ours to shape and remake is not new, of course. In recent work, philosopher Michael Slote (2013) traces the rise of what he calls a "Faustian attitude" back to Enlightenment faith in human rationality. The Faustian attitude emphasizes controlling and planning, directing our own lives and shaping the world around us. What is lacking in this view, argues Slote, is receptivity. Receptivity involves "a capacity for seeing and a tendency to see others' viewpoints ... in the favorable light in which they appear to those others" (195). As such, it is bound up with care and empathy, and with our emotional lives more generally. Slote argues that receptivity is a virtue we overlook as we seek to plan and control our own lives, fail to appreciate the perspectives of others, and exert excessive control over the environments in which we live. Viewed in this way, receptivity is a virtue relevant in both social and environmental contexts: it is a general way of engaging with the world and all its inhabitants. As I will explain, this emphasis on receptivity and openness as virtues that cut across the nature/culture divide may provide a way of thinking through the role and relevance of history for ecological restoration in a changing world.

At this point, it will be helpful to introduce a distinction between the world-as-we-find-it (what we might call the *given world*) and the world-as-we-make it. In connection to Slote's discussion, we might think of Faustianism as emphasizing the world as we make it, and of receptivity as calling our attention to the world as we find it. Following this line of thought, we might expect that the distinction between the world as given and the world as made cleaves along the nature/culture divide. On this view, the given world is the natural world, while the world as we make it is the constructed, cultural world.

I want to understand the division differently, however. Note that Slote's distinction between imposition and receptivity is not tied to a nature/culture divide. The virtue of receptivity is equally at home in contexts involving social interactions as it is in our responses to the natural world. Similarly, for the sake of this chapter, I don't want to draw a contrast between the natural world and the sociocultural world, but between *the world as we remake it through our own agency* and *the world as built by human and natural processes that are independent of us*. What is at issue, then, is not what is produced by human agency as opposed to what is produced by nature, but *how we exert our agency in response to what exists in the world prior to our arrival on the scene*.

The "we" is, of course, a bit slippery here. It can refer either to an individual agent or to a group of agents acting independently or jointly to make and remake the world. Consider the "we," for now, as present generations of human beings. From our perspective as active agents in the world, we can ask ourselves, "To what extent should we defer to the world as constructed by human and natural processes independent of us?" Understanding the world as we find it in this way incorporates not only our natural heritage, but our cultural heritage as well: the world as we find it thus includes mountain ranges, river valleys, diverse plant and animal species, oceans, islands, and coral reefs, as well as farms, cathedrals, cities, and great works of art. The world as we find it, in this sense, is the world we inherit, as built by human and natural forces and their intermingling over time.

In emphasizing the *made* world (and attendant notions such as the "self-made man"), the Faustian approach risks failing to fully recognize the value of the already existing world and the nature of our dependence on and entanglement with that world. Yet the world we enter into as agents is already full of value: valuable persons, animals, plants, ecosystems, infrastructure, institutions, and relationships. The existing world, though far from perfect, is also a world invested with meaning and significance. We will, inevitably, alter and shape the world through our actions. But we should do so in ways that acknowledge and account for the value and significance already present in it.

To take the world as we find it seriously is thus to take both the present and the past seriously. This approach impels us to look at the world not as a blank slate, but as a place full of existing people, places, animals, plants, relationships, and meanings to which some degree of deference is warranted. For ecological restoration, taking the world as we find it seriously might help us navigate the current impasse surrounding historical fidelity, and to clarify how history might productively inform our thinking about restoration, even in a rapidly changing world.

Historical Fidelity in Ecological Restoration

The current debate over historical fidelity seems polarized between two extreme positions: one that embraces the traditional value of historical fidelity as a return to a prior undisturbed state (e.g., Egan 2006), and another that sees historical fidelity as increasingly irrelevant, given rapid environmental change (e.g., Choi 2004, 2007). Defenses of historical fidelity often implicitly appeal to the idea of undisturbed nature as a normative ideal, yet their opponents see this as unjustified, outmoded, and dependent on a sharp but indefensible distinction between nature and culture. Although many restoration projects still aim to restore ecological systems to a natural, predisturbance state, restorationists find themselves under increasing pressure to explain both what should count as natural and why naturalness is what we should seek.

Rather than make a forced choice between traditional models of historical fidelity and newer approaches that dismiss history as largely irrelevant, I suggest that we broaden our emphasis in trying to understand the significance of the past. Rather than fixate on the *natural* world as we find it—or the world prior to human disturbance—as a source of value, we might consider more generally the value of the existing world and its history (see Hourdequin 2013 for further discussion). Maybe there is some more general basis for deference to what preceded us that can help ground respect for the natural world as well as the cultural legacies we inherit.

Such an approach seems particularly apt for layered landscapes, such as renaturalized military sites, where fewer neat lines separate nature from culture. Instead, these hybrid landscapes blend social and ecological histories: nature shapes culture, and culture shapes nature (Whatmore 2002). Although humans have clearly influenced these sites, there may be no single, discrete human disturbance that can serve as the focal point for restoration, and not all human influence should necessarily count *as* disturbance (cf. O'Neill, Holland, and Light 2008, 160). As Holly Deary (chap. 6, this volume) points out, many of the most valued landscapes of the Scottish Highlands are the product of centuries of human use. Similarly, northwestern Europe's botanically diverse chalk grasslands are the product of cattle and sheep grazing (see Allison 2012, chap. 5). To restore these landscapes to their "pre-disturbance" conditions would be faithful to one aspect of their history: traditional forms of ecological restoration can reveal the deep history of a site, for example, setting human influence in a broader ecological and geological context (Drenthen 2009,

294). However, traditional restoration sometimes does so at the expense of more recent layers, generated by ongoing interactions between humans and nature.

Layered landscapes are a valuable context for both exploring and applying new understandings of historical fidelity. This is because neither the traditional model of historical fidelity, which focuses on ecosystems as they existed prior to human influence, nor "futuristic restoration," which advises us to look forward rather than back, seems to fully account for the value of many of these places. History is crucial to the traditional model, but only insofar as it enables us to identify the undisturbed natural state of a place. The second approach, by contrast, places little value on history at all. It is my contention that neither of these approaches provides an adequate answer to the question with which we began: What is the value of the past in thinking about the future in a time of rapid environmental change?[2]

What we need is an account of historical fidelity that calls our attention to the values and meanings embodied in existing landscapes. Such an account will emphasize receptivity rather than a Faustian striving for control, and will enable us to restore landscapes in ways that allow for both continuity and change. Historical fidelity, on this view, does not require allegiance to a particular historical state or to the restoration of landscapes free of human influence. Instead, being faithful to a site's history requires negotiating the diverse meanings, values, and relationships that have emerged there over time.

Narrative, Meaning, and Value in Layered Landscapes

To see why an approach to restoration that takes the world as we find it seriously—whether natural, social, or "socionatural"—may be worth pursuing, it is helpful to vividly understand how value and meaning are embedded in particular places. This understanding will also help to show why neither traditional conceptions of historical fidelity nor contemporary proposals for "futuristic restoration" have the tools to accommodate the diverse values in layered landscapes, such as renaturalized former military sites.

Because of their complex and layered character, naturalized military lands often are sites of diverse meanings and values. At Rocky Mountain Arsenal in Commerce City, Colorado, most visitors come for the wildlife—to see the refuge's many bird species or its reintroduced herd of bison—but others want to see the place where they once worked, or where their families once homesteaded, and how it has been transformed. At Assabet River National Wildlife Refuge in Massachusetts, "bunker tours"—which feature the large concrete munitions storage areas remaining on the site—are highly popular, and outdoor recreation is a bigger draw than the wildlife itself (see Havlick, chap. 9, this volume). The diverse meanings and values of such places is vividly illustrated in a recent book by Kristen Iversen, in which the author describes her experiences growing up very close to the edge of Colorado's Rocky Flats Nuclear Plant, which produced plutonium cores, or "triggers," for the entire US nuclear weapons arsenal (Iversen 2012). This site, too, has been converted to a national wildlife refuge, though it is not yet open to the public, and plans for its future management remain controversial.

Iversen's story, though told from her own perspective, highlights the diverse meanings of the land in and around the Rocky Flats site. There is a striking contrast between Iversen's own understanding of the lands near Rocky Flats and that of decision-makers at the Atomic Energy Commission (AEC). Explaining the AEC's choice of location for the new nuclear plant, Iversen writes:

> The announcement is made simultaneously in Denver, Los Alamos, and Washington, D.C. The plant site in Jefferson County has been chosen for "operational values," including the fact that the land is nothing but an old rocky cow pasture, "virtual waste land." (Iversen 2012, 6)

But to Iversen as a child, the land is anything but a wasteland:

> The first time I ride [my horse] Tonka out to Standley Lake, the wind whips my hair across my face so hard it stings. Tonka is eager to run. I ride bareback with a single leather strap looped around his ears and a rawhide hackamore dropped across his nose, the reins taut, his head tucked and neck arched like a Roman Percheron . . . Let's run! . . . I'm alone. That's the best part, to be alone with the horse and the gently rolling hills and the wind bending the tall prairie grass into long ripples of gold. (Iversen 2012, 70)

Neither of these two perspectives captures the meaning of the area to Iversen's mother, however, or to many others who bought homes in a new development that, for them, represented the American dream of the late 1960s:

Our house begins with a deep rectangular pit. My mother drives us out in the station wagon ... so we can watch. ... There is a lot of pounding. I remember the bones: two-by-fours reaching to the sky, anchored in concrete. Our skeletal house stands on nearly two acres at the end of a road that dips down to a small hill, where our driveway begins ... We look out from the freshly poured concrete of our front porch and see lines of spindly houses: streets laid out for pavement and front yards of raw earth waiting for sod, doors and windows, mortar and bricks. All the pieces waiting to be put together. ... The developer calls it Bridledale. My mother calls it heaven. Bridledale represents the golden dream of suburban life and all its postwar promises. (Iversen 2012, 9)

We thus can see at least three different meanings at this site: a wasteland, open for use as a nuclear plant; a wild place to explore, be free, ride horses, mingle with plants and animals in the open prairie; and a suburban dream, a safe and secure place to raise a family, a solid and comfortable home. Iversen grows up in a place where these images coexist, albeit somewhat uncomfortably. In their outdoor romps, local children jump off the end of a drainage pipe from Rocky Flats into a deep—but likely contaminated—pool, and the developer's daughter dies of cancer at age eleven, likely a result of early childhood exposure to radiation. Her ashes are laced with Pu-239, one of the radioactive byproducts of Rocky Flats.

Given the multiplicity of meanings and values at a place like Rocky Flats, how should restoration proceed at these sites? To what aspects of the past should restoration be faithful? Whose stories and which meanings should be preserved? I take up these questions, arguing that that the narratives we tell about layered landscapes can provide rich, thick descriptions of the values and meanings the sites hold. While the (perhaps conflicting) narratives of a place cannot completely *settle* the questions just raised, they can help us see how better to answer them.

Narratives and Their Role in Restoration

It may ... seem a little counterintuitive, if not downright perverse, to assert that nothing is more vital to the success of land conservation than the stories we tell about it ... But in fact nothing could be more essential. Stories are the indispensable tools that we human beings use for making sense of the world and our own lives. They articulate our deepest values and provide the fables on which we rely as we confront moral dilemmas and make choices about our every action ... [S]tories provide the interpretive compass with which we navigate our lives.

—WILLIAM CRONON (2002, 87–88)

The idea that stories may have an important role in conservation and restoration appears not only in the writings of the environmental historian William Cronon, but in disciplines as diverse as philosophy, environmental planning, geography, and urban studies (see, e.g., O'Neill, Holland, and Light 2008; Goldstein and Butler 2010; Sievanen et al. 2012; Langhorst 2012). Philosophers John O'Neill, Alan Holland, and Andrew Light (2008) have drawn important connections between narrative and restoration, suggesting that a focus on narrative can remedy some of the deficiencies in the traditional approaches to restoration. O'Neill et al. find "new world" approaches to restoration particularly problematic; these tend either to ignore history or to engage with it in the wrong way. Approaches to restoration that attempt to itemize and maximize value, for example, give little attention to history or context. As such, they miss the contextual and temporal dimensions of environmental values. Traditional approaches to restoration, on the other hand, use historical conditions as baselines in determining a given site's "natural state." However, this raises questions about what should count as a site's natural state, given the dynamic changes to which all ecosystems are subject. More fundamentally, insofar as an ecosystem's "natural state" is understood to be its state prior to or independent of human influence, one can ask whether it is really the state that restoration always should seek to achieve (O'Neill, Holland, and Light 2008, 160). Even if one concedes that human influences are sometimes—even often—negative, one may reject the idea "that they are always and in principle so" (O'Neill, Holland, and Light 2008, 160). This point seems particularly important in layered and hybrid landscapes, where humans and nature are often inseparably intertwined and where the land carries important meaning and significance.

In an essay on Wisconsin's Apostle Islands, William Cronon (2003) asks, "How do you manage a wilderness full of human stories?" For here, although the land is wild, there exists a long and layered history of human use. O'Neill, Holland and Light pose a similar question in relation to restoration. In response, they emphasize the importance of *narrative* in setting a course for restoration, particularly in landscapes where humans and nature intermingle. Why narrative? For O'Neill and his colleagues, narrative does just what "new world" approaches do not: it emphasizes context and temporality, and can guide restoration in directions that preserve meaning rather than disrupt it (2008, 155). Thus, narratives can and should play a strong role in developing restoration and management plans. What we ought to consider is "how best to continue the narrative" of a place (Holland and O'Neill 2003, 221).

This, of course, is easier said than done. As O'Neill and colleagues acknowledge, a given place may be subject to a multiplicity of narratives, and some of these may conflict. What's more, even a single narrative can leave significant indeterminacy regarding how best to continue it. Further, narratives may be problematic, warranting disruption rather than continuation (Hourdequin 2013). Racism and sexism, for example, are often supported and reinforced by accompanying narratives of racial inferiority, natural gender roles, and so on. This point about problematic narratives is consistent with a more general observation: although narratives may reveal what people value, what is valued and what is truly valuable can fail to align (McShane 2012; see also Hourdequin 2013).

Given these concerns, "the narrative of a place" cannot serve as a straightforward normative guide for restoration. At the very least, we should seek to identify and critically examine the multiplicity of narratives for a given place before attempting to select a single one to carry forth. This is important, in part, because narratives come in various forms and are mobilized for various purposes. Narratives play a general role in helping us make sense of our lives, but they may do so in diverse ways. For example, at both the individual and the social levels, narratives often bear important ties to *identity* (see, e.g., Arntzen 2008). Relatedly, narratives can serve as a *repository or reminder of values* that individuals and communities hold. For example, for the Western Apache people, stories tied to particular places carry important moral lessons, and these stories are told and retold when someone in the community transgresses a particular boundary or fails to honor core tribal values. Such stories are often told to a group, but with a clear individual target in mind—and for this person, hearing the story is like being shot with an arrow (Basso 1996, 48). The Western Apache also describe stories as "stalking" them: when a person is the target of a place story containing a particular moral lesson or reminder, that story often plays over and over in his or her mind, a reminder of the need to do better. Because stories are tied to place names and to actual, physical places, hearing the place name or passing by the place further reinforces the story's power (Basso 1996, 59).

We see in this case that stories can also *motivate* us to act in certain ways. For the Western Apache, stories play a critical role in the moral ecology, serving as pointed reminders of community expectations. Yet stories can shape choices and actions in more subtle ways. As noted earlier, narratives typically undergird identity, and this, in turn, enables us to think through whether a given choice is consistent with "who we are" as individuals or as a community. Political leaders frequently appeal to narrative identities in motivating support for a particular course of action. For example, the narrative of the American dream emphasizes social mobility and the ability of individuals—no matter how humble their origins—to work hard and achieve a decent quality of life (for discussion of the American dream narrative, see Rowland and Jones 2007). At the personal level, this may motivate individuals to strive to get a good education, work their way up through the ranks, or save money with the goal of some day owning a home. At the level of policy, the American dream narrative can be used to support increased investment in public education or efforts to broaden opportunities for traditionally disadvantaged groups.[3] Narratives can thus serve as an engine of social change; yet they can also motivate resistance to change. Because of their emphasis on continuity with the past, narratives can support the maintenance of the status quo. We hear this when people or institutions appeal to tradition or argue in response to a proposed change, "That's not the way we do (and have done) things around here."

These examples indicate that narratives not only motivate; they also serve to *explain, justify,* and *rationalize* certain values, ways of thinking, and courses of action. The form of justification provided by narratives rarely takes the shape of a deductive argument from explicit premises to explicit conclusions. Instead, narrative justification is more about *fit*. From a philosophical perspective, one might say that narrative justification is more coherentist than foundationalist: it is about how things hang together (see Arras 1997). When O'Neill, Holland, and Light ask us to consider how best to continue the narrative so as to preserve the meaning and significance of a place and its histories, they are directing our attention to these questions of fit.

One might reasonably wonder, though, whether a restoration strategy's coherence with a particular narrative can suffice to justify our choosing it. I have already noted the existence of diverse and often conflicting narratives of a place, citing Rocky Flats as a particular example of this narrative diversity. Narratives reflect particular *perspectives*, whether of individuals, groups, or institutions. Relatedly, all narratives are *selective*: they foreground some things and background others, and their structure and level of abstraction will determine where they fall along a spectrum from simple to complex. Although simple narratives can be appealing, they may overlook the nuanced and conflicting meanings of layered landscapes. For example, military-to-wildlife (M2W) conversion sites frequently employ a "weapons-to-wildlife" narrative that highlights the way in which Army occupation and use of these sites both damaged and protected them. This narrative suggests that following cleanup, M2W sites can serve as important conservation lands and wildlife habitats. While this narrative captures important aspects of many M2W sites, it gives no attention to the historical layers *preceding* military use or to the ties that people have to the land in association with those prior layers. Such ties are often particularly poignant at sites where people were actively displaced to make way for military use, such as the Rocky Mountain Arsenal Wildlife Refuge in Colorado, Big Oaks National Wildlife Refuge in Indiana, and Great Bay National Wildlife Refuge in New Hampshire.

Thus, while narratives may be employed as justifications, the degree to which they are genuinely *justificatory* (whatever that may require) remains open because there is often controversy over which aspects of a place should be foregrounded and which should most strongly guide future choices. Certainly, not all narratives genuinely justify the ways of thinking and acting they commend. History is littered with examples of colonial narratives that worked to justify the oppression and removal of indigenous people, Nazi narratives that worked to justify the extermination of the Jews, and racist and sexist narratives that reinforced and perpetuated inequality and domination. While these examples may represent the extreme, they serve as important reminders of the importance of critical engagement with narratives. There are plenty of narratives that bear no ulterior motive; nevertheless, they remain selective and reflective of a particular point of view.

Now that we have a clearer sense of the multifaceted dimensions and roles of narrative, what does it entail for our thinking about the role of narrative in restoration? One might conclude that narrative has no role to play at all, but I believe that this would be a mistake. Instead, narratives can be used in restoration to explore and negotiate the meanings of complex landscapes, such as former military sites. Narratives can reveal and enable more careful consideration of diverse values. As such, they can play an important role in the process of identifying plans for restoration, management, and interpretation that acknowledge the richness of a layered landscape and the complexities of its past.

Narrative as Method: Exploring and Negotiating Meaning

> [R]esilience is not simply the capacity for change, but an ability to adapt without losing the culture, community ties, and local traditions that make a place home. It is envisioning a kind of change that nurtures communities here and now without tearing them apart. This type of visioning process comes to life through narrative.
>
> —GOLDSTEIN ET AL. (2013)

In the face of complexity, it is often tempting to seek simplicity, and to favor triumphal narratives that celebrate the past as part of an ongoing story of human progress. Yet the meaning of a complex site like Rocky Flats cannot be easily encapsulated in this way. Some see Rocky Flats for its important strategic role in the Cold War, and as representing the willingness of many to undertake risks and make sacrifices to defend their country; others view Rocky Flats as a place cloaked in secrecy and obfuscation. Some see the site as safe, and the remediation operation as an exemplar for future cleanups (see Cameron and Lavine 2006); whereas others see it as greenwashing that leaves a legacy of contamination and danger for generations to come (see Krupar 2011). The weapons-to-wildlife narrative encourages us to downplay these controversies, however, and to embrace the new purpose and meaning of the site as a national wildlife refuge. We see this effort to mark the end of the military story and the initiation of a new identity in senator Mark Udall's remarks about Rocky Flat's sister site, the Rocky Mountain Arsenal Wildlife Refuge, a former chemical weapons plant:

> With today's transfer, the Rocky Mountain Arsenal has truly been converted—it's moved from weapons to wildlife . . . Because of its critically important activities in the defense of our nation, this area has been a secured facility and has thus become a safe haven for a multitude of wildlife species. And thanks to the collaborative effort of so many players, including the workers doing the cleanup and the wildlife officials protecting and enhancing habitat, the legacy of serious environmental harms has been addressed and a new era can begin in earnest. (Udall 2010)

As noted earlier, not all narratives and not all histories are worth continuing along their former paths, and there may be nothing wrong with opening a new chapter in the history of a particular place. Yet it is worrisome when such disjunctures foreclose important conversations regarding the future of a site or cut off important sources of meaning. Rather than construct a simple and univocal narrative of a place, it may in some cases make sense for restoration to attempt to embrace and respond to plurivocal narratives (Goldstein et al. 2013). This, in turn, may require some institutional flexibility and support for creative approaches to restoration, interpretation, and management.

At many M2W refuge sites, there exists the potential to use creative strategies to integrate multiple narratives into interpretation and management. For example, at Aroostook National Wildlife Refuge, a former Air Force base and nuclear weapons storage facility in Maine, managers have worked to transform concrete bunkers into hibernacula for bats, and similar efforts are underway at the Assabet River National Wildlife Refuge and the Great Bay National Wildlife Refuge. These examples of repurposing military infrastructure reflect not only the creative use of resources, but are also opportunities to integrate discussions of a site's natural and sociopolitical histories. Yet integration is not always straightforward, especially at sites whose histories are contested.

Rocky Flats again provides a vivid example. Congress established the Rocky Flats National Wildlife Refuge in 2001, at the initiative of Colorado senators Wayne Allard and Mark Udall (then Representative Udall). In 2005, the US Fish and Wildlife Service (USFWS) completed a comprehensive conservation plan for the refuge calling for prairie conservation and restoration; wildlife habitat enhancement; and the establishment of public access, including parking, trails, and a visitor contact station (US Fish and Wildlife Service 2005). Yet the refuge remains closed to the public. The USFWS lacks the funds to carry out the central objectives in the conservation plan, and the site has been dogged by controversy and lawsuits. Contestation over the site is vividly revealed in the public comments submitted in response to the agency's proposed text for signs at the refuge informing visitors about the site and its history. Commenters raised concerns about the portrayal of the site as critical to nuclear deterrence and to "holding the Soviet Union at Bay," suggesting that it would be disingenuous to treat the US production of nuclear weapons as purely defensive (US Fish and Wildlife Service 2007; Hourdequin and Havlick 2013). In addition, the text was criticized for emphasizing the dangers of tripping and falling while downplaying the risks of residual plutonium contamination (US Fish and Wildlife Service 2007; Hourdequin and Havlick 2013). Many commenters submitted specific line edits to the sign text, striking out passages they disagreed with and inserting alternative language. This attention to detail shows how fraught the portrayal of the site is for various constituents.

At sites like Rocky Flats, narratives can be useful in revealing the rich and nuanced ways in which people understand the site and its role in their lives. Concerns about safety, for example, are not merely concerns about the increased likelihood of contracting a particular disease as a function of plutonium exposure. These particular concerns often are embedded in a much larger set. Narrative allows concerns about safety to be placed in a larger temporal context, and may bring out connections to issues like trust and secrecy. Narratives can be useful here, because the connections that many local people have to Rocky Flats are not unidimensional, but instead tie into a constellation of values and meanings of the site and its history. This is why narrative provides a distinct alternative to aggregative decision-making processes, such as cost-benefit analysis (O'Neill et al. 2008). Because of their attention to thick description, detailed narratives can enable a richer understanding of diverse perspectives and allow for the emergence of values and meanings, rather than work to fit values and meanings into a predetermined frame (cf. Endres 2012). Narratives call attention to the way in which the past sets the stage for discussions of the future.

From a practical perspective, strategies have been developed to incorporate narrative into planning and decision-making processes (see, e.g., Goldstein and Butler 2010; Langhorst 2012), allowing for the creative re-envisioning of possible futures. As Goldstein and Butler explain in relation to controversy over fire management in southern California:

> [C]ompeting narratives were markers of incommensurability of institutional order, ways of knowing, and professional identity. Yet narratives can also provide collaborators with insight into each other's perspectives and values, a way to grapple with complexity and uncertainty while expressing individual and collective identity ... Developing collective narratives permits participants to reassemble familiar ideas, methods, and strategies, trying different combinations until a new story emerges that seems workable and mutually acceptable. (Goldstein and Butler 2010, 6–7; emphasis added)

The fire-management collaborative process employed in this case thus asked participants to construct and contribute their own narratives to bring to the discussion. Bringing these narratives into conversation with one another enabled a shared vision to emerge, and perhaps equally importantly, allowed those engaged with a particular place to identify new roles, or to extend their understanding of their roles in relation to that place.

At Rocky Flats, this process of re-envisioning may be particularly important. Here, the USFWS land managers often find themselves caught in the middle, having inherited a controversy they did not create. Additionally, the USFWS is an agency with extremely limited funding, and refuge staff have minimal capacity for managing residual radioactive contamination, addressing ongoing public safety concerns, or developing management and interpretation strategies that integrate complex socioecological histories. Although USFWS employees often proudly tout their role as representatives of the only US federal agency dedicated centrally to the protection of fish and wildlife, the management of former military sites seems to call for more than this single-minded focus. Military-to-wildlife sites call for careful attention to the world as we find it, as both a social and natural world. Their history in many cases exemplifies the dangers of a Faustian approach and the importance of cultivating receptivity.

For an agency with a single-minded mission, receptivity and attention to the world as we find it may require not altering or straying from core values and priorities, but rather asking what it means to honor those values and priorities in *this* place. M2W sites, insofar as they are wild *and* contaminated, peaceful *and* dangerous, natural *and* cultural, challenge certain traditional concepts and categories. So, too, with the restoration of these sites. Which disturbances are the ones that restoration should seek to reverse or undo? Is undoing or erasing human disturbance always the best thing for nature? For us? In the M2W case, might it be possible to protect wildlife and ecosystems while also acknowledging—even embracing—the human dimensions of these places, and to celebrate the success of restoration while squarely facing the reality, and the shame, that we have the ability to contaminate lands in ways that far exceed our capacity to clean them up?

This question, of course, is one that managers of M2W sites can't really answer on their own. Attention to thick descriptions of the ways in which people value and engage with these sites will, undoubtedly, complexify rather than simplify their management. Yet deep ecologist Arne Naess (1973) makes an important distinction between *complexity* and *complication*. Complication is fragmenting and chaotic, something we should seek to avoid. Complexity embraces diversity but seeks an integration that enables that diversity to persist and contribute to a flourishing system overall. To ignore the complex meanings of a site like Rocky Flats and its local, national, and international significance in order to fit its management into a standard framework, or to provide a neat, happy ending to a story that raises many difficult questions, is to seek simplicity at great cost. And my suggestion here is that we embrace complexity, attend to the world as we find it, and use narratives to stimulate moral imagination and make new possibilities visible. This, in turn, is important for seeing new ways for diverse value puzzles to fit together. In a world characterized by diversity and rapid change, this approach may enable us to preserve meaning and significance in complex landscapes, and to embrace the future without overlooking the past. For restoration of layered landscapes, this may mean reconceiving historical fidelity relationally: to be faithful to history is to take the values, meanings, stories, and relationships that exist in a place seriously, and to determine how best to shepherd these values and relationships going forward.

More generally, a focus on narrative, receptivity, and valuing the world as we find it embodies a relational approach to ethics, and to environmental ethics, that has been backgrounded in the Western tradition but that nevertheless may be crucially important as we attempt to navigate our lives as individuals and societies in a time of rapid environmental change. Rather than treat the world as a blank slate, open to any new inscription, or think of ourselves as free agents building ourselves and our societies from the ground up, we might draw insight from a more relational perspective, such as that found in the work of Japanese philosopher Watsuji Tetsurô. As Robert Carter (2013) describes this view:

> We enter the world already within a network of relationships and obligations. Each of us is a nexus of pathways and roads, and our betweenness is already etched by the natural and cultural climate that we inherit and live our lives within. . . . The study of these relational navigational patterns—between the individual and the family, self and society, as well as one's relationship to the environment—is the study of ethics.

If this is right, then working out how to manage these odd places where eagles soar and sarin bomblets can linger, or where bats roost in concrete military bunkers, may be an important part of a much bigger project of rethinking our concepts and categories in ways that enable us to value the present and the past and the natural and social relationships that emerge in the world over time.

Notes

1. As Wu and Loucks (1995) put it, "[T]he balance of nature idea and the classical equilibrium paradigm have had profound influences on applied ecology, especially on nature conservation, as they have led to the supposition that 'nature knows best.'"

2. In considering this question, we may find that by understanding why we value the world as we find it, including the social world, we can better understand the value of key aspects of the natural world. The restoration of hybrid landscapes prompts us to think beyond the traditional nature/culture dichotomy and its role in ecological restoration, and to develop more thoughtful approaches to restoration in a rapidly changing world. In doing so, we may also discover new reasons to protect and restore the natural environment, even in a "post-nature" world (see Wapner 2010) in which we cannot rely on either the existence of nature in its pure, idealized form or on the assumption that nature always knows best.

3. The complexity of even this familiar narrative is illustrated by the fact that it can be mobilized to support other opposing policy agendas, such as those that emphasize self-sufficiency without government help.

References

Allison, Stuart K. 2012. *Ecological Restoration and Environmental Change: Renewing Damaged Ecosystems*. New York: Routledge.

Arntzen, Sven. 2008. "The Complex Cultural Landscape: Humans and the Land, Preservation and Change." In *Humans in the Land: The Ethics and Aesthetics of the Cultural Landscape*, edited by Sven Arntzen and Emily Brady, 39–74. Oslo: Unipub.

Arras, John D. 1997. "Nice Story, but So What? Narrative Justification in Ethics." In *Stories and Their Limits: Narrative Approaches to Bioethics*, edited by Hilde Lindemann Nelson, 65–88. New York: Routledge.

Basso, Keith. 1996. *Wisdom Sits in Places: Landscape and Language among the Western Apache*. Albuquerque: University of New Mexico Press.

Botkin, Daniel B. 1990. *Discordant Harmonies: A New Ecology for the Twenty-First Century*. New York: Oxford University Press.

Cameron, Kim S., and Marc Lavine. 2006. *Making the Impossible Possible: Leading Extraordinary Performance—the Rocky Flats Story*. San Francisco, CA: Berrett-Koehler Store.

Carter, Robert. 2013. "Watsuji Tetsurô." In *The Stanford Encyclopedia of Philosophy* (Spring 2013 edition), edited by Edward N. Zalta. Accessed November 8, 2013. http://plato.stanford.edu/archives/spr2013/entries/watsuji-tetsuro/.

Choi, Young D. 2004. "Theories for Ecological Restoration in Changing Environment: Toward 'Futuristic' Restoration." *Ecological Research* 19: 75–81.

Choi, Young D. 2007. "Restoration Ecology to the Future: A Call for New Paradigm." *Restoration Ecology* 15: 351–353.

Cooper, Gregory J. 2003. *The Science of the Struggle for Existence: On the Foundations of Ecology*. New York: Cambridge University Press.

Cronon, William. 1996. "The Trouble with Wilderness: Or, Getting Back to the Wrong Nature." *Environmental History* 1 (1): 7–28.

Cronon, William. 2002. "Caretaking Tales." In *The Story Handbook: Language and Storytelling for Land Conservationists*, edited by H. Whybrow, 87–93. San Francisco, CA: Trust for Public Land.

Cronon, William. 2003. "The Riddle of the Apostle Islands." *Orion* 22: 36–42.

Denevan, William M. 1992. "The Pristine Myth: The Landscape of the Americas in 1492." *Annals of the Association of American Geographers* 82 (3): 369–385.

Drenthen, Martin. 2009. "Ecological Restoration and Place Attachment: Emplacing Non-Places?" *Environmental Values* 18: 285–312.

Duncan, S. L., B. C. McComb, and K. Johnson. 2010. "Integrating Ecological and Social Ranges of Variability in Conservation of Biodiversity: Past, Present, and Future." *Ecology and Society* 15 (1): 5. http://www.ecologyandsociety.org/vol15/iss1/art5/.

Egan, Dave. 2006. "Authentic Ecological Restoration." *Ecological Restoration* 24: 223–224.

Endres, Danielle. 2012. "Sacred Land or National Sacrifice Zone: The Role of Values in the Yucca Mountain Participation Process." *Environmental Communication* 6 (3): 328–345.

Goldstein, Bruce E, and William H. Butler. 2010. "The US Fire Learning Network: Providing a Narrative Framework for Restoring Ecosystems, Professions, and Institutions." *Society and Natural Resources* 23 (10): 935–951.

Goldstein, Bruce E., Anne T. Wessells, Raul Lejano, and William Butler. 2015. "Narrating Resilience: Transforming Urban Systems through Collaborative Storytelling." *Urban Studies* 52 (7): 1285–1303.

Higgs, Eric S. 2003. *Nature by Design: People, Natural Process, and Ecological Restoration*. Cambridge, MA: MIT Press.

Hobbs, Richard J., Eric Higgs, and James A. Harris. 2009. "Novel Ecosystems: Implications for Conservation and Restoration." *Trends in Ecology & Evolution* 24 (11): 599–605.

Holland, Alan, and John O'Neill. 2003. "Yew Trees, Butterflies, Rotting Boots and Washing Lines: The Importance of Narrative." In *Moral and Political Reasoning in Environmental Practice*, edited by Andrew Light and Avner De-Shalit, 219–235. Cambridge: MIT Press.

Hourdequin, Marion. 2013. "Restoration and History in a Changing World: A Case Study in Ethics for the Anthropocene." *Ethics and the Environment* 18 (2): 115–134.

Hourdequin, Marion, and David G. Havlick. 2013. "Restoration and Authenticity Revisited." *Environmental Ethics* 35 (1): 79–93.

Iversen, Kristen. 2012. *Full Body Burden: Growing Up in the Nuclear Shadow of Rocky Flats*. New York: Crown.

Kareiva, Peter, Robert Lalasz, and Michelle Marvier. 2012. "Conservation in the Anthropocene: Beyond Solitude and Fragility." *Breakthrough Journal* online. http://thebreakthrough.org/index.php/journal/past-issues/issue-2/conservation-in-the-anthropocene/#. Accessed October 23, 2013.

Krupar, Shiloh R. 2011. "Alien Still Life: Distilling the Toxic Logics of the Rocky Flats National Wildlife Refuge." *Environment and Planning-Part D* 29 (2): 268–290.

Langhorst, Joern. 2012. "Recovering Place: On the Agency of Post-disaster Landscapes." *Landscape Review* 14 (2): 48–74.

Martínez, M. Luisa, and Fabiola López-Barrera. 2008. "Special Issue: Restoring and Designing Ecosystems for a Crowded Planet." *Ecoscience* 15 (1): 1–5.

McShane, Katie. 2012. "Some Challenges for Narrative Accounts of Value." *Ethics and the Environment* 17: 45–69.

Naess, Arne. 1973. "The Shallow and the Deep, Long-Range Ecology Movement. A Summary." *Inquiry* 16: 95–100.

O'Neill, John, Alan Holland, and Andrew Light. 2008. *Environmental Values.* New York: Routledge.

Palmer, M. A., E. S. Bernhardt, E. A. Chornesky, S. L. Collins, A. P. Dobson, C. S. Duke, B. D. Gold et al. 2004. "Ecology for a Crowded Planet." *Science* 304: 1251–1252.

Rowland, Robert C., and John M. Jones. 2007. "Recasting the American Dream and American Politics: Barack Obama's Keynote Address to the 2004 Democratic National Convention." *Quarterly Journal of Speech* 93 (4): 425–448.

Sievanen, Leila, Rebecca L. Gruby, and Lisa M. Campbell. 2012. "Fixing Marine Governance in Fiji? The New Scalar Narrative of Ecosystem-Based Management." *Global Environmental Change* 23 (1): 206–216.

Slote, Michael. 2013. *From Enlightenment to Receptivity: Rethinking Our Values.* New York: Oxford University Press.

Udall, Mark. 2010. "Udall Celebrates Cleanup of Rocky Mountain Arsenal, Completion of National Wildlife Refuge." Press Release. October 15, 2010, available at: http:// gatewaynews-government.blogspot.jp/2010/10/udall-celebrates-cleanup-at-rocky. html. Accessed June 25, 2015.

US Fish and Wildlife Service. 2005. "Comprehensive Conservation Plan, Rocky Flats National Wildlife Refuge." Commerce City, CO. http://www.fws.gov/ mountain-prairie/planning/ccp/co/rfl/rfl.html. Accessed September 15, 2013.

US Fish and Wildlife Service. 2007. Rocky Flats National Wildlife Refuge, Final Rocky Flats Signage. Last updated 12 December 2011. http://www.fws.gov/nwrs/threecol-umn.aspx?id=2147530249. Accessed July 1, 2015.

Wapner, Paul K. 2010. *Living through the End of Nature: The Future of American Environmentalism.* Cambridge, MA: MIT Press.

Whatmore, Sarah. 2002. *Hybrid Geographies: Natures Cultures Spaces.* London: Sage.

Williams, Gerald W. 2000. "Introduction to Aboriginal Fire Use in North America." *Fire Management Today* 60 (3): 8–12.

Williams, John W., and Stephen T. Jackson. 2007. "Novel Climates, No-Analog Communities, and Ecological Surprises." *Frontiers in Ecology and the Environment* 5 (9): 475–482.

Wu, Jianguo, and Orie L. Loucks. 1995. "From Balance of Nature to Hierarchical Patch Dynamics: A Paradigm Shift in Ecology." *Quarterly Review of Biology* 70 (4): 439–466.

CHAPTER 3 | # The Different Faces of History in Postindustrial Landscapes

JOZEF KEULARTZ

Introduction

Measured by expenditure and scale, the reclamation of industrial brown-fields and industrial ruins is currently one of the largest infrastructure undertakings in Europe and America. The legacy of the industrial era, from 1850 to 1950, saddles landscape planners and designers with multiple problems. Should they aim for demolition, preservation, or the transformation of decommissioned military sites, derelict factories, and decayed piers? How should they treat former industrial sites as sites of public memory—as "memoryscapes"? What role should history play in the regeneration and revitalization of postindustrial landscapes? To answer these questions, I make use of Friedrich Nietzsche's essay "On the Use and Abuse of History for Life." But first, I discuss the problem of history in ecological restoration, especially of hybrid landscapes where natural and human histories have been closely intertwined.

The Problem of History in Ecological Restoration

Because the idea of restoring something is to return it to a prior state, "no general account of restoration would be complete without some attention to history" (Higgs 2003, 77). The role of history in ecological restoration has proved to be very intricate. In the early 1990s, when ecological restoration was emerging as a recognized discipline, ecological restoration was generally considered to be "the return of an ecosystem to a close approximation of its condition prior to disturbance," to cite the very influential definition issued by the US National Research Council (1992). However, the idea of returning ecosystems to predisturbance conditions by reversing human impact soon ran into difficulties.

The first problem was caused by the shift within ecology from equilibrium theory to nonequilibrium theory, and the associated change in perception of ecosystems from static entities with a linear and predictable development to dynamic entities that evolve along nonlinear and unpredictable trajectories. This shift from the balance to the flux of nature has diminished the significance of the notion of predisturbance conditions: whereas in equilibrium theory "stability was the norm, and disturbance was bad" (Wallington et al. 2005, 12), in nonequilibrium theory disturbance is considered to be an inherent feature of the internal dynamic of ecosystems. The concept of stability is being replaced by the notion of contingency. This notion means that restoration ecologists will have a variety of reference states to choose from. "Contingency establishes a whole range of systems, not just one 'climax' or predisturbance state" (Pickett and Parker 1994, 76).

The second problem concerns the idea, inherent in equilibrium theory, of a pristine wilderness devoid of human effects. This idea was deflated as it became apparent that many wilderness areas were profoundly affected by humans before European conquest and settlement. A case in point is one of the great symbols of American wilderness, Yosemite Valley, established in 1864 as the nation's first natural park. The valley was occupied by the Ahwahneechee Indians until 1853, when they were evicted from the valley in the interest of gold miners. Soon after their expulsion it became clear that their land-management practices, especially those involving burning, had an important ecological impact. The lack of burning led to the accumulation of detritus and brush, which in turn made for much more violent fires and ruined the very scenic views that were meant to be preserved (Olwig 1996).

The realization that even an archetypal wilderness area such as Yosemite Valley had been substantially shaped by human activity has brought about a breakdown of the dichotomy between nature and culture. Thinking in terms of clear-cut boundaries between nature and culture has been generally replaced by thinking in terms of a broad continuum of mixtures or mélanges, creating a hybrid zone in which it is no longer a question of "either/or" but of "less or more." The idea of a continuum or spectrum ranging from the purely wild on one end to the purely civilized on the other was put forward by Roderick Nash in his 1973 book *Wilderness and the American Mind.* Nash calls this idea of a scale useful "because it implies the notion of shading and blending" (1982, 6).

The idea of hybrid intermediary landscapes further complicates the role of history in ecological restoration because, in addition to natural history, we now have to take human history into account. In the nineteenth century, the "continent of history" was opened up to scientific investigation on the model of the modern natural sciences, adopting the position of a neutral and indifferent observer outside or above time and history. Historical knowledge was supposed to be an objective account of "how things actually happened" (*wie es eigentlich gewesen*), to cite the famous dictum of Leopold von Ranke, the most important historian to shape the historical profession as it emerged in Europe and the United States in the late nineteenth century. According to von Ranke, the historian must renounce all judgment and refuse to take sides. He should extinguish his self in order to let the facts speak for themselves.

Von Ranke's view of history as an objective, impartial, and unprejudiced enterprise soon came under attack. One of the most truculent and eloquent critics was Friedrich Nietzsche. In his essay "On the Use and Abuse of History for Life," published in 1874 as the second of his *Untimely Meditations*, Nietzsche compared von Ranke–style historians, with their sterile neutrality, to "a race of eunuchs" (1954, 238).[1] These historians let themselves "be turned into an 'objective' mirror of all that is" (263), and thus into a "purely passive medium" (246). They have reversed the relationship between historical inquiry and life, under the motto *fiat veritas pereat vita* (let there be truth and may life perish [230]).[2]

Historical inquiry, according to Nietzsche, is, rather, more about subjective interpretation than about objective observation. In stressing the irreducibly interpretative and hence creative nature of historical inquiry, Nietzsche introduced a problematic that has occupied historians to this day and strongly influenced the development of the twentieth-century hermeneutic philosophy of Hans-Georg Gadamer and Paul Ricoeur, among others (Sinclair 2004; see also Drenthen, chap. 13, this volume). Not unlike the aforementioned shift within natural history, the emphasis on interpretation and creativity has brought about a shift in human history, from stability and permanence to change and contingency, with the result that there is not just one single history but a variety of histories.

In "On the Use and Abuse of History for Life," Nietzsche distinguishes three ways in which history belongs to the living person: "[I]t belongs to him as an active and striving person; it belongs to him as a person who preserves and admires; it belongs to him as a suffering person in need of emancipation" (Nietzsche 1954, 218). These three relationships correspond to three kinds of history: the *monumental,* the *antiquarian,* and the *critical.* While each of these uses of history can be put in the service of life, each may also degenerate into a threat to life. This happens when one form of history gains supremacy at the expense of the other two. Nietzsche's ideal is that of a balance, in which the different forms of history may complement and correct each other.

To highlight the role and significance of human history in restoring layered landscapes, this chapter provides an overview of Nietzsche's triad of forms of history and applies them to different forms of the design and management of postindustrial landscapes, using examples from England, Belgium, Germany, the Netherlands, and the United States.

Antiquarian History

Antiquarian history appeals to a person's or a people's inclination toward the preservation and admiration of the past. The antiquarian looks back at the origins of his existence with love and loyalty. He wants to preserve the conditions under which he came into existence for those who will come after him. Nurturing what has stood from time immemorial provides antiquarians with a sense of continuity and collective identity. Nietzsche mentions the example of the antiquarian for whom the history of his city becomes the history of his self: "He looks on the walls, the turreted gate, the city council, and the folk festival as an illustrated diary of his youth, and sees himself in it all—his strength, industry, desire, reason, faults and follies" (1954, 225).

The antiquarian sense of history offers man the assurance that his existence is neither arbitrary nor accidental but, rather, a link in a chain of events extending from the past and, therefore, justified. Nietzsche compares this historical sense with "the sense of well being of a tree for its roots," and "the happiness of knowing one's growth to be . . . the fruit and blossom of a past" (226).

The antiquarian has an instinct for nuance and detail. This devotion to specifics may, however, lead to a narrowed vision in which things are looked at too closely and in isolation. In the absence of a measure, the antiquarian tends to level all differences and to perceive everything old and past as equally worthy of respect. Insofar as antiquarian history does not make any distinction between what is truly important and what is less important, it tends to degenerate into a "blind mania for collecting, a restless compiling of everything that ever existed" (Nietzsche 1954, 227).

Nietzsche cautions against the possibility that the antiquarian approach to history may become too powerful, invading the territory of the other approaches. Because antiquarian history knows only how to preserve life, not how to create it, it is always in danger of overestimating everything old and undervaluing everything new. When this happens, when things of the past are valued more than things of the present, antiquarian history no longer serves life, but mummifies it. If this happens, "then the tree dies unnaturally, from the top gradually down to the roots, and at last even the roots are generally destroyed" (228). As it threatens to paralyze the present with its reluctance to replace the old with the new, antiquarian history leads to an ongoing musealization of the past.

Postindustrial Sites as Open-Air Museums

In England, a country that is proud of its history and cherishes nostalgic sentiments, the emphasis is often on the preservation and restoration of the industrial past. The Geevor Tin Mine Heritage Centre (figure 3.1) on the coast of Cornwall is a good example of the preference to turn former industrial sites into open-air museums that invite visitors to relive the past as concretely and authentically as possible.

Tin mining has long been the main economic activity in Cornwall, and in many respects it has formed the landscape and its residents. The mining activities in the area date back to the seventeenth century. The Geevor Tin Mine was one of the largest in the Cornwall area, employing up to 400 people, with workings that extended far out under the sea. In 1990, the mine was closed, resulting in high unemployment. On the initiative of former miners, in collaboration with the local government, the area was transformed into a heritage center. It is now the largest mining-history site in the United Kingdom, where visitors can follow the story of the mining and processing of tin. The site now functions as an open-air museum: the buildings and machinery have been returned to their original state as much as possible, and parts of the former mine shafts have been pumped dry again. Visitors can take guided tours led by former miners, and thereby experience life as an underground laborer. There is a unique collection of mining artefacts, mineral displays, and photographs of the mine and miners at work.

FIGURE 3.1 The headframe above the Victory shaft at Geevor Mine in Cornwall. England. Courtesy of Nilfanion under Creative Commons License.

With its strong emphasis on the preservation and admiration of the past, the Geevor Tin Mine Heritage Centre provides an example of antiquarian history. There is an imminent danger that the center will not be able to inspire "the fresh life of the present." The mine has not really received a second life, but has only had its first life prolonged after retirement. It is questionable whether this is sufficient to provide the region with new impulses or direction.

Of course, England is not the only country with an antiquarian approach to the industrial past. An excellent example of this approach in Continental Europe is offered by a series of four mining sites in Wallonia (Belgium) that were included in the World Heritage List in 2012. These sites—the Grand-Hornu, Bois-du-Luc, Bois du Cazier, and Blegny-Mine—form a strip 170 kilometers long by 3 to 15 kilometers wide, crossing Belgium from east to west, and covering the same chronological period, from the early nineteenth century to the end of the twentieth. The ensemble of the four Walloon mining sites provides an eminent and complete example of the world of industrial mining in Continental Europe, at various stages of the Industrial Revolution.

In the United States, the antiquarian approach to industrial heritage is certainly not a common one. "Unlike Britain, where ruins are made symbols related to national myths, the United States finds its initial identity in its freedom from ruin" (Briante 2006, 11). An interesting exception is the Sloss Furnaces in Birmingham, Alabama, the only twentieth-century blast furnace in the United States being preserved as a historical industrial site. The pig-iron factory, established in 1881 by James Sloss, was redeveloped as a "Museum of Modern Times" after it closed in the 1970s. "Short of wearing costumes recalling the late 1800s, its organizers have left the site and its buildings intact" (Hardy 2005, 37).

Monumental History

Monumental history opposes the mummification of life and the musealization of the past and offers a counterbalance to a degenerated antiquarian history that no longer gives inspiration to the fresh life of the present. Monumental history can serve life by inspiring contemporary generations to creatively and courageously shape their present and future. It examines the past with the explicit intent of finding teachers and role models to be emulated and surpassed, encouraging and empowering humanity to attain excellence and greatness. Monumental history is concerned with the greatest moments in the history of humanity that serve to indicate that greatness was once attained and is therefore possible again. This knowledge offers strength and power, and takes away the self-doubt, which frustrates creativity, that humans might perhaps be wishing for the impossible. Thus monumental history can serve as a weapon against resignation.

It is important to realize that Nietzsche uses the term "monumental" in a metaphorical sense. The greatness and grandeur of exemplary individuals and their excellent works are seen as analogous to the extraordinary spatial dimensions of ancient structures such as megaliths, temples, and statues. If we want to apply Nietzsche's account of monumental history to our industrial heritage, these spatial dimensions have to play an important role. Because of their monumental size, buildings and other objects are experienced as sublime. In his *Critique of Judgment* (sec. 26) from 1790, Immanuel Kant (1963) associates the sublime with the colossal, "which is almost too great for any presentation." He mentions the pyramids in Egypt and St. Peter's Basilica in Rome as examples of the sublime, "which in its ultimate form is the 'absolutely great.'"

Monumental history can serve life by inspiring us to great actions and works, but, similarly to antiquarian history, it can also deteriorate into a threat to life. Whereas antiquarian history tends to get bogged down in little details and fine distinctions, monumental history has a tendency to overlook or tone down differences in motives and occasions. To draw strength from historical examples, the uniqueness and individuality of the past will usually be forced into a general formula. As long as the past is mainly used as a model worthy of imitation, it is in constant danger of becoming deformed and distorted and degenerating into a miscellaneous collection of "effects in themselves," a grab bag, from which forms, concepts, and structures, et cetera, can be drawn opportunistically.

The monumentalist sees history as a chain of peaks connecting the great moments of humanity through the ages. In such a view, history always runs the risk of being beautified and of coming close to free poetic invention. Especially in times when monumental history dominates the other forms of history—the antiquarian and the critical—it is often impossible to make a distinction between monumental history and mythical fiction. Monumental history will then entice the brave man to rashness, and the enthusiastic man to fanaticism. "If we imagine this history in the hands and heads of a gifted egoist or an infatuated scoundrel, then we see empires overthrown, princes murdered, war and revolution instigated, and the number of historical 'effects in themselves' increased once more" (Nietzsche 1954, 222).

Monumental history can not only cause serious harm in the hands of powerful and active men but also and above all when the powerless and inactive take hold of monumental history for their own ends. As his most common example, Nietzsche mentions the case of inartistic or half-artistic natures who turn the canon of monumental art against the great artistic spirits of their time. Their instinct tells them that art can be struck dead by art, Nietzsche says. Their glorification of the past as a series of accomplishments that are impossible to emulate can have a paralyzing effect on the ambition and creativity of the artistic spirits. To prevent greatness from arising, they say, "See! Greatness is already there!" (Nietzsche 1954, 223). Their motto is: let the dead bury the living. In this way, monumental history no longer offers inspiration and loses its function as an antidote to quietism.

Conservation through Development

The Netherlands offers many examples of a monumental approach to the industrial past. The Dutch management style with respect to derelict industrial sites is often less conservative than the English style. Perhaps because the Netherlands is a very densely populated country where space is scarce, the Dutch have developed a pragmatic style, giving new functions to old buildings and structures. The Western Gas Factory (figure 3.2), a coal gas factory complex near the historic center of Amsterdam, is a case in point.

The Western Gas Factory was built in 1883 by the Imperial Continental Gas Association (ICGA) of London. It was the largest gas extraction plant in the Netherlands. Gas was extracted from coal and used for street lighting. Gas production at the Western Gas Factory ceased in 1967.

Many of the buildings on the site were designed by architect Isaac Gosschalk in the Dutch Neo-Renaissance style, which was introduced by Gosschalk and was popular between 1870 and 1915, a period of economic growth often likened to the Golden Age in the seventeenth century. After 1992, the buildings were renovated and are now used for a variety of creative activities and cultural events. Artists set up studios in the smaller buildings. The large spaces, such as the gasholder, are regularly used for exhibitions, house parties, fashion shows, and festivals. On the site there

FIGURE 3.2 Western Gas Factory. Courtesy of Arjen Veldt, with permission from the Westergasfabriek.

are also various small companies with a permanent lease, such as a traditional bakery, a coffeehouse, and a cinema.

The park surrounding the buildings was designed by the landscape architect Kathryn Gustafson. Her design, called "Changement," shows the gradual transition from city to countryside. The use of the park is intensive and varied: big concerts, information markets, neighborhood parties, picnics, football, and the like. The park also has attractive green cycle and walking routes.

The successful redevelopment of the Western Gas factory is a good example of monumental history. It reminds one of the motto "conservation through development" from the Dutch "Belvedere Memorandum," a government strategy to integrate cultural heritage in the future spatial development of the Netherlands (1999). The memorandum argues for a new balance or synthesis between the preservation of existing cultural-historical values and the creation or development of new spatial values and new forms of use. The intrinsic value of the past is less important than its usefulness and relevance for the present and the future. The renovation of the Western Gas Factory was carried out with the intention to give the local community new social and economic vitality by attracting business enterprises and cultural ventures.

In contrast to the Geevor Tin Mine Heritage Centre, the Western Gas Factory has received a second life, but insofar as the monumental approach tends to rule over both the antiquarian and the critical approaches and as the past is only opportunistically used because of its monumental effects, its new life may be in danger of becoming shallow.

The Western Gas Factory certainly has a monumental character, but its greatness and grandeur are hardly determined by the size of its structures.[3] A curious example of industrial heritage that owes its monumental character to size is Ferropolis—"the city of steel"—at the former brown coal mine Golpa-Nord near Dessau in central Germany (figure 3.3).

Ferropolis is located on a peninsula in the lake that was created in 2000 when the former mining area was flooded. The city of steel consists of five giant lignite excavators—monuments to the machine age—that were placed in half a circle, within which an open-air theater was built. These excavators have been given nicknames: Medusa, Mad Max, Gemini, Mosquito, and Big Wheel. They are among the largest moving structures mankind has ever made, and are even larger than the moving platforms used for the rocket flights to the moon at Cape Canaveral. The biggest giant—Gemini—weighs 1250 tons, and is 30 meters high and 125 meters long. The iron mastodons provide a breathtaking setting for international

FIGURE 3.3 Bucket wheel excavator in Ferropolis. Courtesy of Rmollik under Creative Commons License.

festivals and big concerts. In *The Guardian* (London) of May 15, 2007, Sarah Philips described her impression of the site as follows: "From the second I set eyes on Ferropolis, I was completely blown away. The cranes have an ominous beauty, shooting up into the sky like gothic spires. Later when it gets dark, they are lit up by brightly coloured lights, and seem both dangerous and thrilling at once, like a fairground ride."

Critical History

Critical history serves as remedy for the pathologies of antiquarian history and monumental history. To overcome the paralyzing obsession with the past, without relapsing into a superficial pursuit of monumental effects, one must have the strength to shatter and dissolve a past and to erase its memories. This is achieved, says Nietzsche, "by dragging history to the bar of judgment, interrogating it meticulously and finally condemning it; every past is worthy of condemnation" (1954, 228). To characterize this critical attitude, Nietzsche quotes the famous verse from Goethe with which Mephistopheles introduces himself to Doctor Faust:

I am the Spirit that denies!
And rightly too; for all that doth begin
Should rightly to destruction run;
'Twere better then that nothing were begun.
Thus everything that you call Sin,
Destruction-in a word, as Evil represent—
That is my own, real element. (Goethe n.d.)

According to the critical attitude and the spirit of denial, everything that is experienced as an injustice, such as a privilege, a caste, or a dynasty, merits destruction. But the critical analysis of history can also be productive. Through this analysis, it is possible for man to discover knowledge that conflicts with his nature; critical history then gives him the power to utilize this new knowledge to his advantage and "implant a new habit, a new instinct, a second nature so that the first nature withers away" (Nietzsche 1954, 229).

Cutting ties to the past thus gives us a sense of liberation and emancipation. It allows us to move forward toward growth and progress, and raises hope for a future without suffering and injustice. But though condemnation of the past is useful for the present, it can also degenerate into a dangerous practice for life itself, because it is difficult to find a limit to the denial of the past and because second natures are generally weaker than the first. Just because we destroy the past does not mean we can escape the past; for we derive from the past. We are merely the products of previous generations, with all their aberrations, passions, errors, and crimes, and we are unable to shake off that chain entirely. If we deny this fact, our hope for a fair and decent future may turn out to be a false hope.

Denial of the Past: From Demolition to Ruination

The critical approach to history is typical of modernity: a revolution is needed to unleash the power of progress and to undermine the counterforces of the past. Down with tradition—tabula rasa—and up with the "great leap forward." Especially after the First World War, a revolutionary climate prevailed in architecture. Modern architecture (Bauhaus, De Stijl, CIAM [Congrès internationaux d'architecture modern]) cleared away all local, regional, and national traditions in the most radical fashion. The old regime, with its aristocratic and elitist traditions, was rejected as outdated. Modern architecture's ideal was a classless society without secrets and privileges. Hence its preference for transparent materials such as glass. The German philosopher Walter Benjamin has noticed that "glass is generally an enemy of secrecy; it is also the enemy of possessiveness" (2005, 734). Modern architecture is no longer about security and secrecy, but aims at "converting human habitations into the transitional spaces of every imaginable force and *wave of light* and air" (Benjamin 1999, 264).

The aggressive will to renewal, so typical of modern architecture, was also at work in the historical avant-garde movements, such as futurism, Dadaïsm, constructivism, surrealism, and situationism. Italian writer Filippo Tommaso Marinetti provides a telling illustration of the pronounced destructive and iconoclastic fury of these movements. In his first manifesto of futurism of 1909, he proposed to free Italy from its "cancer of professors, archaeologists, tourist guides and antiquaries" by demolishing museums and libraries (quoted in Gamboni 1997, 259). Another example is offered by Russian painter Kasimir Malevich, who in 1919 wrote that the only concession to be made to preservationists was "to let all periods burn, as one dead body" and put the resulting powder on one medicine shelf (quoted in Gamboni 1997, 259). And Marcel Duchamp, in an interview in *Arts and Decoration* in 1915, praised the harmonious growth of New York City, which he deemed "a complete work of art," and declared, in a similar vein to Nietzsche's description of critical history: "I believe that your idea of demolishing old buildings, old souvenirs, is fine ... The dead should not be permitted to be so much stronger than the living. We must learn to forget the past, to live our own lives in our own times" (quoted in Gamboni 1997, 260).

Today, especially in Europe, there is little of this urge for destruction and iconoclasm still at work in the reclamation of postindustrial sites. Hugh Hardy mentions the Tate Modern in London and the Dia Beacon in New York as examples of buildings from which everything except the basic structure was removed. Hardy argues that both buildings offer visitors no clue to their original uses—as a power station and a box-printing facility of the former National Biscuit Company, respectively. "Their minimalist design produces large, simple volumes, but they lack identity with the industrial past, making big, but bland, places" (Hardy 2005, 37).

What is most remarkable in today's critical approach to postindustrial sites is the shift from demolition to ruination. Currently, we are witnessing a marked "ruinophilia," or *Ruinenlust* (DeSilvey and Edensor 2012). This postindustrial fascination with ruin differs from the romantic obsession with ruination and decay. Modern, postindustrial ruins have generally been created within the past sixty years; whereas romantic, picturesque ruins are relics of another, more distant time and culture. But most importantly, postindustrial ruins are seldom objects of nostalgic longing, but usually evoke feelings of catastrophe and provoke a critical attitude toward the relics of the machine age.

Quite a few scholars quote Walter Benjamin's "Theses on the Philosophy of History" to capture the way postindustrial ruins are generally perceived and valued. The ninth thesis is a meditation on a drawing by Paul Klee called "Angelus Novus," interpreted by Benjamin as the "angel of history," whose face is turned toward the past:

> Where we perceived a chain of events, he sees one single catastrophe which keeps piling wreckage upon wreckage and hurls it in front of his feet. The angel would like to stay, awaken the dead, and make whole what has been smashed. But a storm is blowing from Paradise; it has got caught in his wings with such violence that the angel can no longer close them. This storm irresistibly propels him into the future to which his back is turned, while the pile of debris before him grows skyward. The storm is what we call progress. (Benjamin 1992, 257)

In their decay, ruins unmask the modernist idea and ideal of history being a progressive, linear sequence of events as a cruel illusion. Ruins are symbols of the failed promises and broken dreams of the industrial age. They cast a critical light on the capitalist faith in a future of unlimited prosperity, as well as on the socialist hope for a fairer and more equal society. Ruins may be used to critically examine capitalist and state manifestations of power or, in other words, as political "counter-sites to forces of state violence, totalitarianism and colonial repression" (DeSilvey and Edensor 2012, 5; see also Edensor 2005a, 2005b, and 2005c).

The Protection of Destruction

If we look for examples of a critical attitude toward postindustrial sites, then Germany immediately comes to mind. After the fascist regime of the 1930s and 1940s and the Stalinist regime in East Germany after the Second World War, this country is anything but proud of its history. Here the emphasis is not on the conservation or restoration, much less the monumentalization, of derelict and decayed factories.

An excellent example of a critical attitude toward the industrial past is the Landscape Park Duisburg Nord (figure 3.4). The park site is the location of a former steelworks plant built in 1901 by the famous German industrialist August Thyssen, whose son was impressed by Hitler and claimed to have donated one million marks to the Nazi Party. Until it was closed in 1985, when an overcapacity in the European steel market had to be reduced, the plant produced millions of tons of pig iron. The decline in coal and steel production left behind an industrial wasteland of 230 hectares (570 acres), a bizarre landscape of rail beds, smokestacks, slag heaps, polluted soil, industrial ruins, and re-engineered waterways.

A citizens' action group successfully protested against the demolition of the old iron and steel works, and from 1989 to 1999 a new type of landscape park was created. This park is one of the best-known public spaces within the 80-kilometer-long corridor known as Emscher Park, the site of a unique planning initiative coordinated by the International Building Exhibition (IBA). It receives a high number of visitors: approximately 700,000 every year (Winkels and Zieling 2009, 28).

FIGURE 3.4 Landscape Park Duisburg Nord © Christa Panick. Reprinted with permission from LATZ+PARTNER.

It was not the intention of landscape architect Peter Latz, the leading designer of the park, to idealize the industrial past and turn the site into an open-air museum.[4] The park was supposed to tell a story of hard labor and, above all, of the decay of the site and the takeover by nature. Soon after the plant had been shut down, the buildings and structures became overgrown by vegetation. With over 1,800 plant and animal species, including many red-listed species, the site currently shows a very rich biodiversity. The reoccupation of the site by nature was not to be stopped but should be stimulated. To draw attention to this process, Peter Latz deliberately opted for tight patterns in the additions he made, thereby stressing the contrast between spontaneous and designed nature.

Remarkably, there are also lots of exotic plant and tree species, which traveled to the site with the iron ore. Surveying the park, ecologists found some 200 plants that are not native to northern Germany. The emergence of this unusual vegetation as a byproduct of industrial waste led Peter Latz to claim that "destruction has to be protected so that it isn't destroyed again by recultivation" (quoted in Beard 1996, 35). He considered the interplay of industrial relicts and spontaneous nature—"*Industrienatur*"—as "an archetypical dialogue between the tame and the wild" (Latz 2000, 97).[5] As Elissa Rosenberg explains, Latz recognized that the fantastic forms that resulted from the site's aberrant processes and materials "could not be created by either art or nature alone but lie somewhere in between" (Rosenberg 2009, 216).

Here, one is reminded of Georg Simmel's famous essay, "The Ruin." Simmel considered architecture to be the only art in which the great struggle between the upward-striving power of the spirit and the downward-dragging force of nature is held in balance. This unique balance breaks down and shifts in favor of nature the instant a building crumbles. A new characteristic whole emerges in the ruin, in which the hierarchy of nature and spirit is reversed. "Nature has transformed the work of art into material for her own expression, as she had previously served as material for art" (Simmel 1958, 381).[6]

Nietzsche's Trinity Realized

The reoccupation of Duisburg Nord by nature was not the only spontaneous event that occurred there. Another was the discovery of the huge 12-meter-high walls of the former ore storage bunkers as a climbers' paradise. Since 1990, the Duisburg section of the German Alpine Club has built its own "climbing garden" in the landscape park. The walls of varying degrees of steepness and the well-preserved towers are ideally suited to climbing. There is also a *via ferrata* (a fixed climbing route) created in authentic Alpine style and secured with a steel rope, which mountain climbers use when training for tours in the Alps. With over 2,000 members, the Duisburg section of the club is one of the largest, despite the fact that its climbing garden is also the club's lowest-lying training center.

In a similar vein, the Duisburg North Park Diving Club transformed the gasholder or gasometer into a large indoor diving basin center. The club members filled the gasometer with 21 million liters of rainwater and created a new underwater landscape by sinking an artificial coral reef, a ship wreck (11.5 meters long), two car wrecks, and an aircraft wreck (a Cessna). The diving gasometer is Europe's largest artificial diving pool. Water-sports enthusiasts can dive to depths of 13 meters, and the gasometer has a diameter of 45 meters.

Whereas the focus on nature reclaiming the landscape testifies to a critical attitude, the reuse of these buildings and structures by climbers and divers also reveals something of a monumental attitude. This attitude is most evident in the conversion of the former halls of industry into locations for theaters, concerts, conferences, and conventions. In this regard, Duisburg Nord has been a major inspiration for the "conservation through development" of the Western Gas Factory.

Duisburg Nord owes its monumental character to a large extent to the gigantic size of the industrial relics. As Judith Stilgenbauer explains, to Latz, "the abandoned colossuses of steel production also spoke a language of the sublime" (Stilgenbauer 2005, 7). In Latz's own words, "The blast furnace is not only an old furnace, it is a menacing dragon rising above frightened man, and it is also a mountain top used by climbers, rising above its surroundings. The former ore bunkers become the rock faces of a mountain scenery" (Latz 2001, 151).

In addition to a monumental attitude, one can detect an antiquarian attitude here, insofar as the park is not only about reusing but also about remembering and respecting important historical values. Although Latz wanted the sense of decay and depletion to remain intact, Duisburg Nord still serves as a kind of open-air museum that shows visitors important aspects of the history of modern steel and iron industry. The park is part of the European Route of Industrial Heritage (ERIH), a network of the most important industrial heritage sites in Europe.[7] The—virtual—main route is built by the so-called Anchor Points, the milestones of European industrial heritage that are the most historically important and attractive for visitors. Today there are eighty-two Anchor Points—they include not only Duisburg Nord but also Geevor Tin Mine and Blegny Mine, one of the four Walloon mining sites mentioned earlier.

Unlike all the previous examples of postindustrial sites, Landscape Park Duisburg Nord presents a design in which all three of Nietzsche's forms of history can be identified. As mentioned by Vollmer and Berke (2006, 60), the park "is not only a gigantic monument, but also an open-air museum, a free climbing and scuba-diving venue, and an illuminated work of art." It is also, I would add, a unique nature park.

Final Thoughts

According to Nietzsche, each of the three uses of history proves advantageous to life: the antiquarian, by inspiring pride in his origins and cultivating an attitude of reverence for the past of his people; the monumental, by highlighting humankind's greatest achievements and providing us with suitable models for emulation; and the critical, by equipping us with the tools to critically reassess the present and to negate the past when necessary.

But each of these uses of history may deteriorate into a threat to life when it becomes too powerful and begins to dominate the other two. The antiquarian is always in danger of mummifying life and crippling the active person; the monumental is constantly at risk of blurring the line between history and fiction, on the one hand, and losing its function as antidote to resignation, on the other; and, finally, the critical may go too far in its denial and destruction of the past, thereby ultimately losing the opportunity to achieve a more just and less oppressive future.

Nietzsche's ideal is that of a balance, in which the antiquarian, the monumental, and the critical approaches to history may complement and correct each other. The enormous appreciation by international experts and the general public of Landscape Park Duisburg Nord, where such a balance seems to be achieved, offers testimony of the value and validity of Nietzsche's ideal.

Notes

1. Nietzsche borrowed this metaphor from the historian Johan Gustav Droysen, who in his 1868 book *Grundriss der Historik* condemned historians a la von Ranke for their "eunuchische Ojektivität."

2. The translations of Nietzsche's text are based on Ian Johnston (https://records. viu.ca/~Johnstoi/nietzsche/history.htm) and Adrian Collins (http://www.gutenberg.org/ files/38226/38226.txt).

3. The tallest building is the gasholder. At the time of its construction in 1903, it was the largest gasholder in Europe, with a capacity of 100,000 cubic meters. But nowadays the height of the structure is only 15 meters, one-quarter of its original height.

4. Latz was the recipient of the Grande Medaille d'Urbanisme from the Académie d'Architecture in Paris (2001), the first European Prize for Landscape Architecture (2002), the EDRA Places Award (2005), and the Green Good Design Award (2009).

5. "Walking through the park with Latz, I could feel a melting away in my mind of the distinction between what is natural and what is artificial" (Lubow 2004).

6. See Gross (2009) for an account of ruins and restorations inspired by Simmel.

7. See www.erih.net.

References

Beard, Peter. 1996. "Peter Latz, Poet of Pollution." *Blueprint* 130: 28–37.

Belvedere Memorandum. 1999. "A Policy Document Examining the Relationship between Cultural History and Spatial Planning." The Hague: VNG Publishers.

Benjamin, Walter. 1992. "Theses on the Philosophy of History." In *Walter Benjamin: Illuminations*, edited and introduced by Hannah Arendt, 253–264. New York: Harcourt, Brace and World.

Benjamin, Walter. 1999. "The Return of the Flaneur." In *Walter Benjamin: Selected Writings 1927-1934*, edited by Michael W. Jennings, Howard Eiland, and Gary Smith, 262–267. Cambridge, MA: Harvard University Press.

Benjamin, Walter. 2005. "Poverty and Experience." In *Walter Benjamin: Selected Writings 1931-1934*, edited by Michael W. Jennings, 731–744. Cambridge, MA: Harvard University Press.

Briante, Susan Carol. 2006. "American Ruins: Nostalgia, Amnesia and Blitzkrieg Bop." PhD diss., University of Texas, Austin.

DeSilvey, Caitlin, and Tim Edensor. 2013. "Reckoning with Ruins." *Progress in Human Geography* 37 (4): 465–485.

Edensor, Tim. 2005a. "The Ghost of Industrial Ruins: Ordering and Disordering Memory in Excessive Space." *Environmental Planning D: Society and Space* 23: 829–849.

Edensor, Tim. 2005b. "Waste Matter: The Debris of Industrial Ruins and the Disordering of the Material World." *Journal of Material Culture* 10 (3): 311–332.

Edensor, Tim. 2005c. *Industrial Ruins: Space, Aesthetics and Materiality*. Oxford and New York: Berg.

Gamboni, Dario. 1997. *The Destruction of Art. Iconoclasm and Vandalism since the French Revolution*. London: Reaktion Books.

Goethe, Wolfgang. *Faust, Part I*. Translated by George Madison Priest. The Alchemy Website. Levity.com. http://www.levity.com/alchemy/faust04.html.

Gross, Matthias. 2009. "Further Towards a Continuum Between Nativism and Cosmopolitanism." In *New Visions of Nature. Complexity and Authenticity*, edited by Martin Drenten, Jozef Keulartz, and James Proctor, 257–263. Dordrecht: Springer.

Hardy, Hugh. 2005. "The Romance of Abandonment: Industrial Parks." *Places* 17 (3): 32–37.

Higgs, Eric. 2003. *Nature by Design*. Cambridge MA: MIT Press.

Kant, Immanuel. 1963. *Kritik der Urteilskraft*. Stuttgart: Reclam.

Latz, Peter. 2000. "The Idea of Making Time Visible." *Topos* 33: 94–99.

Latz, Peter. 2001. "Landscape Park Duisburg-Nord: The Metamorphosis of an Industrial Site." In *Manufactured Sites. Rethinking the Post-Industrial Landscape*, edited by Niall Kirkwood, 150–161. New York: Taylor & Francis.

Lubow, Arthur. 2004. "The Anti-Olmsted." *New York Times*, May 16.

Nash, Roderick. 1982. *Wilderness and the American Mind*. New Haven, CT: Yale University Press.

Nietzsche, Friedrich. 1954. *Werke in drei Bänden*, Band 1, München: Carl Hanser Verlag.

Olwig, Kenneth. 1996. "Reinventing Common Nature: Yosemite and Mt. Rushmore." In *Uncommon Ground: Rethinking the Human Place in Nature*, edited by William Cronon, 379–408. New York: W. W. Norton.

Philips, Sarah. 2007. "Who Needs a Field to Have a Festival?" *The Guardian*, May 15.

Pickett, S. T. A., and V. Thomas Parker. 1994. "Editorial: Avoiding the Old Pitfalls: Opportunities in a New Discipline." *Restoration Ecology* 2 (2): 75–79.

Rosenberg, Elissa. 2009. "Gardens, Landscape, Nature: Duisburg-Nord, Germany." In *The Hand and the Soul: Aesthetics and Ethics in Architecture and Art*, edited by Sanda Iliescu, 209–230. Charlottesville: University of Virginia.

Simmel, Georg. 1958. "Two Essays: The Handle, and The Ruin." *Hudson Review* 11 (3): 379–385.

Sinclair, Mark. 2004. "Nietzsche and the Problem of History." *Richmond Journal of Philosophy* 8: 1–6.

Stilgenbauer, Judith. 2005. "Landschaftspark Duisburg Nord." *Places* 17 (3): 6–9.

US National Research Council. 1992. *Restoration of Aquatic Ecosystems*. Washington, DC: National Academy Press.

Vollmer, M., and W. Berke. 2006. *Ruhr Picturebook. Industrial Heritage: New Life in Old Buildings*. Essen: Klartext Verlag.

Wallington, Tabatha. J., Richard J. Hobbs, and Susan A. Moore. 2005. "Implications of Current Ecological Thinking for Biodiversity Conservation: A Review of the Salient Issues." *Ecology and Society* 10 (1): 15. http://www.ecologyandsociety.org/vol10/iss1/art15/.

Winkels, Ralf, and Günter Zieling. 2009. *Landschafstpark Duisburg-Nord. Vom Eisenkochtopf zum Erlebnispark*. Duisburg: Mercator-Verlag.

CHAPTER 4 | Nature and Our Sense of Loss

ALAN HOLLAND

Introduction

In the final chapter of his book on meaning, David Cooper refers us to the heroine of Michael Ondaatje's novel *Anil's Ghost*, who is no longer able to believe that "meaning allowed a person a door to escape grief and fear." He comments that this is a belief that "most of us are reluctant to abandon" (2003, 126). In what follows I propose to put a reverse spin on this belief and advance the hypothesis that grief at any rate—or, more generally, our sense of loss—is the price we pay for meaning.[1] Hence meaning, rather than being a way of escape from grief, is precisely what opens the door to grief and, more generally, to our sense of loss. Stated crudely, the contention is this: that the more meaningful our lives become, the more we stand to lose. So meaning, rather than being the means through which we can escape loss, is precisely what makes us vulnerable to loss. But, as we shall see, the fact that meaning is not a way of escape from loss in no way entails that it does not have a vital role to play in our attempts to come to terms with loss. In fact, this "dance" between meaning and loss, we might say, pretty well epitomizes the human condition.

My specific aim is to suggest that a fruitful way to understand the kinds of restoration project with which this volume is concerned is in terms of just such a dance between meaning and loss. For why are we moved to undertake restoration projects in the first place? An initial suggestion is that the very project of restoration is motivated by a felt need to recover our composure in the dance. We look to restoration precisely because of a sense that something is awry, that some damage has occurred that needs to be made good, that in some sense we have lost our balance. And if someone should ask, "What exactly do we think we have lost, and what exactly is it that we are attempting to restore?," this approach affords a simple and single answer: meaning. An alternative answer that has commonly been proffered is value, and in particular, natural or intrinsic value. But this response is fraught with difficulties, aired most recently and with particular force by Eric Katz (2012). And it faces particular difficulties in the case of "layered landscapes," where culture and nature intermingle. For on this alternative analysis, cultural and natural values tend to be at odds: any advancing of cultural values will be seen as occurring "at the expense of" natural value. The advantage of looking at such situations in terms of meaning is that, inasmuch as they involve both natural and cultural meanings, these are not necessarily viewed as being at odds. Indeed, we might even frame as a shorthand objective for many such restoration projects the devising of a state of affairs in which cultural and natural meanings mutually reinforce one another.

In what follows, I shall first present an anatomy of loss, and attempt to show in more detail how it connects with meaning. I shall then present an account of the kinds of loss, and of meaning, that are to be met with in nature. Finally, I intend to show how the "meanings" approach can be deployed to deal with the interplay of culture and nature that characterizes what we are here referring to as "layered landscapes."

Meaning and Loss: Some Conceptual Groundwork

I

We can develop the position I want to sketch here further by considering and contrasting it with the outlook on nature that was characteristic of the ancient Stoics. For nature was above all their "bag," so to speak. "What do I want?" asks Epictetus rhetorically. And he replies, "To understand nature and follow her" (Epictetus 1995, 304, Handbook 49). Or again, as Seneca says in his fifth letter to Lucilius: "Our motto, as everyone knows, is to live in conformity with nature" (Seneca 1969, 37). But what, exactly, does this entail? We learn more from letter nine, in which Seneca enthusiastically endorses the words and actions of a certain Stilbo.[2] This Stilbo, when his home town was captured and ransacked by Demetrius (known, not surprisingly, as Demetrius the Sacker of Cities), emerges from the ruins—his city, his home, his belongings all gone, his wife and children dead—and is asked by Demetrius whether he has lost anything. He replies: "I have all my valuables with me"—literally, "all my goods are with me" (Seneca 1969, 52). What an active and courageous man, enthuses Seneca, victorious over the very victory of the enemy, who says in effect "I have lost nothing" (1969, 52).

What has this to do with nature? Well at its simplest we can say that the Stoics looked to understand and "follow" nature as a way of making themselves invulnerable and, in particular, immune to loss. We get some inkling of how this is supposed to work from an everyday example offered by Epictetus:

> If you are going out for a bath, put before your mind what commonly happens at baths: some people splashing you, some people jostling, others being abusive, and others stealing. So you will undertake this action more securely if you say to yourself, "I want to have a bath and also to keep my choice in harmony with nature" . . . So, if anything gets in your way when you are having your bath, you will be ready to say, "I wanted not only to have a bath but also to keep my choice in harmony with nature; and I shall not keep it so if I get angry." (Epictetus 1995, 288–289, Handbook 4)

More chilling perhaps is this: "If you kiss your child or your wife, say to yourself that it is a human being that you are kissing; and then you will not be disturbed if either of them dies" (Epictetus 1995, 288, Handbook 3). We find a similar sentiment in Seneca letter 104:

> [T]he falling of the leaves is not difficult to bear, since they grow again, and it is no more hard to bear the loss of those whom you love . . . for even if they do not grow again they are replaced. 'But their successors will never be quite the same.' No, and neither will you. (Seneca 1969, 187)

What seems evident from these and similar remarks is that the Stoics understood their injunction to follow nature in something very close to what Holmes Rolston (1979, 25–30) identifies as the "tutorial sense": in working out how to live their lives, they took lessons from nature.

What we also see here clearly is the tendency that Bernard Williams (1985, 197) has described as typical of ancient thought—namely, "the desire to reduce life's exposure to luck." For the Stoics this was a matter of reducing our dependency on "externals"—"things that are not up to us"—to a minimum. In fact, Williams himself is rather severe on the Stoics for adopting this attitude. But this strikes me as a mite unfair, given that these were people for whom there was so little that could be assured, so little that could be relied upon. (We shall return to this point later.)

Reference to the Stoic attitude affords a salutary reminder of how others might view these matters, but our specific purpose in setting out the Stoic view is to offer a counterpoint to the alternative perspective that we shall now attempt to articulate, and whose motto (with apologies to Socrates) might be stated thus: the invulnerable life is not worth living.

II

In its most general formulation, the main claim I want to advance is that there is some correlation—indeed some kind of conceptual correlation—between the meaning that we find in things and our sense of loss when they are no longer available to us. On the basis of this claim, together with the evident sense of actual or imminent loss that assails us when we reflect on the current state of the natural world,[3] it will be argued that nature's importance lies, above all, in the meanings to be found there, and in the meaningful engagements that nature affords, and that if we fail to recognize this fact, we sell nature short. A cautious version of the claimed correlation between meaning and loss would be that degree of loss felt is some function of degree of meaning. The bald, and bold, linear claim would be that the more meaning we find in things, the greater our vulnerability to loss.

But the claim needs to be understood with some care. For at first blush one might respond (Stoically) that if meaning makes us vulnerable to loss, then the less meaning we find the better. But here the distinction between loss and vulnerability to loss is crucial. Loss remains all it ever was—something we try to avoid if we possibly can; though even here, as we shall see, some forms of clinging on are inappropriate, and we often have to learn when to let go. But just now the thought is that it is precisely because loss is what it is that vulnerability to loss generates the meaning that it does.

Examples, or illustrations, of loss and our vulnerability to loss and their connection to meaning are—sadly—only too easy to find. If you have held in your hands the body of a newly dead kitten, already beginning to stiffen and no longer able to exhibit that liquid motion so characteristic of the kind, you will know what I mean. Our previous interactions were so full of meaning—hopefully on both sides—that the sense of loss is all the more keenly felt. In opting to bring a kitten into our lives, into our family, we increased our vulnerability to loss. That, in a nutshell, is one example of the nexus of relations that I believe can, in principle, be broadened out to encompass the whole of our relations to nature.

III

Clearly, in our attempt to characterize loss, there are many more distinctions to be drawn and nuances to be observed; here I shall mention just one or two of them. For one thing we are referring here to a loss that is tragic—in part because it is a loss of something irreplaceable. And losses are of a different order, and perhaps, too, of a different quality, depending on whether they involve the loss of something that is (i) recoverable (in principle)—such as the umbrella left on a train; (ii) irrecoverable but replaceable—such as the umbrella inadvertently tossed into the incinerator; or (iii) neither recoverable nor replaceable—such as a species. The distinction between the replaceable and the irreplaceable is one reason why conservation never should, indeed never can, truly put things back. The reason is that such a view entails treating what is irreplaceable as replaceable, or even recoverable. But so far as the connection with meaning is concerned, there is probably some continuity between the different contexts in which we speak of loss. "I was quite attached to that umbrella," we might say: it had come to mean something to us, so that we feel its loss more keenly.

Also, the example of the kitten happens to depict a personal loss, but loss can be impersonal too. We come upon a blackbird whose foot had become entangled in some baler twine. It had been unable to escape and now hangs limp, its throat that once throbbed in song now stilled. There is loss here, too, impersonal loss—or at least not "our" loss. One less voice in the dawn chorus, at best, a one-parent family left behind or perhaps orphaned nestlings destined to die. And this points to a difference from the case of the kitten. There, the sense of loss was tied to an already existing relationship, now severed. In the case of the blackbird there was no preexisting relationship. Now, it is true that meanings tend to reside in what I have elsewhere called a nexus of relations—meaningful relations (Holland 2012). ("Tend to," in light of one's possible attachment to an umbrella, where it may not seem appropriate to speak of a "relationship"; compare Aristotle's remark that one "cannot be friends with a bottle of wine.") But, it seems to me, the relations do not have to be ones in which we are personally involved for them to generate a sense of loss—a sense that meaning has been sucked from the world. The blackbird himself belonged to a nexus of relationships, now severed; hence the orphaned nestlings. However, this is not yet to explain the sense of loss experienced in this case. Orphaned nestlings are probably the rule rather than the exception, and we could not possibly absorb loss of such magnitude and still retain the will to live. True, actual encounters set some limit to what we have to absorb, but there are probably other elements in the situation as described that are relevant. One is the human involvement in the loss. Another is the "senseless" character of the loss. Had the blackbird simply fallen prey to some predator, for example, we might have felt sad, but might not have felt the sense of loss in the same way or to the same extent. (The existence of such "senseless loss" was always among the more powerful objections to the design argument for the existence of God.)

More important, perhaps, is the fact that examples of shared or common loss are equally, and regrettably, only too easy to find. On October 21, 1966, it took just five minutes for the coal tip above Aberfan in Wales to slide down the mountain and engulf a farm, several houses, and a school. One hundred and sixteen children died, along with twenty-eight adults. The reverberations of the disaster are felt even now—and felt indeed worldwide. The children were described as the "lost generation"—a hole in the fabric that was Wales. Similar examples may be cited from the United States.[4] Reverberations are still felt from a disaster that struck the small town of New London, Texas, on March 18, 1937, when a spark ignited a cloud of natural gas that was escaping from a faulty heating system at the London Consolidated School. Around 300 people died, most of them children. "How does a community recover from such a loss?" asks Sarah Mosle (2012) who writes about the event in the *New York Times Magazine*. She refers to recovery, not, of course, of what has been lost, but of the community that has directly experienced the loss, and, in doing so, highlights another feature of the dance between meaning and loss—how loss itself can radically undermine meaning. Families who undergo a tragic loss—the death of a child perhaps—are not always brought together by the experience; they are sometimes torn apart. Nor, again, can the boundaries of the relevant community—the community that "experiences" the loss—be delineated: schoolchildren as far afield as Brazil and Poland sent letters of sympathy.

IV

Another aspect of most of the examples considered so far is their focus on the young. And loss of the young, invariably an untimely loss, almost always has a particular poignancy. Very crudely, it is the loss of a future rather than the loss of a past. To this distinction some words of Nozick seem particularly pertinent:

> The young live in each of the futures open to them. The poignancy of grow-
> ing older does not lie in one's particular path being less satisfying or good
> than it promised earlier to be—the path may turn out to be all one thought.
> It lies in traveling only one (or two, or three) of those paths. . . . When all the
> possibilities were yet still before us, it felt to us as if we would do them all.
> (Nozick 1981, 596)

As Mosle (2012) puts it, "[T]he incomprehensible horror and grief at the death of a child is also for the milestones not reached, the moments unshared . . . it's for the lives unlived we mourn." And although those lives, had they been lived, would have had just one trajectory, unlived, they remain open-ended (Nozick's point).

On the other hand, when our sixteen-year-old cat goes, we shall miss the old boy terribly. But this appears to be a loss of a different kind or, at any rate, a different quality. If anything, it is a loss that enhances meaning rather than undermining it: though a reminder of mortality, it is "timely." And were he to have proved immortal, his life would not have been one whit more meaningful. (For similar remarks comparing the beauty of Helen, whose face "launched a thousand ships," with that of Aphrodite, see Holland 2011, 1.) Thus, for those humans who complete their three-score years and ten, the memorial service is often an occasion for celebration. The reasons for this are various. For example, the old, both human and nonhuman, are survivors in the face of vicissitudes, who themselves bear the marks of many meaningful engagements. They are meanings realized rather than meanings foreclosed. But there is still loss: we shall "miss" them, and the sense of their absence will linger on. The Welsh priest-poet R. S. Thomas expresses this as well as any:

> She left me . . .
> . . . Impalpable,
> Invisible, she comes
> to me still . . .
> There is a tremor
> of light, as of a bird crossing
> the sun's path, and I look

up in recognition
of a presence in absence. (Rogers 2006, 297)

At the same time, these are not losses we should wish to prevent; they are the price we pay for our meanings, and are glad to pay.

Meaning and Loss in Nature

V

A feature of the examples just discussed is the role that nature itself plays in setting the parameters: of who is "old," who is "young," which of our expectations are appropriate, which are unrealistic, and so forth. I hope I am not misappropriating Charles Taylor's (1992, 35–41) notion of a "horizon of significance" therefore, if I appropriate it to suggest that nature's role in the search for meanings in our own lives is in part akin to a horizon of significance.[5] And this is very different from the tutorial sense to which the Stoics subscribed. In this sense, nature is the measure of all things, one might say—or at least of most of them. But if nature sets the parameters of significance, this is not yet to establish that nature itself has meanings. Nor does it exhaust the meaningful potential of the interplay between cultural and natural horizons, which will be explored later.

We certainly do speak of loss in connection with nature. First, and most obviously, the loss of biodiversity comes to mind. Equally obviously, this is hardly to be thought of as something we have simply mislaid. Oliver Rackham fills in some of the detail in this way:

> There are four kinds of loss. There is loss of beauty, especially that exquisite beauty of the small and complex and unexpected . . . There is loss of freedom . . . There is loss of historic vegetation and wildlife, most of which once lost is gone forever . . . In this book I am specially concerned with the loss of meaning. The landscape is a record of our roots and the growth of civilization. Each individual historic wood, heath etc. is uniquely different from every other, and each has something to tell us. (Rackham 1986, 25–26)

So this is countryside rather than "nature," if you want to be pedantic about it, but extrapolation is not difficult. Think of the fossil record or, more fundamentally, of what Erwin Schroedinger ([1944] 1992, 21) calls the "code-script" that is written into every single living organism; we are only just beginning to understand "what it has to tell us."

But Schroedinger also has something else to say that is equally important and equally pertinent to our topic. If nature teaches us anything, it is that loss—as they say about the poor—is always with us. And this is a fact that has its basis in the laws of physics, in particular the "natural tendency of things to approach the chaotic state" (1992, 73). It seems reasonable to assume that meaning presupposes some degree of order, so that a state of chaos is devoid of meaning—a state of absolute loss in which there is nothing more to lose. Effectively, what we have called the dance between meaning and loss reflects what is, at this more basic level, a dance between negative entropy and entropy. Thanks in good measure to the hereditary mechanism, life has the ability not exactly to defy this tendency but at least to delay it. Thus "the device by which an organism maintains itself stationary at a fairly high level of orderliness ... really consists in sucking orderliness from its environment" (73). Let us just say, for the moment, that these observations seem to indicate that restoration projects conceived as some form of making good, or making up for, loss would be misconceived. They had better be conceived as some form of coming to terms with loss.

It may well be true, if not obvious, as W. G. Hoskins (1955, 17) remarks, that "poets make the best topographers." It is both true and obvious that they afford numerous avowals of the sense of loss that interests us, and of the correspondingly copious meanings present in nature.[6] We might add in passing that if the advice we need is how to come to terms with loss, then poets probably also make better advisers than policymakers, who must always present themselves, it seems, as somehow "making things better."

"What would the world be, once bereft / Of wet and of wilderness?" asked Gerard Manley Hopkins (1953, 51) in his poem "Inversnaid," addressed to a "burn," or stream, of that name. If there is ambiguity here as to whether it is we, or the world, that would be bereft (i.e., experience loss), there is no ambiguity about the "lament" that the Northamptonshire poet John Clare puts into the mouth of a piece of land he knew as "Swordy Well":

And me they turned me inside out
For sand and grit and stones
And turned my old green hills about
And pickt my very bones. (Clare 1984, 148)

Even R. S. Thomas, who had trouble finding meaning anywhere—and thought his God to be "that great absence In our lives, the empty silence Within" (from "Via Negativa," quoted in Rogers 2006, 255)— experienced a moment when he came upon a copse that was alive with goldcrests and was transfixed: "[F]or a timeless moment the birds thronged me, filigreeing me with shadow, moving to an immemorial rhythm on their way south" (from "A Thicket in Lleyn," quoted in Rogers 2006, 307). I pause only to note how important is the transience of this moment to its meaning. Whether one takes the idea that nature itself can undergo loss literally, or whether one has to understand this as metaphor, appears a moot point. But I see no reason to resist the literal interpretation, even though an entity that is incapable of sensitivity cannot actually experience a sense of loss. Forests, wetlands, rivers, however, can lose one or more of their characteristic denizens—be they goshawk, spider, or otter—and, for a while at least, their meaning seems diminished thereby.

VI

How far one can, or even must, rest the evidence for meanings in nature on personal testimony is unclear. One thing, though, does seem clear. Thus far we have spoken of loss mostly in relation to ourselves, our families, our community, to our society perhaps. But if it is legitimate to speak of meanings in nature, then what we might call the "reference community" that undergoes the loss, or experiences the sense of loss, will be correspondingly wider, and must likely include past, present, and future generations.

Furthermore, if we recognize future generations among the potential "community of losers," so to speak, we now glimpse another form of loss that is distinct from those that have already been mentioned. Peter Railton (2003, 188) refers to it in this way: "It seems reasonable to say that an individual can experience a loss in being alienated from nature, for example, without assuming he was ever in communion with it, much as we say it is a loss for someone never to receive an education or never to appreciate music." Here, crucially, we are thinking not of the foreclosure of something that has already started but the foreclosure of something that has not even begun. And if we consider climate change, for example, described as "the biggest problem facing humanity," it is arguable that it is just the prospect of loss of this last kind that we have identified that so exercises us. And it exercises us just insofar as we think of ourselves as forming a community with future (and past) generations, sharing values in common and sharing, above all, our sense of loss. It is precisely this potential "community of losers" toward whom Bill McKibben (1990, 55) gestures when he writes that "a child born now will never know a natural summer, a natural autumn, winter, or spring"—a sentiment further clarified by the remark that "the *meaning* of the wind, the sun, the rain—of nature—has already changed" (44).

Distinct again is a related, though quieter, form of loss whose identification we owe to another poet—this time Edward Thomas. It is succinctly captured in the title of his poem "First known when lost," whose first stanza runs:

> I never had noticed it until
> 'Twas gone,—the narrow copse
> Where now the woodman lops
> The last of the willows with his bill (Thomas 2003).

This is not the loss of something we shall never experience but the loss of something we have experienced but whose meanings we failed to appreciate until it was lost.

But there is more, if we can build again on some of Railton's further observations. Noting that "ethical philosophers have continued to speak of the meaning of life in surprisingly private terms," he suggests that there is a "worthwhile analogy between meaning in lives and meaning in language" (2003, 185). His point is that just as meaning in language has to be something shared, something embedded indeed in a set of social and historical practices, so also "[a] system of available, shared meanings would seem to be a precondition for sustaining the meaningfulness of individual lives" (187). What this adds is that we should not think of the meanings that are so important to us in "private" terms but as things that are communal and shared; which further entails, as I understand it, that they occupy an intersubjective critical space. What this means in turn is that the Humpty Dumpty theory of meaning (a word "means just what I choose it to mean"[7]) applies no more to meaning in our lives than to meaning in language. The meanings that we claim to find are open to critical scrutiny.

VII

To conclude this section of the chapter, and draw together some of our reflections so far, I shall attempt a preliminary characterization of the notion of meaning that I believe can be the basis for the policy applications that are the focus of discussion in the third section. I suggest that it has two elements.

First is the connection with loss that I have been at pains to articulate. What this attempts to capture is a particular quality of the meanings that make our lives worth living, and that we often find in our engagements with nature—what I can only call their "visceral" character.

But second, I believe this to be coupled with "opportunities for understanding." In other words, it is not clear to me that there is merely an "analogy" between meaning in language and meaning in life. Underlying both, it might be argued, is the notion of understanding. Thus, meaningful relations are, among other things, those that enhance our understanding. But note that where there can be understanding, there can also be misunderstanding. Hence, and as a corollary, it might be argued that we are not necessarily, individually at least, the final arbiters of nature's meanings. Our understandings must always be open to the possibility of "correction."

Meanings, therefore, can be viewed as combining both visceral and cognitive elements; they might be described as forms of understanding that we cannot bear to be without, and without at least some of which life is not worth living.

Meaning, Loss, and Restoration in Layered Landscapes

VIII

In light of our discussion so far, what are the prospects for making meanings a more central focus for environmental policy in general, and for the restoration of layered landscapes in particular? If the connection between meaning and loss that has been argued for here has any foundation, then one can at least point out that loss and the threat of loss are great mobilizers of concern. Following the school tragedies referred to earlier, for example, Sarah Mosle (2012) speaks of the "galvanizing conversations" that ensued. Within days of the disaster in New London, the legislators had decreed that a "malodorant" be added to natural gas.

But aren't meanings, private, slippery, subjective things? How can they provide a basis for public policy? We have already prepared the way for a response. In the first place, meanings are not private and slippery, but public and intersubjective—matters for critical scrutiny. And against the charge that meanings are "subjective" I am inclined to mount a Humean defense. We need to distinguish clearly between the subjective in the sense of the personal or idiosyncratic, and the subjective in the sense of the experienced. For it seems to me that the experienced response of loss is, or is capable of being, pretty well universal. And another reason for dwelling on the case of the Stoics is to suggest that in some fundamental way, they are evidence for, rather than evidence against this universality. We can perfectly well understand their quest for invulnerability, and we can see it not as evidence that their instincts were different from ours but that their situation was.

IX

In order to see more clearly how the notions of loss and meaning might be deployed in the case of layered landscapes, let us first consider a small-scale but instructive example of how one individual sought to honor both cultural and natural meanings in the aftermath of the First World War—the so-called Great War.

Sir Walter Newman Flower (1945, 69) writes of how, after the 1914–1918 war had ended, he decided that he "would make a patch of remembrance in flowers—flowers that would go on and on, as one Summer succeeded another—to those who died that we should retain our gardens in our own keeping." In the Autumn of 1919, he went out to the battlefields, which he found "coloured with flowers," to gather seeds: "I gathered a large packet of poppy seed from the trenches of the Somme ... In Fricourt I found some poppies that had grown round a patch of bandages stained russet now with blood, and I carefully took their seed ... In what remained of Delville Wood I found these lanky blue chicory flowers ... I passed on to Vimy Ridge, and there in the untouched trenches the wild antirrhinum was flowering as if in rejoicing that War had departed" (69–70). In consequence, "My War Garden is a pageant of scarlet and blue as I write [sc. 1945], with the Vimy Ridge yellow antirrhinums as an undergrowth, and the scarlet-eyed creeping flowers from Trones Wood, and a great flood of red Somme poppies sweeping over the whole" (71).

Several features of this account bear remark, and bear, further, on how we might approach restoration projects involving layered landscapes. First, though an act of remembrance might seem at first sight to be very different from the project of restoration, they have this feature in common: both are prompted by, and are a response to, loss. From his description we see clearly how this act of remembrance functions as a way that Sir Walter has found of acknowledging and coming to terms with loss. So it is with restoration, which, we have argued, is to be seen precisely as a way of responding to, and coming to terms with loss.

But secondly, there is, of course, a more specific connection. What Sir Walter's act of remembrance commemorates is among the most painful cultural acts of which humans are capable—war. And among the layered landscapes with whose restoration this volume is concerned are precisely those that bear the marks of war.[8] What is important to note here is that Sir Walter does not in any way seek to mask or obscure the pain: on the contrary, he carefully gathers seed from poppies that had grown around bandages "stained russet with blood." Thus, he picks up the threads, and makes a meaningful fabric out of them. Just so, what is being urged here is that restoration projects should seek to gather up the significant residues of a site, however painful, and rebuild their meanings. They might even follow Newman Flower's lead and begin ecological restoration with surviving remnants or upstart colonizers. But the similarities do not end there: they extend to the *way* in which both remembrance and restoration respond to loss.

For, third, we may be struck by how this act of remembrance functions as an act of honoring both cultural and natural meanings. The garden that Sir Walter creates is a token of those (culturally created) gardens kept safe by the sacrifice of those who fell. At the same time, it is populated by plants naturally occurring at the site of their falling. It can be argued that restoration, too, should be seen as just such an act of honoring the cultural and natural meanings that it aims to address.

Fourth, we see how the act is not only expressive of concern but also a focus of continuing attention. The act of remembrance does not simply dwell on the past but has continued meaning in Sir Walter's own life. He commits himself, in other words, not so much to an act of remembrance as to a life of remembrance. Likewise, it can be argued, restoration projects should not simply look backward but should aim to have continuing relevance and meaning in people's lives.

Fifth, we see how both natural and cultural meanings receive their due, not separately but intertwined in a way that enables each to enhance the other. It is just such a prospect that seems within reach of those attempting the sensitive restoration of layered landscapes, and in the next section we shall briefly explore one way in which this mutual enhancement might be achieved.

Sixth, we note the parallel importance of historical continuity in both cases. The flowers in Sir Walter's "little quiet corner" are the direct descendants of the flowers from the trenches. Likewise, restoration projects will manifest varieties of historical continuity—or else must, presumably, forfeit their title of "restoration" project. But this by no means exhausts the role of history. It is only by understanding both the ecological and cultural history of a place that we understand how it has come to be as it is. Without this history we would be blind to the meanings that it represents, and hence unable to rebuild those meanings, which, we have argued, is what restoration should aim to do.

But finally, all this is not to say that there is only one way of (re)building meanings. For example, Newman Flower kept his patch carefully weeded so that "no vagrant wild flower" would come in and "assume a glory they have never earned" (1945, 70). Others may feel this detracts from rather than enhances meaning.

X

The "Great War" brought terrible loss in its wake. We have just seen how one individual set about addressing this loss. I have suggested that restoration projects, too, are to be seen as attempts to come to terms with loss, and hence that Newman Flower's exercise in remembrance may have much to teach us. I want now to suggest, in particular, that a key element in the effectiveness of the act of remembrance lies in the contrasting significance that attaches to individual lives in the natural and cultural domains, respectively. Essentially, as Tennyson wrote, nature is "so careless of the single life" ([1850] 2007, lv). In culture, on the other hand, we attach supreme importance to the individual. Hence the importance attached to the "loss" of an individual in the two domains is very different.

We have seen how the Stoics in effect sought to bring solace by assimilating the two domains. They invite us to regard the death of our spouse or our child as we might regard the falling of leaves from a tree. Now, in cultures where human life is cheap, where disease, famine, and early death are rife, this is quite possibly an effective strategy. In our contemporary culture, however, this is no longer something we can contemplate. War is terrible precisely because, among other things, it is a cultural act in which individual lives are treated as of no more account than they are in the natural world. It is for this reason that it joins death, famine, and—on one interpretation—disease, as one of the four horsemen of the apocalypse (Rev. 6).

But it is possible to view nature's indifference to the individual in another, and altogether more positive, light. For it is precisely because the identity of the particular natural individual is a matter of indifference that a succession of natural individuals can symbolize perpetuity. And this is exactly how Newman Flower sees it when he speaks of making a patch of remembrance in flowers—"flowers that would go on and on, as one Summer succeeded another." Thus it is exactly the "carelessness of the individual" that enables the poppies and antirrhinums, individually short-lived, to symbolize perpetuity and thus make a "patch of remembrance." And historical continuity plays its part because later populations of flowers are descendants of earlier ones and, in this case, of some significant original population. This is one way then in which the mutual enhancement of cultural and natural meanings is achieved. And the restored plot, or patch of remembrance, achieves a meaning richer than that of any stone monument (which is, of course, another way of symbolizing endurance) because it is alive and dynamic. It develops a life of its own, and this is one reason why, unlike Sir Walter, we might welcome the "vagrant wild flowers" that come along; they are nature's own unbidden contribution, so to speak.

XI

An alternative to the approach outlined here is to see restoration projects as an exercise in environmental ethics aimed at preserving or restoring value, intrinsic or otherwise. Hence they constitute not so much a visceral response to loss as an ethical call to duty. We have already noted how this approach tends to set the claims of nature and of culture at odds with one another, at the same time giving little by way of guidance as to how these tensions are to be resolved. (For further critical comment, see Marion Hourdequin, chap. 2 in this volume.)

But in any event the claim that nature makes ethical demands on us ultimately proves hard to vindicate: it tends to rely on appeals to the "interests" of natural beings, or to the value of their "flourishing." But if the Stoics can be criticized for making human morality dance to the tune of nature, then the environmental ethicists can be criticized for making nature dance to the tune of human morality.

So far as interests are concerned, it would be difficult to improve on what Bernard Williams has written in this regard:

The idea of ascribing interests to species, natural phenomena and so on, as a way of making sense of our concern for these things, is part of a project of trying to extend into nature our concerns for each other, by moralising our relations to nature. I suspect, however, that this is to look in exactly the wrong direction. If we are to understand these things, we need to look to our ideas of nature itself, and to ways in which it precisely lies outside the domestication of our relations to each other. (Williams 1995, 237)

So far as flourishing is concerned, we need to think long and hard about how minimal is the flourishing that nature permits before we pronounce that the value of nature lies in the flourishing of wild things. As E. O. Wilson (1992, 329) observes, "Each species . . . was sculpted and burnished by an astronomical number of events in natural selection, which killed off or otherwise blocked from reproduction the vast majority of its member organisms before they completed their life-span." In a word, the flourishing of individuals is far and away the exception. For countless numbers of members of countless numbers of species their fate is, and always will be, failure to flourish. Nor can the point be evaded by stepping up to the level of ecosystems. True, ecosystems can flourish. But it then becomes a moot point whether we can, or should, endorse such flourishing, which in so many cases depends precisely upon the discarding of countless individuals.

Nature is the context within which we practice ethics; but it has to be a moot point whether it itself should be thought of as subject to ethics. When Bill Shankley, former manager of Liverpool Football Club, was admonished for his overenthusiastic attitude to the game, and was told that it was hardly "a matter of life and death," he hastened to agree, adding, "I can assure them it is much more serious than that" (*Sunday Times* [UK], October 4, 1981). Just so, I am inclined to think that to talk of individual and collective moral failings in relation to the threatened collapse of the natural world hardly cuts the mustard. We must speak rather of collective folly, myopia, and insanity, and try to understand how the worst manifestations of these collective failings might be averted.

Conclusion

Restoration, it has been argued, should be conceived not as an attempt to restore some lost value but as a response to certain sorts of threat to meaning—a response which has as its objective the rescuing and reinvigoration of meanings so that they resonate now and will resonate in the future. It will not look to return to the past but will look to the future as a meaningful way of building on and continuing what has gone before. It will not play favorites with natural as opposed to cultural meanings, but will look for ways in which they can mutually enhance each other. Above all, it is an attempt to deal with loss, both natural and cultural, not through some vain attempt to replace or compensate for what has been lost, but through coming to terms with loss. It involves a recognition that the loss in question has both visceral and cognitive ramifications, and a recognition, too, that loss is among the most basic conditions of life. So restoration projects, best seen as exercises in what Aristotle called "practical wisdom," require us to grasp not only what features or elements in a situation must at all costs be retained but also, and of equal importance, what features or elements in a situation must be relinquished. It is, to repeat, a matter of finding our balance in the dance between meaning and loss.

Notes

1. It may indeed be that fear, too, is a price we pay for meaning, especially what Bernard Williams (1995, 239) calls "Promethean fear"—"a fear of taking too lightly or inconsiderately our relations to nature."

2. Stilbo was actually a Cynic, but no matter; historically, Stoicism has its roots in Cynicism.

3. A sense that receives overwhelming corroboration from empirical sources. See, for example, *State of Nature,* the recently published report by the Royal Society for the Protection of Birds (RSPB 2013).

4. I thank Marion Hourdequin for drawing my attention to these.

5. For Taylor, a horizon of significance is a horizon "against which things take on significance for us" (37); they constitute a "background of things that matter" (40). In order to do this they must be "given" (39), and they must emanate from "beyond the self" (40). Nature satisfies both these conditions and is indeed cited by Taylor himself, along with history and society, as among the "background of things that matter" (40).

6. Compare Simon James (2014) for some similar observations.

7. Lewis Carroll, *Through the Looking Glass.*

8. See, for example, chapters 8, 9, and 10.

References

Clare, John. 1984. *The Oxford Authors: John Clare.* Edited by E. Robinson and D. Powell. Oxford: Oxford University Press.

Cooper, David. 2003. *Meaning.* Chesham, UK: Acumen.

Epictetus. 1995. *The Discourses of Epictetus.* Edited by C. Gill. Translated by R. Hard. Everyman Library. London: Dent.

Holland, Alan. 2011. "Why It Is Important to Take Account of History." *Ethics, Policy & Environment* 14 (3): 1–16.

Holland, Alan. 2012. "The Value Space of Meaningful Relations." In *Human-Environment Relations,* edited by Emily Brady and Pauline Phemister, 3–15. Dordrecht: Springer.

Hopkins, Gerard Manley. 1955. *Poems and Prose of Gerard Manley Hopkins.* Edited by W. H. Gardner. Harmondsworth: Penguin.

Hoskins, W. G. 1955. *The Making of the English Landscape.* Harmondsworth: Penguin.

James, Simon. 2014. "Green Managerialism and the Erosion of Meaning." In *Old World and New World Perspectives in Environmental Philosophy*, edited by Martin Drenthen and Jozef Keulartz, 139–150. Dordrecht: Springer.

Katz, Eric. 2012. "Further Adventures in the Case against Restoration." *Environmental Ethics* 34: 67–97.

McKibben, Bill. 1990. *The End of Nature*. Harmondsworth: Viking.

Mosle, Sarah. 2012. "The Lives Unlived in Newtown." *New York Times Magazine*, December 30. http://www.nytimes.com/interactive/2012/12/30/magazine/the-lives-they-lived-2012.html.

Newman Flower, Sir Walter. 1945. "The War Garden." In *Through My Garden Gate*, 69–71. London: Cassell & Co.

Nozick, Robert. 1981. *Philosophical Explanations*. Cambridge, MA: Harvard University Press.

Rackham, Oliver. 1986. *The History of the Countryside*. London: Dent.

Railton, Peter. (1984) 2003. "Alienation, Consequentialism and the Demands of Morality." In *Consequentialism*, edited by Stephen Darwall, 160–196. Oxford: Blackwell.

Rogers, Byron. 2006. *The Man Who Went Into the West: The Life of R. S. Thomas*. London: Aurum Press.

Rolston, Holmes. 1979. "Can and Ought We to Follow Nature?" *Environmental Ethics* 1: 7–30.

RSPB. 2013. *State of Nature*. Sandy, Bedfordshire, UK: Royal Society for the Protection of Birds.

Schroedinger, Erwin. (1944) 1992. *What Is Life?* Canto Classics. Cambridge: Cambridge University Press.

Seneca, Lucius Annaeus. 1969. *Letters from a Stoic*. Edited by Robin Campbell. Harmondsworth: Penguin.

Taylor, Charles. 1992. *The Ethics of Authenticity*. Cambridge, MA: Harvard University Press.

Tennyson, Alfred Lord. (1850) 2007. "In Memoriam." *Selected Poems*. Edited by Christopher Ricks. London: Penguin Classics.

Thomas, Edward. 2003. *The Poems of Edward Thomas*. Haddington, Scotland: Handsel Books.

Williams, Bernard. 1985. *Ethics and the Limits of Philosophy*. London: Fontana.

Williams, Bernard. 1995. *Making Sense of Humanity*. Cambridge: Cambridge University Press.

Wilson, E. O. 1992. *The Diversity of Life*. New York and London: Penguin.

CHAPTER 5 | Layered Industrial Sites
Experimental Landscapes and the Virtues of Ignorance

MATTHIAS GROSS

Introduction

Open-cast mining activities and the industrial contamination of landscapes are among the most dynamic drivers of landscape change in human history. Perhaps more so than with other kinds of landscape transformation, the radical alterations associated with these phenomena pose a challenge to science and policy. This chapter discusses some of the "experimental strategies" that are deployed in the restoration of landscapes altered by industrial activities. To examine the issue of continuity and change in ecological restoration projects more closely, I focus especially on situations of ignorance faced by practitioners and stakeholders in such projects, framing their strategies for moving forward despite not knowing as a form of experimental practice, which seems increasingly normal and perhaps appropriate in twenty-first century society.

Furthermore, due to their long history of human-nature interactions, layered landscapes appear to be particularly ripe for an experimental approach to restoring or redesigning. Layered landscapes inherit many alternating phases of mainly human activity and "natural" processes hardly understood by human actors. These lead to many sets of *nonknowledge*—that is, not merely unknown unknowns (complete unknowns), but more or less clear knowledge of what is not known (e.g., it is unknown exactly what type of chemicals are in the ground, but it is known that they are there). This invites an experimental lens in addition to the lenses of narrative, meaning, and different ways of engaging with history presented in the previous three chapters. An experimental approach takes seriously the idea that a clear acknowledgment of what is not known is a form of hypothesis that is needed for trying out things diligently and responsibly. This, however, means that it is not historical fidelity, which has often been used as a major quality in ecological restoration, that is aimed for, but as a naturally occurring surprise stemming from the layered piece of land "itself." Thus, historical data are used, at best, as starting points, not as goals to be reached. Quite the contrary, to give credit to the natural powers involved, the unexpected is fostered in order to surprise the experimenters and stakeholders involved.

From an experimental perspective, ecological restoration can balance continuity as well as, sometimes, radical change. This is crucial since experiments and sudden social changes share crucial similarities. An experiment in the most general sense can be defined as a cautiously observed venture into the unknown. An experiment is deliberately arranged to generate unexpected events: the surprising effects derived from the experimental setup can be seen as the driver behind the production of new knowledge. Surprises help scientists become aware of what they did not know. Or, as Bazon Brock (2010, 180) puts it, "In the natural sciences experiments are the best way of falsifying hypotheses. If the experiment fails, we know that the hypotheses are unusable, thus the scientist was working successfully."

Viewed in this way, only experiments that fail can be called successful experiments. To put it in more general terms, sudden, unexpected changes that make the experimenters aware of their own ignorance (a falsified hypothesis) provide the impetus for new knowledge. The difference is that such abruptness is welcomed in a laboratory experiment; whereas in the everyday world of modern society, it normally is not.

This chapter will build on this idea of locating the planned unexpectedness of experiments at the core of modern science and its application in the real world by using the restoration of industrially altered landscapes as a test case. Industrially transformed sites seem especially telling when it comes to providing insights into the complex histories of layered landscapes shaped by the ongoing interaction between industrial activities, human communities, and ecological processes. Here, the different layers of history are lurking in the ground waiting to burst into the open; as Barbara Adam has noted, "[T]he visible phenomena making up the landscapes have the invisible constitutive activities inescapably embedded within them" (1998, 54). In contrast to approaches that externalize ignorance by analyzing risk assessments or that sidestep it by using rhetorics of certainty, I suggest that the unexpected aspects of knowledge production can be described using the notion of experimentality. This is important given that calls for greater certainty and safety are being sounded ever more loudly in contemporary political debates; at the same time, empirical research on decision-making can be seen as indicative of an increase in "experimentalities" and as a reaction to unavoidable uncertainty and ignorance, the reverse side of modernist beliefs in scientific certainty. This resonates with observations made by Brian Wynne (2005) regarding different types of complexity and of awareness of the limits of predictability, which are readily apparent within different genomics research and practitioner cultures yet largely denied by the scientists themselves. Thus, perhaps the experimental strategies observed in real-world decision-making are indicative of a change in practical ways of coping with uncertainty and ignorance, even though official rhetorics still suggest otherwise.

Referring to contemporary initiatives in science and research as "experiments" should thus be understood as a cautionary reminder that decision-making and interventions are never completely reliable. In this sense, *experimentality* is an appropriate term for the realities within which decision-making and policy strategies operate. After all, everybody knows that in everyday life a whole host of things may happen unexpectedly. However, the theoretical tools available for framing what everybody seems to know are only in their infancy.

I will first briefly discuss the centrality of ignorance or, as I call it here, *nonknowledge,* as a central aspect of knowledge-making and application, in order to knit it together with the idea of everyday experimentation. In the second half of the chapter I look at two cases of real-world experimentation: the revitalization of industrially contaminated sites and the restructuring of former open-cast mining pits. This is done to carve out some patterns suited to describing the "flow" of experimentality and thus the contours of what has been called the experimental society. This appears to be important since unlike in the traditional orientation toward historical data, an experimental strategy takes historical data into account as part of hypothesis building (i.e., specifying ignorance) but also points to the unpredictability and thus, often, the "falsification" of historical data, where the interconnections between human and natural histories do not allow a return to the past. Even more so, this experimental falsification is built on the expectation that the "naturalness" of the landscape develops differently from the expectations of the planners and stakeholders. Unexpected turns in the development of a layered industrial landscape thus become processes of learning and experimentation that are full of surprises built on nature's unpredictability. In a way, an experimental strategy in ecological restoration allows for natural activities as a pushing back against human control and thus a more natural (in the sense of being independent from humans) strategy than ideals of returning to some pristine nature allow for.

Beyond Risk: Experimenting with the Unpredictable

The pivotal aim of concepts of risk developed from the second half of the twentieth century onward increasingly has been to make the future predictable by means of probability calculations, thereby rendering it amenable to human intervention and planning. Understood this way, risk can be seen as a means of rationalizing an uncertain future. Although many different conceptions of risk are available, risk is most widely understood as the probability of a harmful event multiplied by the amount of harm the event is expected to inflict. Classical risk assessments assume that the probabilities of the relevant events occurring in a certain area under consideration are known. In these terms, dealing with ignorance clearly differs from taking or limiting risks, since the risk of a certain event occurring presupposes knowledge of both the character of events that may occur and the probability that they will do so.[1] Although many other notions of risk exist, some authors, such as Jack Dowie, have argued in favor of abandoning risk completely. Dowie (1999, 59) states succinctly, "There is no need to use the word 'risk' in the process of identifying the best course of action and trying to assess anything about 'risk' per se is a waste of time—largely because there isn't a *se*" (emphasis in the original). Instead of abandoning risk altogether, I would argue for a constructive alternative to these criticisms and would add that when either scientists or lay people talk about risks, it would in many cases be empirically and theoretically more useful and meaningful to frame decisions, utterances, and practices according to different shadings of ignorance. In other words, it can be argued that it is often things that are not known that are most important for decision-makers and thus more important for empirical analysis. Risk and ignorance should be kept apart so as not to water down the two notions. Recently, a large number of sociologists, anthropologists, economists, philosophers, and legal scholars have begun exploring the ways in which ignorance is not simply the obverse of knowledge. Ignorance has a social life and a political economy of its own. Efforts to harness and to deploy ignorance are increasingly seen as important and profitable strategies within economic and political institutions (e.g., Hess 2010; McGoey 2012). The positions put forward in this research depart from the still-common view that sees ignorance as necessarily detrimental, pointing instead to the broader challenges and (in some cases) the merits of not knowing and to the ways in which ignorance can even serve as a productive resource.

Taking this line of thought further, in order to be able to act in an experimental setting, the actors involved need to agree on what is not known and to take this into account for future planning. They need to decide to act in spite of (sometimes) well-defined ignorance, or *non-knowledge* (Gross 2010a, 2012, 2015). The aim is thus to specify ignorance so that it can be used in a meaningful and constructive way. Whereas having faith in the total control and complete knowledge of ecological systems and social processes implies an ability to act only when everything is known in advance, an "experimental approach" makes it possible to accommodate different factors despite the presence of gradations of the unknown.

From the Experimenting to the Experimental Society

The idea to conceptualize processes *outside* the laboratory as experiments goes back to Francis Bacon's reflections on the relationship between the experimental method and society. On the one hand, Bacon was highly influential in shaping the world view that sees the experimenter's realm as distinct from the world of the objects experimented upon and that privileges (rational) human beings over all others as masters of a world to which they essentially do not belong. Moreover, in Bacon's natural philosophy only those with the "interpretative key"—that is, scientists in scientific institutions—can access the secrets of nature (cf. Clody 2011). At the same time, Bacon's most provocative proposal was the idea that approval of the experimental method in science by the dignitaries of the state would turn society itself into a large-scale experiment (Krohn 2009). In this view, modern society should give the experimental method an experimental chance, since the promise of gains reaped by modern science cannot be backed up by anticipatory arguments but only by practicing and implementing the new method in the larger society. There is good reason to buy into this Baconian argument. Ideally, the laboratory confines the problems and risks of research within its four walls, away from the wider society. Real-world experimentation at least partially unloads some of the uncertainties of research onto social and ecological systems. This being the case, it is possible to regard ecological restoration processes outside the laboratory, for example, as experiments—a view that poses a clear challenge to the premises of ecological (scientific) predictability and certainty.

Some classical notions of social experiments can be found in Jane Addams's Hull-House (Gross 2009) and the 1920s Chicago School of sociology (Gross 2010a), but some can also be traced to ideas put forward by John Dewey (Haworth 1960).[2] The term and concept "experimenting society," however, was developed by Donald Campbell (1917–1996) and his associates from the early 1960s onward (cf. Campbell 1998). Departing from this notion, and as a critical commentary on the way research processes and their related hazards were increasingly (and often unintentionally) extended beyond the limits of the laboratory into wider society during the 1980s, Wolfgang Krohn and Johannes Weyer (1994) outlined an understanding of scientific research that sees it as increasingly erasing the boundaries between the laboratory and wider society. Taking this rather critical stance as a point of departure and developing it further, twenty-first-century debates on real-world experiments (Gross and Hoffmann-Riem 2005), experiments in living (Marres 2012), and collective experiments (Latour 2011) have attempted to frame experimental practices as potentially useful strategies for coping with unavoidable uncertainty. If it is true that society has become a laboratory (Krohn and Weyer 1994), then we may want to look for examples of how to deal successfully with the issues that arise in this extended laboratory. This calls for a notion of the experimental society that is based on a conceptualization of social processes as experimental endeavors undertaken to cope with the structural complexity and surprising dynamics of modern social life—in other words, a modern society conducting experiments on itself.

An experimental approach in this sense can be conceived of as a way of coordinating the contingent activities of diverse actors and of enabling them to continue without interruption despite an acknowledged awareness of ignorance. In relation to the examples presented here, the message is that it is not science alone but also diverse nonscientific stakeholders that are called on to play a crucial role in articulating values, concerns, and perhaps even such things as aesthetic preferences in the course of restoring and redesigning a piece of land. The same applies to the many other issues associated with technological choice and social agency.

In the view presented here, today's experimentality in modern knowledge societies did not emerge from social scientists' recommendations in the service of society and government but is understood as an indicator of societal strategies aimed at dealing with uncertainties, surprising events, ignorance, and situation-specific experience.

However, "experimentation is not a word that comes easily to the minds and lips of political leaders," as Guy Peters (1998, 126) remarked, summarizing his reflections on the barriers to learning in policymaking. This stance resonates with a well-known West German slogan for an election campaign, *Keine Experimente* (No Experiments), where the term *experiment* was used often, albeit in a clearly derogatory sense. "No Experiments" was the slogan used by West German chancellor Konrad Adenauer of the Christian Democratic Party in a 1957 election campaign to urge that the successes of postwar Germany should not be gambled away with the reform plans put forward by the other parties. This was more than a half century ago. Recent observers, by contrast, seem to detect a change toward a more experimental type of political regulation and decision-making, often referred to as European experiments or as a new mode of experimentalist governance (cf. Felt et al. 2007; Sabel and Zeitlin 2010). One of the central claims is that increasingly successful policymaking and regulation rest on "experimental" frameworks that give actors wide-ranging freedoms to try out novel innovations, modes of implementation, and legal regulations, which, in turn, need to be evaluated so that the results can be compared with other experimental settings in order to make learning possible (cf. De Schutter 2010). Whereas most interpretations of the precautionary principle try to delay action before proof or, at best, to think about preventive actions in face of uncertainties, the precautionary principle does not spell out what should be done to move forward in the face of unavoidable unknowns. A truly experimental approach needs to be understood as one that knowingly moves into the unknown by trying to specify what is unknown (e.g., hypothesis building) as clearly as possible and then use unavoidable failures or mishaps as a basis for learning measures.

If we now agree that experimentality in various forms is already part of modern society, what could this potentially mean for ecological restoration and landscape development? Using some results from research on the restoration of former industrial sites as a basis, the next two sections offer case studies of the layered aspects involved in redesigning former open-cast mining pits and cleaning up contaminated industrial sites.

Open-Cast Mining Pits: Setting the Stage for Postindustrial Landscapes

All over the world, former coal mining fields are being regenerated in a variety of ways. In most cases, however, there is a desire to redesign these areas to become more natural sites. Of course, such landscapes are substantially different from the landscapes that existed before mining was begun. Especially noteworthy here is the area to the south of Leipzig in eastern Germany, where a completely new landscape has arisen and is still emerging, including sixteen new lakes, natural habitats, as well as hills, recreation areas, and sites for local green tourism. In this so-called New Lake District, where, until 1989, sixty million of East Germany's three hundred million tons of coal produced per year were extracted, a completely new landscape has come into existence. How did this come about?

In the years following 1990, in which the area's coal industry was suddenly exposed to world market prices, most of the surface mines were closed because they did not operate efficiently.[3] The region to the south of Leipzig experienced a period of economic and social breakdown unprecedented in Central European economic history. Nearly 40,000 people lost their jobs. Despite the problems posed by this situation, the post-mining landscapes south of Leipzig represented a unique opportunity to master the ecological and structural changes by means of creative landscaping. In 1991, after the various proposals and models drawn up in a competition among landscape planners and architects had been screened and assessed, and citizen hearings held, a first overall framework for the New Lake District was developed by the Regional Planning Department of West Saxony. The city council issued licenses for specific parts of the general framework plan and adopted a resolution containing measures aimed at attracting new investors. All the planned developments and technical aspects of implementation came under German mining law, which regulates not only the recovery of natural resources but also the potential future restoration and use of post-mining landscapes in open-cast mining pits (cf. Kremer and Neuhaus 2001). Since the guidelines for such procedures in German mining law do not constitute a strict, official directive, the responsibilities of other authorities are not affected (Züscher 1998, 43), so that the actors involved have a certain degree of freedom to create their own schedules and organize their own work. This was important since the original plans from 1991 frequently had to be adjusted to changing social and natural conditions. Lake Cospuden, the first of the lakes, was named after a village that was resettled in 1978–79 to make way for the brown coal excavators. Today, the restored lake attracts some 600,000 visitors a year.

The fact that the lake was flooded successfully was due to several cycles of experimental activity involving the gradual and careful integration of both scientific and social goals. In the first few years following the termination of mining activities, the Cospuden mine became partially filled with rising groundwater from a glacial terrace aquifer. For more than fifty years, the groundwater level had been lowered to 80 meters below ground during mining activities, so in a sense, the water returned naturally after 1990. From 1996 to 2000, the Cospuden open pit was more actively recultivated and flooded more rapidly using groundwater from other active mining areas in the region.

The challenges faced in the early 1990s stemming from flooding via groundwater were the endangering of slope stability, acidification of the rising groundwater, and the mobilization of heavy metals from spoil heaps. Furthermore, project workers encountered severe soil contamination caused by harmful emissions from the now-closed power plants, chemical refineries, and briquette factories. As the groundwater rises and even when neighboring pits are flooded, these areas can be affected by groundwater circulation. As expected, the acidity of the water changed notably, though to widely varying degrees. On the basis of available knowledge, it became clear that the flooding of Lake Cospuden had to be accelerated to avoid further acidification. Consequently, possibilities for speeding up the process of flooding were explored early on. With natural groundwater alone it would have taken some thirty years or more to fill the pit. In several meetings with investors, town planners, and concerned citizen groups, it was soon decided that natural flooding should be supplemented by lowering the groundwater levels in the neighboring surface mines in Profen and Zwenkau, two of the few mines still active during the 1990s.

The original plan, including efforts to identify funding sources, was deliberately premised on changing external conditions and on a process of accommodating these changing conditions. One important external influence was the designation of the lake as a project to be presented at Expo 2000, the World Exhibition held in Germany. The plan was to finalize flooding by summer 2000 in order to attract both media attention and tourists to this major design project.

Legal liability issues around rehabilitation often make it difficult, if not impossible, for government agencies and mining companies to act in the face of any uncertainty. Companies want governments to underwrite rehabilitation efforts so that they themselves can relinquish all liability. Governments do not want to do this in order to avoid absorbing significant liabilities themselves. Public expectations and aspirations around future resource use only seem to make them more nervous—particularly when a significant degree of direct public access to potentially hazardous sites is proposed. Yet this was different in the case discussed here—why so? The answer is not simple or clear-cut. However, what *can* be said is that it was easier to reach a decision in this case despite the knowledge gaps because the whole area fell under German mining law. Hence, the responsibility for dealing with possible failures lay in the hands of mining companies as the successors of the privatization agency appointed by the German Ministry of Finance. Unsurprisingly, the main actors involved in the revitalization process refer to the years up to 1997–98 as a time of activity and innovation, simply because many things were not known and different options were tried out. What was well known was that the problems induced by flooding included the acidification of the rising groundwater (cf. Schreck 1998). Yet in the early 1990s, there was felt to be too little time to conduct laborious hearings or to indulge in implementing the full planning repertoire. The only solution, it was believed, was to get as many experts and stakeholders to one table as quickly as possible, to figure out how things *could* work, and then decide whether to go ahead despite the many obvious uncertainties. In the end, this is what was done. But the question of why it was possible, given that in many other cases the expectation of surprises and the acknowledgment of ignorance are often so prominent as to induce paralysis, is still not answered.

To get closer to answering this question, I would like to refer to a study on the bureaucracy of the former East Germany by Garcia-Zamor (2004) to highlight an implicit cultural aspect involved in the process. Garcia-Zamor has referred to a certain type of "GDR-pragmatism" that was still prevalent in many decision-making processes in eastern Germany during the 1990s. This refers to the fact that, before 1990, "each individual case was decided in a discretionary way. If a decision turned out to be a mistake, it was possible to correct it, regardless of what the rule (the abstract norm) demanded" (2004, 15, see also Wollmann 2003). This behavior, however, according to Garcia-Zamor, was not compatible with the standards of the official rule of law in the long run. However, it could very well be part of the explanation for an attitude that facilitated innovative experimentation within the framework of German mining law, including an openness to the unexpected and a willingness to learn from failure.

Acting in the face of ignorance thus appeared to be a feasible way to move forward. By 1998, however, decisions still had to be made on the basis of a considerable amount of nonknowledge. Rapid flooding via a pipe from the open-cast mine in Zwenkau was done on the basis of stakeholders' agreeing that unexpected incidents were likely. However, this type of unknown is fundamentally different from a total lack of knowledge. It also differs from general knowledge about the limits of knowledge in a certain area, as is inherent in the word *ignorance*. Instead, the actors involved in the design of the new lake apparently agreed on what was not known and took it into account in future planning, meaning that they decided to act in spite of well-defined nonknowledge.

This development was met with disfavor by some of the engineers and companies constructing the lakeshores, foundations, and dikes and restoring the natural habitats, since they had to speed up their work considerably. In general, rapid flooding has a positive impact not only on slope stability but also on water quality (Berkner 2001, 53). However, the speed of the flooding forced the engineers and scientists to experimentally extend their knowledge about what was not known (nonknowledge) and thus to experience a new kind of learning. The whole project can thus be seen as an example of what Chandra Mukerji (2009) has called "impossible engineering." These are projects that start out as "impossible" because they exceed existing knowledge and the expertise of the scientists and engineers involved, but then turn into successful projects without exact knowledge about why it happened. This knowledge can only be produced post hoc.

The Impossibility of Avoiding Ignorance: Experimenting with Contaminants

Estimations indicate that between 500,000 and 1.6 million contaminated sites exist in Europe (EEA 2000, Frauenstein 2010), some 20,000 of which can be classified as "megasites" because of the complexity of the soil and groundwater contamination found on them. These megasites pose a range of tricky technical and management challenges. Some of the challenges relate to having to cope continuously with ignorance in the face of multiple sources of contaminants and plumes from previous industrial activities. Since much of the contamination on deserted brownfield sites originates from industrial production in the early twentieth century, records of accidents and waste disposal leading to contamination are often rare to nonexistent. Very little documentation (archive materials or maps) about the chemicals dumped into the ground exists today. Worse still, the buffering capacities of many soil types and their ability to filter chemicals mean that contaminants are often not perceived until the damage is far advanced.

Given the predetermined time frames of most cleanup and restoration projects, and their limited budgets, actors nowadays are usually aware that they will have to make decisions based on nonknowledge.[4] They realize that it is useless to try to know things that cannot yet be known. To wait for proper knowledge would mean extending operations beyond project time frames and frittering away the chance to promote new investments and further economic development. However, this means that the actors on the ground have to expect that surprising things might happen. As soon as construction workers remove the topsoil, it is possible that they will find something that runs contrary to their expectations. The actors involved, then, learn to know in advance what they do not know (positive nonknowledge) and are able to use this knowledge as a basis for further planning and action. This positive nonknowledge can emerge from a general state of ignorance. Based on this nonknowledge, for instance, planners will consult engineering companies (because now they know what the unknowns are), who will then take samples and evaluate the soil; they may subsequently conclude that an area is heavily contaminated with, say, liquid tar and various solvents. Commenting on such an incident, the representative from the engineering company in charge of a major revitalization project on contaminated land in the eastern German state of Saxony-Anhalt stated, "The discovery of tar meant that the whole philosophy of the project had to be rethought. A completely new plan had to be drafted ad hoc." In a similar vein, a representative from the project management explained:

> Construction and cleaning-up has to be understood as a continuous process. They [the workers on the ground] started to remove the material, and when they did so they found that the subsoil was totally different from what we expected. The problem is that tar, which turns to liquid at a certain temperature, makes it necessary to use another type of water barrier for the rain storage reservoir. (as cited in Bleicher and Gross 2012, 200)

For many stakeholders this means that they have to act first and then get the official permits later. Thus the actors involved often had to act ad hoc and, in so doing, they moved into a legal gray area. This phenomenon is not unusual, and it shows that the impossibility of knowing everything was taken seriously and turned into a constructive strategy. This is an important point. Doing otherwise would have slowed down the overall process significantly and would perhaps even have brought the project to a halt if the normal legal procedures for investigating mistakes had been triggered—one of the main reasons there are so many deserted brownfields in Europe and elsewhere (cf. BenDor et al. 2011; Sardina et al. 2013; Schädler et al. 2013). In the case discussed here, the actors were prepared for unexpected events and so were able to make decisions quickly and flexibly. In other words, we can say that the actors involved agreed on what was not known and took this into account in their subsequent activities; that is, they decided to act on the basis of their (positive) nonknowledge. Positive nonknowledge, however, can become new knowledge to be fed into the next stage of the real-world experiment in order to subject it to further observation and assessment. And to be sure, every set of new knowledge again opens new horizons of unknowns.

Experts' willingness to disclose the limits of their knowledge in their communications with other stakeholders can thus be understood as an important part of implementing successful landscape design and cleanup processes. This entails altering permits (administration), changing plans (engineering companies and research institutes), and last but not least, being flexible in redeploying capital for remediation. In addition, special clauses in the contracts and permits between the actors—so-called collateral clauses—make particular mention of the unknown. Collateral clauses are agreements between joint contractors to pool their guarantees in handling a large landscape restoration project. The objectives are that others will also have recourse to the contractor's warranty to continue the project in the face of unexpected changes. This is possible through supplementary provisions, and the ability of both the contractor and the customer to demand a supplementary quote or a follow-up proposal that may deviate from the original specification.

A further important issue in successfully coordinating such projects is the institutionalization of contacts and information exchange. Although this might seem obvious, regular consultation among all institutions and actors involved for the purpose of exchanging information, discussing new developments, and agreeing on strategies for adapting to new situations is not always standard procedure. Consultation also implies that all the actors involved must communicate their own nonknowledge, understood not in terms of failure or sloppy investigation but rather as a normal way of dealing with contaminants. The approach taken to cope with this phenomenon is one that accommodates project activities despite the presence of unknown factors. Put another way, dealing with ignorance is not simply a process of trial-and-error or of learning from failure, as failures suggest that mistakes have been made. Instead, stakeholders and actors in the restoration of industrially contaminated land take seriously the impossibility of avoiding ignorance, so that there is no target for blame and no "finger pointing." The activities in contaminated-site management presented here seem to include ignorance and nonknowledge explicitly as part of their forward planning. This seems to encourage the development of innovative strategies and to make full use of the potential and resources of the actors involved to achieve a common goal. New knowledge may emerge from these "failures." Unlike probabilistic risk assessments, which often gloss over the unknown, "successful failures" can help to specify areas of ignorance so that the limits and the borders of knowing are intentionally taken into account in acting or planning. Given the enormous number of unknown factors involved in the dynamic layers of contaminated landscapes, acting in spite of ignorance by acknowledging nonknowledge can be seen as a crucial factor in our understanding of the experimentalities of landscape restoration.

Outlook: Decision-Making and the Experimentalities of Landscape Design

The situation in old, industrialized regions seems to prompt a more urgent need for action than in economically prosperous regions. Remediation has to be carried out quickly to safeguard economic investments. When new knowledge is acquired about ground contaminants, it often leads to greater knowledge about what is *not* known. When it comes to the planning and handling processes involved in restoring or revitalizing industrially altered landscapes, however, it is still common for both policymakers and scientists to say officially that decisions are based on reliable scientific knowledge ("the facts"). Only these known and observable "facts" are included explicitly in policy and risk-assessment deliberations. This leads to a gap between the official rhetoric and the situation on the ground for practitioners, for whom dealing experimentally with ignorance almost becomes the norm.

This means, however, that new forms of governance are at once important and yet difficult to achieve. This is because to be able to act, the actors involved need to agree on what is not known and to take this into account for future planning. Furthermore, if it appears meaningful to characterize contemporary modern societies as leading toward more experimentality, and if experimentality is becoming a "key trope" of modern society (as has been proposed by such observers as Guggenheim 2012; Last 2012; Lorimer and Driessen 2014), then public experimentation and the acknowledgment of nonknowledge are set to become more important than ever before. This transition would mean moving away from an orientation based on previous experience and historical extrapolations in nature, technology, and society (e.g., risk assessments) and shifting instead toward prospective and temporary notions of knowns and unknowns. The aim of this shift would be to enable active intervention in the form of experimentally coping with the inherently uncertain, multilayered character of industrially morphed landscapes.

Thus understood, allowing the unpredictable elements in a formerly degraded ecosystem, or at least a landscape once presided over by humans, via the experimental strategies laid out here, means to better understand how nature is able to shake off human influence as much as possible and gradually return to its own independent state. In this way, the setting of restoration goals would be treated as "working knowledge" (cf. Nowotny 2008), knowledge developed to make a next step, while remaining open to the realization that it may not have been the right knowledge (hypothesis falsified), since it has been called into question by a new answer arising from the unpredictability inherent in the layered ecosystem; it has fostered the actors to move into different directions. Seen in this way, dealing with the unknown in the restoration of large-scale landscapes appears to be a crucial and unavoidable part of the overall process, rather than as an anomaly or an indicator of failure.

Perhaps it is no coincidence, after all, that the case study examples of contaminated sites that have been cleaned up "experimentally" are from Germany. On the one hand, Germany is what has been called an "adversarial society," that is, one that does not allow mistakes and failures without clear attribution to decision-makers and culprits—the antipode to an experimental society. On the other hand, the fruitfulness of an experimental approach to moving forward in the face of acknowledged ignorance presupposes a pragmatic attitude toward the future in order not to write off degraded landscapes, but to help reveal unrealized possibilities and opportunities for redesigning and "restoring" a piece of land (cf. Havlick 2014). This also helps to free restoration processes from some pristine or virgin ideal and instead considers both nature and humans as valuable actors in an ecosystem, and it thus serves as a positive and creative model for ecological restoration and design beyond the negative connotation of debates on the Anthropocene.

Despite the discourse on European experimentalist governance, one can still expect a strictly anti-experimentalist attitude from administrations and state agencies in Germany. Official rhetoric calls for more certainty and more safety measures. Decision-making based on nonknowledge would be regarded as irresponsible tinkering—which certainly it sometimes can be—but at least as often it appears inevitable and should not be excluded from official statements. Despite this, real-world decision-making in a strictly regulated bureaucracy seems, quite paradoxically, to foster a positive engagement with ignorance and surprise, because in clearly defined spatial settings the experimental activities can be rendered an accepted part of an adversarial society because they define legal spaces for failure, mishaps, and risk-taking. In this context, actors are able to harness the great potential entailed in moving forward along an experimental path. Indeed, actors dealing with the types of landscapes discussed in this book are used to unexpected events. This, of course, may also invite corporations or individual actors with unsavory motives to use this an excuse and to ensure the ability to change course if their initial actions prove disastrous. This may be a reason why experimental strategies are mostly found in innovation projects and ecological design projects, like the ones discussed here. In this sense, experimentality is no romantic idea of incrementalism, of muddling through, or of some type of adaptive management where actors passively adapt to changing external conditions ("roll with the punches"); instead, it demonstrates in stark manner that dealing with unknowns can become a reality not by choice but by necessity for the sustainable future of a region. One is tempted to speculate that at a local or regional level experimental strategies may thrive best when there are strict state regulations in place that provide the freedom to experiment and also to "fail." However, an important prerequisite for successfully failing through experimentation is that the actors involved are prepared to make decisions despite the existence of ignorance. To make use of Friedrich Nietzsche's (1982, 453) famous aphorism, an experimental society means that "we are experiments: let us also want to be them!"

Notes

1. Concepts of risk in many of the social and engineering sciences range from traditional actuarial analysis, classical probabilistic risk assessments (e.g., fault and event trees, scenarios, and model building) to different psychological and sociological approaches. For useful overviews and critical reflections see Aven (2014); Measham and Lockie (2012); Pidgeon et al. (2003); Zinn (2008).

2. It should be noted, however, that Dewey's notion of experimentalism was a very loose one that had to do with the reconstruction of experience in the sense of

learning from previous experience in order to improve one's decision-making in the future (cf. Ansell 2012, Hlebowitsh 2006).

3. This section draws on Gross (2010b). For further details of the case and other literature on the subject, please also consult Gross (2010a, chap. 5). For enlightening reflections on landscape developments at former open-cast mining pits in eastern Germany in the context of recent energy transitions and the "post-normal science" debate, see Pielke (2012).

4. This section draws in part on Gross and Bleicher (2013). The examples and interview quotes presented stem from different research projects on "experimental strategies" in the revitalization of industrial sites in Germany, especially the SAFIRA II program on remediation research in regionally contaminated aquifers, funded by the German Federal Ministry of Education and Research (BMBF) from 2006 to 2012. On the program and its transdisciplinary organization, see Behrens and Gross (2010).

References

Adam, Barbara. 1998. *Timescapes of Modernity: The Environment and Invisible Hazards.* London: Routledge.

Ansell, Chris. 2012. "What Is a 'Democratic Experiment'?" *Contemporary Pragmatism* 9 (2): 159–180.

Aven, Terje. 2014. *Risk, Surprises and Black Swans: Fundamental Ideas and Concepts in Risk Assessment and Risk Management.* London: Routledge.

Behrens, Vivien, and Matthias Gross. 2010. "Customisation of Transdisciplinary Collaboration in the Integrated Management of Contaminated Sites." In *Collaboration in the New Life Sciences,* edited by John N. Parker, Niki Vermeulen, and Bart Penders, 139–160. Burlington: Ashgate.

BenDor, Todd K., Sara S. Metcalf, and Mark Paich. 2011. "The Dynamics of Brownfield Redevelopment." *Sustainability* 3 (6): 914–936.

Berkner, Andreas. 2001. "Geburt eines Sees." *Südraum Journal* 12: 50–55.

Bleicher, Alena, and Matthias Gross. 2012. "Confronting Ignorance: Coping with the Unknown and Surprising Events in the Remediation of Contaminated Sites." In *Vulnerability, Risks, and Complexity: Impacts of Global Change on Human Habitats,* edited by Sigun Kabisch, Anna Kunath, Petra Schweizer-Ries, and Annett Steinführer, 193–204. Cambridge, MA: Hogrefe Publishing.

Brock, Bazon. 2010. "Cheerful and Heroic Failure." In *Failure: Documents of Contemporary Art,* edited by Lisa Le Feuvre, 180–182. Cambridge, MA: MIT Press.

Campbell, Donald T. 1998. "The Experimenting Society." In *The Experimenting Society: Essays in Honor of Donald T. Campbell,* edited by William N. Dunn, 35–68. New Brunswick, NJ: Transaction.

Clody, Michael C. 2011. "Deciphering the Language of Nature: Cryptography, Secrecy, and Alterity in Francis Bacon." *Configurations* 19 (1): 117–142.

De Schutter, Olivier. 2010. "The Role of Evaluation in Experimentalist Governance: Learning by Monitoring in the Establishment of the Area of Freedom, Security, and Justice." In *Experimentalist Governance in the European Union,* edited by Charles F. Sabel and Jonathan Zeitlin, 261–296. Oxford: Oxford University Press.

Dowie, Jack. 1999. "Against Risk." *Risk, Decision & Policy* 4(1): 57–73.

EEA. 2000. *Down to Earth: Soil Degradation and Sustainable Development in Europe: A Challenge for the 21st Century.* Environmental Issue Series no. 16. Copenhagen, Denmark: Publication of the European Environment Agency.

Felt, Ulrike, Brian Wynne, Michel Callon, Maria E. Gonçalves, Sheila Jasanoff, et al. 2007. *Taking European Knowledge Society Seriously*. Luxembourg: Office for Official Publications of the European Communities.

Frauenstein, Jörg. 2010. *Stand und Perspektiven des Nachsorgenden Bodenschutzes*. Dessau, Germany: Umweltbundesamt.

Garcia-Zamor, Jean-Claude. 2004. "The Bureaucracy of the Former East Germany: A Difficult Transition from Communism to Democracy." In *Bureaucratic, Societal, and Ethical Transformation of the Former East Germany*, edited by Jean-Claude Garcia-Zamor, 1–26. Lanham, MD: University Press of America.

Gross, Matthias. 2009. "Collaborative Experiments: Jane Addams, Hull-House, and Experimental Social Work." *Social Science Information* 48(1): 81–95.

Gross, Matthias. 2010a. *Ignorance and Surprise: Science, Society, and Ecological Design*. Cambridge, MA: MIT Press.

Gross, Matthias. 2010b. "Ignorance, Research and Decisions about Abandoned Opencast Coal Mines." *Science & Public Policy* 37 (2): 125–134.

Gross, Matthias. 2012. "'Objective Culture' and the Development of Nonknowledge: Georg Simmel and the Reverse Side of Knowing." *Cultural Sociology* 6 (4): 422–437.

Gross, Matthias. 2015. "Journeying to the Heat of the Earth: From Jules Verne to Present-Day Geothermal Adventures." *Engineering Studies* 7 (1): 28–46.

Gross, Matthias, and Alena Bleicher. 2013. "'It's Always Dark in Front of the Pickaxe': Organizing Ignorance in the Long-Term Remediation of Contaminated Land." *Time & Society* 22 (3): 316–334.

Gross, Matthias, and Holger Hoffmann-Riem. 2005. "Ecological Restoration as a Real-World Experiment: Designing Robust Implementation Strategies in an Urban Environment." *Public Understanding of Science* 14 (3): 269–284.

Guggenheim, Michael. 2012. "Laboratizing and De-laboratizing the World: Changing Sociological Concepts for Places of Knowledge Production." *History of the Human Sciences* 25 (1): 99–118.

Havlick, David. 2014. "Opportunistic Conservation at Former Military Sites in the United States." *Progress in Physical Geography* 38 (3): 271–285.

Haworth, Lawrence. 1960. "The Experimental Society: Dewey and Jordan." *Ethics* 71 (1): 27–40.

Hess, David J. 2010. "Environmental Reform Organizations and Undone Science in the United States: Exploring the Environmental, Health, and Safety Implications of Nanotechnology." *Science as Culture* 19 (2): 181–214.

Hlebowitsh, Peter S. 2006. "John Dewey and the Idea of Experimentalism." *Education and Culture* 22 (1): 73–76.

Kremer, Eduard, and Peter U. Neuhaus. 2001. *Bergrecht*. Stuttgart: Kohlhammer.

Krohn, Wolfgang. 2009. "Francis Bacons literarische Experimente." In *"Es ist nun einmal zum Versuch gekommen:" Experiment und Literatur I, 1580–1790*, edited by Michael Gamper, Martina Wernli, and Jörg Zimmer, 33–52. Göttingen: Wallstein.

Krohn, Wolfgang, and Johannes Weyer. 1994. "Society as a Laboratory: The Social Risks of Experimental Research." *Science & Public Policy* 21 (3): 173–183.

Last, Angela. 2012. "Experimental Geographies." *Geography Compass* 6 (12): 706–724.

Latour, Bruno. 2011. "From Multiculturalism to Multinaturalism: What Rules of Method for the New Socio-Scientific Experiments?" *Nature and Culture* 6 (1): 1–17.

Lorimer, Jamie, and Clemens Driessen. 2014. "Wild Experiments at the Oostvaardersplassen: Rethinking Environmentalism in the Anthropocene." *Transactions of the Institute of British Geographers* 39 (2): 169–181.

Marres, Noortje. 2012. "Experiment: The Experiment in Living." In *Inventive Methods: The Happening of the Social*, edited by Celia Lury and Nina Wakeford, 76–95. London: Routledge.

McGoey, Linsey. 2012. "The Logic of Strategic Ignorance." *British Journal of Sociology* 63 (3): 553–576.

Measham, Thomas, and Stewart Lockie, eds. 2012. *Risk and Social Theory in Environmental Management*. Canberra, AUS: CSIRO Publishing.

Mukerji, Chandra. 2009. *Impossible Engineering: Technology and Territoriality on the Canal du Midi*. Princeton, NJ: Princeton University Press.

Nietzsche, Friedrich. 1982. *Daybreak*. Cambridge: Cambridge University Press. Originally published in 1881.

Nowotny, Helga. 2008. "Designing as Working Knowledge." In *Creating Knowledge*, edited by Hille von Seggern, Julia Werner, and Lucia Grosse-Bächle, 13–19. Köln: Jovis Verlag.

Peters, B. Guy. 1998. "The Experimenting Society and Policy Design." In *The Experimenting Society: Essays in Honor of Donald T. Campbell*, edited by William N. Dunn, 125–139. New Brunswick, NJ: Transaction.

Pidgeon, Nick, Roger Kasperson, and Paul Slovic, eds. 2003. *Risk Communication and Social Amplification of Risk*. Cambridge: Cambridge University Press.

Pielke, Roger A., Jr. 2012. "Post-Normal Science in a German Landscape." *Nature and Culture* 7 (2): 196–212.

Sabel, Charles F., and Jonathan Zeitlin, eds. 2010. *Experimentalist Governance in the European Union*. Oxford: Oxford University Press.

Sardina, Idalina Dias, Daniela Craveiro, and Sérgio Milheiras. 2013. "A Sustainability Framework for Redevelopment of Rural Brownfields: Stakeholder Participation at Sáo Domingos Mine, Portugal." *Journal of Cleaner Production* 57 (1): 200–208.

Schädler, Sebastian, Michael Finkel, Alena Bleicher, Maximilian Morio, and Matthias Gross. 2013. "Spatially Explicit Computation of Sustainability Indicator Values for the Automated Assessment of Land-Use Options." *Landscape and Urban Planning* 111: 34–45.

Schreck, Peter. 1998. "Environmental Impact of Uncontrolled Waste Disposal in Mining and Industrial Areas in Central Germany." *Environmental Geology* 35 (1): 66–72.

Wollmann, Hellmut. 2003. "Rebuilding Local Democracy and Administration in East Germany: A 'Special Case' of Post-Communist Transformation?" In *Local Democracy in Post-Communist Europe*, edited by Harald Baldersheim, Michal Illner, and Hellmut Wollmann, 29–59. Opladen: Leske und Budrich.

Wynne, Brian. 2005. "Reflexing Complexity: Post-Genomic Knowledge and Reductionist Returns in Public Science." *Theory, Culture & Society* 22 (5): 67–94.

Zinn, Jens, ed. 2008. *Social Theories of Risk and Uncertainty*. New York: Wiley.

Züscher, Albert-Leo. 1998. "Die Wiedernutzbarmachung im Bergrecht und die Umsetzung im Betrieb." In *Braunkohlentagebau und Rekultivierung*, edited by Wolfram Pflug, 42–48. Berlin: Springer.

PART II | Approaching Layered
Landscapes

Restoration in Context

CHAPTER 6 | # Restoring Wildness to the Scottish Highlands

A Landscape of Legacies

HOLLY DEARY

Introduction

Landscape-scale restoration has received increasing attention in the European context over the past decade (Fisher et al. 2010). In Scotland, the ambition is largely manifested as an aspiration to restore "wilderness values." Explicit in its alliance with naturalness and wilderness, "rewilding" is founded on ideology and values which guide all traditional restoration discourses: authenticity, purity, and historical fidelity. However, while these values represent conceptual discord at the best of times, when they are applied to the hybrid landscapes of the Scottish Highlands, with their history of use, abandonment, and reuse, a number of philosophical quandaries are revealed. The complex nature of these layered cultural landscapes, which evolved *in* the presence of humans, challenges the relevance of typical restoration values, such as authenticity and historical fidelity, as the parameters of naturalness and wildness are increasingly elusive.

This chapter presents the results of research done with eighteen Highland estates (large rural landholdings) engaged in the restoration of wilderness values. It aims to explore and evaluate rewilding frameworks to understand how the authentic state of naturalness is conceptualized in Scotland's emergent wild land movement. The following discussion is therefore largely focused on practitioner viewpoints and provides insight into on-the-ground perspectives on debates that have largely been the domain of environmental philosophers. The chapter explores:

i. The degree to which notions of authenticity and historical fidelity in restoration are capable of confronting the complexity of the layered Highland landscape
ii. The place of cultural heritage in the restoration of wilderness qualities in history-laden landscapes
iii. The potential for restoring wilderness qualities while interpreting, and celebrating, a shared history between humanity and nature

Supporting quotes from the interview transcripts are used at intervals throughout this discussion to reinforce specific points. These are extracts from semistructured, face-to-face interviews with land managers from the above-mentioned Highland estates. Interviews were conducted over a two-month period, and then fully transcribed and thematically coded using QSR Nvivo software.

History of the Highlands: "*Un*wilding the Wilds"

The "mist-shrouded mountain; the solitary pine; the distant sunset" are recurring motifs used to depict the Scottish landscape (MacDonald 1998, 241). Scotland is a country of remote mountains, secluded lochs, dramatic coastlines, and exposed heathland; it is a natural backcloth estimated to be worth GPB£5 billion to the nation's tourism economy (Warren 2009). This *Highland wilderness* is etched into the Scottish psyche, symbolizing the foundations of its finest industries, from mountaineering to multimillion-pound whisky distilleries. Scottish cultural identity is founded on a long and enduring relationship with the land and with the wild (Samuel 2000; Toogood 2003). However, beyond the romanticism, the Highlands are far from this mythic ideal. The Scottish Highlands have a checkered environmental history, from both a climatic perspective and a human-interactions perspective. Indeed, teasing out the intricacies of natural environmental change and human-induced change is an issue that continues to perplex academics (Brown 1997; Smout 2000). One point of assurance, nonetheless, is that *Homo sapiens* settled in Scotland throughout postglacial time, and there was most likely a permanent population of hunter-gatherers from 9,000 BP onward. Despite their occupation, it is widely accepted that early Mesolithic settlers were too technologically primitive to have had a significant impact on the environmental conditions of the land they inhabited. It was only with the arrival of agriculture and technological advancement during the Neolithic that the onslaught of environmental degradation began (Smout 2000). As Neolithic settlers advanced to subsistence farming with grazing animals, Scotland's temperate climax ecology started to suffer substantial losses. This trend continued with the onset of the Highland Clearances in the eighteenth and early nineteenth centuries, when many Highland communities were forcibly displaced from the land to make way for industrial numbers of sheep (Smout 1993). The latter part of the nineteenth century was no more favorable for the natural environment. As the aristocracy followed Queen Victoria in pursuing sporting opportunities, the landscape was subject to extensive species extirpations, which cataloged the demise of predatory species, such as eagles, hawks, ospreys, pine martens, and wildcat (Warren 2009). Over this long history, Scotland metamorphosed from a living, forested ecosystem, with thriving species abundance, to the barren, treeless "wet desert" that is a Highland glen today (Darling 1955). Perhaps "a fast forward history of land-use in the Highlands should be accompanied by a pibroch lament"[1] as the artifice of Scotland's "wilderness" is exposed (Lister-Kaye 1994, 8).

Restoring Scotland's Wildness

Despite their culturally fashioned nature, the Scottish Highlands exhibit very little visual evidence of human influence and continue to be celebrated for their wild character (Mackay 2002; Scottish Wild Land Group 2012). To manage the distinct complexity of a profoundly altered landscape still cherished for its wild quality, Scottish Natural Heritage (the Scottish Government's adviser on natural habitats and landscape) has developed a distinct "wild land" framework that recognizes the idiosyncrasies of these seminatural landscapes (Scottish National Heritage 2002). "While the term 'wilderness' is often used to describe the wilder parts of the globe, it is best avoided in Scotland because it implies a more pristine setting than we can ever experience in our countryside, where most wild land shows some effects from past human use" (6) However, regardless of such pragmatism, the ideological foundations of wilderness continue to manifest themselves in the wild land restoration rhetoric that currently dominates Scottish conservation discourses (McMorran et al. 2008). Aspirations to expand and enhance Scotland's wild quality by restoring missing components and processes are increasingly discussed as part of rewilding initiatives. There is currently a strong native woodland restoration movement concerned with restoring the archetypal treeless Highland Glens back to vibrant, wild forest (Hobbs 2009). Supported by pollen analysis suggesting that Scotland's ancient ecosystem, the Caledonian Pine forest, covered 15,000 km² of Scotland at its maximum in approximately 5,000–6,500 years BP, conservationists aim to restore native pinewoods from today's meager 180 km² (Featherstone 2010). Alongside the restoration of Scotland's ecologically denuded condition, conservationists are adopting a landscape emphasis through their aspiration to also restore the experiential aesthetics of wildness. To date, this has resulted in instances of the removal, or at least declining maintenance, of human artifacts in wild land (McMorran et al. 2008).

Using Authenticity as a "Restoration Guide"

Whether managing ecosystems for ecological integrity or an experiential landscape quality, unconscious choices concerning different levels of authenticity and historical fidelity are unavoidable. Such axiological nature conservation concepts, which imply "a state of nature that existed at some previous point in time," are wholly inescapable in landscape conservation and management (Hull et al. 2001, 327; Gustavsson and Peterson 2003). Scotland's rewilding narratives are no exception. Notions of authenticity and historical fidelity are undeniable in visions of rewilding; the "re" prefix itself is indicative of the retrospectivity implicit in restoration paradigms generally, while the "wilding" implies a reference condition that is vaguely considered to be the era before significant human disturbance (ca. 6,000 years BP). Where restoration means the recovery of presettlement conditions, wilderness provides the ultimate standard. Wilderness is the natural antithesis of settled, humanized landscapes; "it is the ultimate landscape of authenticity" (Cronon 1996, 16). Through rewilding narratives, therefore, the loss of authenticity in wilderness is marked by the onset of human modification and influence.

The rich cultural and social history associated with the palimpsest Highland landscape is therefore unquestionably problematic in Scotland's emergent rewilding narratives. The Highlands were shaped by thousands of years of human/environment interactions, the evidence of which is still present in today's landscapes in the form of hill forts, cairns, old field systems, and abandoned crofts. Furthermore, a number of traditional and contemporary Highland land uses continue to etch a human signature onto this already complex manuscript (e.g., muir-burn, peat cutting). Indeed, as these landscapes continue to evolve, renewable energies infrastructure will perhaps be considered the present-day contribution to the cultural landscape. Nonetheless, as Scotland's wild land discourse conveys, the Highland landscape unquestionably exhibits a quality of wildness that remains uncompromised by these legacies. In fact, the history of abandonment, clearance, and forced migration associated with a deserted croft arguably exacerbates this sense of wildness through its portrayal of a landscape too savage, and too wild, to support human existence.

The complex interface between this natural and cultural heritage in terms of contemporary conceptions of wildness in the Highlands makes restoring an authentic condition of wildness extremely difficult. The socially constructed nature of wilderness, coupled with the historical longevity of this degraded ecological condition, means that in popular rhetoric, the Scottish heather moorland is considered to be "wild." This moorland is commonly mistaken to be the natural condition of the Highlands and with its barren, untamed appeal is often lamented as "Britain's last wilderness" (Mackay 1995). Despite striving toward ecological integrity, the current push to restore woodland cover could potentially degrade public conceptions of wildness in Scotland. Authenticity, therefore, takes on a very malleable meaning at the interface between a historically complex landscape and socially constructed discourses of "wild" and "natural." If the Highlands exhibit a quality of wildness, then the historical, and contemporary, role of management in manifesting such a quality must be recognized. The Highlands "are celebrated and protected for their wild land qualities, and yet the emptiness of many glens is the result of forced evictions during the infamous Clearances of the early nineteenth century" (Warren 2009, 257). Scotland's cultural heritage is woven into these perceptually wild and natural settings to the point that the natural and human histories of these places are inseparable and indistinguishable. For example, as woodland cover has become increasingly fragmented and integrated with commercial forestry, the present-day natural tree line and species distribution have become increasingly obscured (Brown 1997). Ultimately, where "culture is the agent [and] the natural area is the medium, the cultural landscape is the result" (Sauer 1925).

In the wilderness context, historical fidelity and authenticity are paragons of virtue: untouched, virginal, and primeval. Consequently, when applied as a restoration target, wilderness implies the loss and removal of cultural values and artifacts. Therefore, while authenticity and historical fidelity are the conceptual anchors of ecological and landscape restoration, they are unable to grasp the complex history of the Highlands and result in the privileging of perceptions of the "unaltered" over the land's true history (Cronon 2003). The quandary is how to manage these cultural wilds as a "historical wilderness, in which we commit ourselves not to erasing human marks on the land, but rather to interpreting them so that visitors can understand just how intricate and profound this process of rewilding is" (Cronon 2003, 38). Restoration, under the aegis of authenticity and historical fidelity, in a wilderness context will inevitably result in legible signs of past land uses being lost. In many instances, these signs are intrinsically linked to "sense of place." The following section therefore considers the relevance of traditional restoration values—where *historical fidelity* describes the wholeness of natural systems relative to how they functioned in the past (Hobbs et al. 2010), and *authenticity* implies "natural" in terms of prehuman influence conditions (Ridder 2007)—to the Scottish Highlands and whether such erosion of meaning is inevitable in the restoration of hybrid landscapes.

The "Authenticity Challenge" in the Scottish Highland

Establishing Baselines: Highland Reference Conditions

Restoration is heavily reliant upon environmental guidelines. Most definitions of wildness and naturalness assume that some sort of putative original ecosystem existed against which comparisons for restoration can be formulated (Warren 2007). The dualistic frameworks through which such values are conceived are founded on the dichotomy between "natural" versus "compromised" that forms the foundation of notions of authenticity. Consequently, restoration strategies, particularly in a wilderness context, rest upon the tacit assumption that what is natural and what is unnatural are easily discernible; that the "pristine" can be separated from the "altered" (Warren 2009). In reality, "it is not obvious when something changes from being natural to being unnatural" (Hull et al. 2001, 332). Alteration is, by its very nature, a process rather than an absolute. Marking the point of transition from wild and natural to unwild and unnatural in any ecosystem is something of a logical impossibility; but it becomes ever the more challenging in the Highland context, where the process of modification occurred over a 6,000-year history of occupation, resulting in an inherent subtlety to human impacts (Habron 1998). Establishing reference conditions in a landscape that coevolved in the presence of people is "arbitrary and, as such, is an ethnocentric act that can marginalize and diminish the reality of those people who were present or moved through the landscape before the baseline was set" (Crifasi 2005, 627). This is particularly pertinent given the cultural sensitivities surrounding the Highland Clearances in Scotland, which remain an immensely sensitive issue today (Toogood 2003; Warren 2009). Add to this already complex history the fact that, due to ongoing natural climatic variability, woodland was already in retreat at the onset of human modification, and reference conditions for the demise of *uncultured nature* become even more elusive. Assigning causation in Scotland's trajectory from naturally forested ecosystem to one dominated by peat and heathland to anthropogenic forces is incredibly challenging when "changing climatic conditions and other environmental factors mean that many of today's 'natural' ecosystems developed after *Homo sapiens* was already on the scene" (Dudley 2011, 14). The unwilding of the Scottish Highlands was neither temporally nor spatially discrete or absolute, which exacerbates the deceptive wild and natural quality of the Highlands. As one land manager pointed out in our interview, *"All these trees here which conservationists say are native pinewood were actually planted between 1869 and 1877 by Sir John Ramsdon."* Sometimes the beguiling beauty of nature can disguise the fact that "the environment that we appreciate, and think of as natural, is often the creation of earlier human actions" (Postrel 1999, 155). In reality, the hybrid nature of the Highland landscape does not offer any temporally relevant baselines for restoring authenticity and historical fidelity. The search for appropriate baselines of naturalness and authenticity in any instance can be "disorientating," but nowhere is this more perplexing than in the Scottish Highlands (Crifasi 2005, 627). No baseline could encapsulate the full complexity of these storied landscapes.

Embracing Cultural Heritage

Given that postglacial Highland ecosystems have never really existed in the absence of humans, a number of land managers are uncomfortable with applying the purist values implicit in authenticity and historical fidelity. Notions of restoring "wild, untouched nature" in the Highlands were viewed as overly ambitious and fallaciously reasoned; in the words of one land manager, "What you've got in Britain is a cultural landscape, what you'll end up with is a cultural landscape." The historical longevity of many of Scotland's traditional land-use practices, for instance, those associated with the management of grouse moors for sport, have delivered multiple unintended nature conservation benefits which notions of authenticity and historical fidelity are unable to acknowledge (Thirgood et al. 2000). Scotland's paradoxical situation whereby a number of management practices arguably retain Scotland's landscape in an artificial condition of "pseudo-wildness" causes substantial tensions with authenticity. *"The managed system that we live in in the Highlands has had many decades, well hundreds of years in some cases, of testing and refinement"* (respondent quote). Managing for authenticity in the Highlands is, therefore, perceived by some land managers as leading to a reduction in nature conservation value. An almost synergistic relationship has developed between Scotland's natural and cultural heritage, adding a layer of complexity that the overly simplistic narratives of authenticity and historical fidelity are unable to account for. Traditional restoration perspectives do not acknowledge the thriving species abundance and habitat quality that cultural landscapes can exhibit. Where natural and cultural heritage is fully integrated, *"you can have a cultural landscape which is a self-functioning ecosystem"* (respondent quote). The capercaillie (*Tetrao urogallus*)—a large woodland grouse that is an iconic symbol of Scottishness and an important focus of conservation efforts—exemplifies this very well. Given the historical decline in its native habitat—the Scottish pinewood—concerns over the potential extinction of the capercaillie have afforded it a high degree of protection. But despite being a symbol of all that is natural and pure in Scotland's natural heritage, this species can actually do very well in nonnative spruce forests, as opposed to simply native pinewoods (Summers et al. 2004), such as *"spruce thickets, which are nonnative, are actually favored by capercaillie, particularly in winter"*(respondent quote). Accordingly, forestry practices founded on authenticity could actually lead to the decline of this charismatic conservation species. The coevolution of Scotland's natural and cultural heritage means that natural processes and natural conditions do not always produce the "best results." In fact, many land managers assert that the quality of Scotland's natural heritage is intrinsically linked to a number of cultural practices. *"We're a National Park because of the quality of the landscape and the biodiversity, and that is largely a consequence of management. Landowners can't be doing everything badly and we need to remember that"* (respondent quote). Authenticity is not necessarily good for conservation; management does not necessarily cause degradation.

Moreover, beyond the conservation benefit of traditional land-management practices, a number of Scottish land managers assert the value and significance of cultural heritage in its own right. The folklore associated with the Highlands provides a significant amount of revenue to Scotland's economy through tourism. Scotland's cultural landscapes are of immense value and are worthy of conservation in their own right; as one land manager pointed out, *"To have big areas of heather moors as a cultural landscape is something very special and something very Scottish"* (respondent quote). Such hybridity of natural and cultural heritage cannot be celebrated under an authenticity mandate. Authenticity in restoration affords such distinct assemblages no protection. Although Britain's cultural heritage has always received more attention in nature conservation than elsewhere in the world (Gustavsson and Peterson 2003), it is evident that Scottish land managers are concerned that the current Scottish wild land movement prioritizes natural heritage over cultural heritage. Where managing for wildness has resulted in the removal of cultural artifacts, such as disused bothies[2] or sheepfolds,[3] symbols of immense socioeconomic resonance have been lost. Fundamental discussions about what cultural heritage brings to the overall landscape character were called for. Consequently, while popular understandings of wilderness suggest that historical evidence of human land use reduces wild value, this research supports Feldman's (2011) assertion that actually, such historical context deepens people's understandings of wild nature. Consequently, "to acknowledge past human impacts ... is not to call into question their wildness; it is rather to celebrate, along with the human past, the robust ability of wild nature to sustain itself when people give it the freedom it needs to flourish in their midst" (Cronon 2003, 38). Ironically, restoration and enrichment of landscapes is all about the meaning of "place," and yet the simplistic narratives that romanticize particular historical geographies result in dogmatic restoration frameworks which are incapable of interpreting the subtlety of this "sense of place."

Living Working Landscapes

The cultural elements of Highland landscapes are not reserved for history. Being part of a small island, nature conservation must coexist with other land uses. A freeze frame favoring a particular historical context, as the management objectives of authenticity and historical fidelity imply, is incapable of incorporating today's contemporary management practices. To ignore and exclude the extensive history of the Highlands out of some misguided effort to portray them as authentic refuges for prehuman disturbance conditions is to ignore the fact that many of these historical legacies are still present in the landscape today in the form of traditions. As discussed above, the presence of cultural heritage, in the form of traditional practices, is not always destructive to the conservation value of the experiential parameters of wildness. Many land managers therefore described the authenticity of the Highland landscape in terms of trueness to its history as opposed to presettlement conditions. From this perspective, cultural practices and traditions contribute to the authenticity of these places. The Highlands have a deep history of use and work. Living communities are therefore an immensely important part of their cultural heritage (MacDonald 1998). Similar to Cronon's (2003) discussion of the Apostle Islands archipelago in the United States, the general public in Scotland rarely recognize the evidence of "past human efforts to yield bounty from this soil" (38). Authenticity in restoration implies previous exploitation, degradation. and destruction, the negative impacts of which are evidenced in the landscape and must be "cleaned up." This implies recovery and healing, but the narrative of destruction is too severe for a context in which not every human impact is an act of degradation. As Feldman (2011) explores, if the artifacts and practices of cultural heritage did not, and do not, lead to degradation, then restoring such landscapes to prior natural conditions cannot accurately be described as a recovery.

The cultural baggage associated with the "emptying" of the Highlands during the eighteenth and nineteenth centuries is enduring. The results of the Clearances have been long lasting and have resulted in hypersensitivity toward retrospectivity in the management objectives among Scottish land managers. *"Looking at the Highlands and Scotland as a whole, there's still—very understandably—massive sensitivity about the fact that the Highlands are so depopulated . . . the Clearances is still a big issue for the Highlands"* (respondent quote). The barometer for authenticity in the wilderness context is controlled by the onset of human activity and modification. Restoring authenticity to the Highlands is therefore culturally entrenched in notions of re-enacting the Clearances and re-emptying a once emptied landscape (Toogood 2003). The current sociopolitical context of traditional practices such as hill sheep farming, already struggling to survive against a backdrop of stringent European Union bureaucracy, makes rewilding a chilling prospect for many land managers and Highland communities. Despite a long trend of depopulation, the Highland landscape continues to support marginal rural communities, many of which have experienced significant degrees of economic strife due to the rugged nature of this wild landscape, but continue to make a living from the land (Mackenzie 2004). Nature conservation in the Highlands has therefore long been allied with notions of sustainability, which restoration frameworks founded on authenticity are not. Such a complex socioeconomic history profoundly complicates contemporary restoration frameworks which must understand, and account for, these cultural sensitivities.

Postmodern Context: The Crystallizing Effects of Environmental Change

Adding to an already complex story, the postmodern context provides a strong case against seeking to achieve historical fidelity in restoration projects. Although not specific to the plurality of the Scottish landscape, the ideals of authenticity and historical fidelity are undermined by the ambiguous borderless context in which we live. The dichotomous values of natural/unnatural and wild/unwild are unrepresentative of this pluralistic world, and are incompatible with the current state of disorientation. *"If global warming is something that happens in the next thousand years then we could have different types of plants and things establish . . . different trees could actually go to different altitudes, so it is not actually a restoration"* (respondent quote). Conventional restoration values cannot be maintained within the weak frameworks offered by globalization and rapid environmental change. Regardless of the complexity of reading the Highland landscape, against the current Anthropocene narrative, a vision of nature as untangled from the human is not helpful in guiding nature conservation. Today's world is a very different place from that which earlier settlers found, and land managers in Scotland appear increasingly aware of this: *"you can't look back into the postglacial epoch and identify some point at which you wish to go back to"* (respondent quote). Nature does not have to be pristine to be natural. If it does, then conservationists must accept that we have no nature left (Cronon 1996).

Authenticity in Highland Rewilding Frameworks: How Do Rewilding Estates Conceptualize Authentic Wildness?

It is evident that conventional restoration frameworks present problematic targets for Scotland's emergent wild land movement. They induce management prescriptions based on the value of "natural," and the disvalue of "cultural" that radically oversimplify the complexity of these hybrid landscapes. Conventional restoration goals assume the existence of unmodified reference conditions and continuity in how ecosystems function throughout time (Callicott 2002). Consequently, authenticity and historical fidelity in rewilding rests on two myths that are inappropriate for Scotland's hybrid, but wild, landscapes: (1) the colonial myth of wilderness, which asserts that nature is compromised by human intervention, and (2) the scientific myth of climax ecology, which labels humans as an artificial disturbance in the pervasive equilibrium of natural ecosystems (Callicott 2002). Applying these values to the moving baselines offered in cultural landscapes necessitates arbitrary, and therefore meaningless, management decisions. For instance, to use Scotland's enlightening capercaillie example again, having faced extinction in 1975 this highly protected conservation symbol was actually reintroduced into Scotland in the nineteenth century (Hobbs 2009). Under the auspices of authenticity, is this iconic species native, nonnative, naturalized, or a fake? Such practical discord abounds.

The practitioner perspective presented in this chapter stresses the fact that a significant amount of value is placed on cultural history, which conventional restoration frameworks seeks to deny and conceal (Feldman 2011). The storied nature of the Highlands brings meaning to these ambiguous landscapes—meaning that land managers are keen to preserve and, above all, respect (Toogood 2003). While this leaves a host of practical questions relating to how much historical evidence should be left on the landscape, and how it should be managed, it raises some more immediate conceptual questions, such as, how can the "wilderness" rhetoric be reconciled with the Highland's narrative of use? Although unrefined, and often improvised, Scotland's emerging rewilding frameworks may have something to offer this conceptual debate. Light (2000) calls for a more practically oriented philosophical perspective on ecological restoration issues. The wild land rhetoric employed by a number of Scottish land managers currently offers the degree of pragmatism and alternative perspectives on the meaning of "authenticity," which are needed to develop rewilding discourses that are more capable of incorporating the land's cultural and social histories.

Scotland's Wilding Continuum: Employing Pragmatism

As Cronon (1996, 10) famously declared, wilderness "is entirely a creation of the culture that holds it dear, a product of the very history it seeks to deny." Wilderness managers are often, therefore, considered to be "principal vandals of historic structures," as they seek to erase past history to create an illusion of pristine landscapes (Cronon 2003, 40). The pragmatism through which Scotland's wild land rhetoric is conceived is therefore crucial to enabling Highland estates to conceive authenticity as being the product of its long relationship with human occupation, thereby valuing cultural heritage rather than seeking to suppress it. According to Scottish land managers, wild land discourses—as opposed to wilderness—enable them to value the wild character of the Highlands, while acknowledging their anthropogenic genesis. The longevity of the human relationship with this land has resulted in a process of naturalization. *"A lot of these old archaeological remains are almost naturalized themselves. They're covered in lichens and mosses and I think they do add something to the effects, so you could have a cultural aspect to the wild land"* (respondent quote). Consequently, wild land in Scotland is as much about the history and practices that bring meaning to the landscape as it is about the land itself. Not only is the degree of wildness remaining in these areas the outcome of past and present management policies, this history of use and abandonment is central to contemporary cultural connections with these places as "wild" (Scottish Natural Histories 2002). Authenticity in a Highland context cannot be derived from presettlement conditions; instead the "wild primitivism" that is sought through rewilding frameworks is found in the preservation of this ancient sense of dependency on the land rather than an earlier stage of evolution. It is apparent, therefore, that in terms of the ontological roots of wildness, individuals concerned with the restoration of Scotland's wild land are willing to accept an "authentic illusion . . . as a probable realistic concept for conservation and landscape management when applied in practice" (Gustavsson and Peterson 2003, 319). While the juxtaposition of "wildness" and "civilization" means that enhancing wildness necessitates "decreasing culturalness," moving beyond such a dualistic perspective results in wildness and cultural heritage becoming far more reconcilable. Land managers in Scotland assert that wildness is a continuum concept, and therefore, rather than being characterized as one end of a dualism, it is characterized as a multitude of positions between pristine wilderness and humanized landscape. Where wildness is a continuum, not an absolute, the natural and cultural facets of the landscape cannot be directly juxtaposed. Consequently, while the storied landscapes of the Highlands may not represent the gold standard in terms of wildness, they can claim a position on this continuum.

From Composition to Process

It was evident during my discussions that in some of Scotland's rewilding frameworks, ecological notions of authenticity and the historical are being replaced with a new set of values: ecosystem health, autonomy, and resilience. Aplet's (2000) distinction between naturalness and freedom is particularly helpful in understanding this emergent conceptual framework. While *naturalness* is typically understood to mean "wholeness" relative to historical norms, *freedom* means the extent to which the ecosystem is beyond human control. A more process-oriented (as opposed to composition-oriented) restoration target in the form of a "wild ecology" is the focus of conservationists' aspirations for Scotland's wild lands. This process emphasis, concerned with restoring nature's autonomy and self-regulation rather than a particular baseline in time, remains largely uncompromized by the traces of other histories on the landscape.[4] Simply providing opportunities for constituent parts and processes to re-establish themselves enables land managers to adopt a forward-looking conservation strategy which can acknowledge the distinct blend of natural and cultural heritage that characterizes the Highlands. This conceptual framework, described by one land manager as "future naturalness," is concerned with allowing the landscape to reach its full ecological potential, while embracing today's altered baseline. While lacking conceptual clarity—and most likely conscious endorsement in many instances—this conceptual shift can acknowledge that the Highlands are the product of coevolution and remove the culturally entrenched notions of "emptying" the land through its acknowledgement of the fact that *"seminatural landscapes is the best we will have"* (respondent quote).

Conclusion

Paradoxically, the uplands of Scotland are still considered to be "wild" in popular narratives, despite evidence to the contrary (Habron 1998). In reality, the unmodified, natural Highland wilderness is the product of a largely feudal tenure system in which humans were excluded from the Highland ecosystem and replaced with sheep (Smout 1993). The Highlands therefore present a particularly challenging restoration context; while the natural heritage value of the Highlands, coupled with its popularity as a "wild adventure" destination, may provide an argument for conventional restoration based on presettlement conditions, this approach obscures historically and culturally significant events. The conventional restoration values of authenticity and historical fidelity are too simplistic to account for the complexity of these hybrid landscapes. They subscribe to the largely toppled nature/culture binary and involve baselines that "create arbitrary boundaries across otherwise continuous human action on the landscape" (Crifasi 2005, 627). However, there is a danger that in this postmodern, postnatural climate, conservationists might jump from thinking that authenticity does not provide a clear way forward for natural systems to thinking that authenticity is not important at all. Authenticity remains a useful concept when considered from a landscape-evolution and historical-continuity perspective (see Hourdequin, chap. 2, this volume). The history of landscape provides considerable meaning. Therefore, while it is important not to focus on the past in a dogmatic way, history should not be dismissed as normatively irrelevant. The natural and cultural heritage of the Highlands are so tightly woven that it is wholly inappropriate to tease them apart. Restoration frameworks in Scotland must, therefore, foster a more open-ended interpretation of landscape history. The fact that the cultured nature of Scotland's wild places is recognized by most land managers provides a good starting point; Scottish land managers appear overtly prepared to embrace the idea of socionatural landscapes. The current struggle to reconcile the restoration of wilderness values with rich cultural heritage in Scotland consequently presents an immense opportunity for considering ways of reframing our ideas of wilderness and history to ensure that the future restoration, aimed at bringing "new value," does not always result in the loss of another value.

Notes

1. *Pibroch* is a type of music associated with the Scottish bagpipes. It is often, but not exclusively, slow and stately in style.

2. A *bothy* is a basic, most commonly stone-built, shelter found in the more remote mountainous areas of Scotland, most notably the Scottish Highlands. Elsewhere across the globe, bothies are better known as backcountry or wilderness huts.

3. A *sheepfold* is a dry stone-walled sheep pen commonly found in rural parts of the UK. They are typically historical as opposed to contemporary, and are commonly semiruinous.

4. The degree to which continuing contemporary cultural influence remains in tension with this wild land restoration framework is very context specific and concerned with the degree to which the continuing human action impedes natural processes.

References

Aplet, G. H. J. Thomson, and M. Wilbert. 2000. "Indicators of Wildness: Using Attributes of the Land to Assess the Context of Wilderness." In *Wilderness Science in a Time of Change*, edited by Frank McCool, David N. Cole, William T. Borrie, and J. O'Loughlin, 89–98. Ogden, Utah: Proceedings RMRS-P-15-VOl-2.

Brown, N. 1997. "Re-Defining Native Woodland." *Forestry* 70 (3): 191–198.

Callicott, J. B. 2002. "Choosing Appropriate Temporal and Spatial Scales for Ecological Restoration." *Journal of Biosciences* 27: 410–420.

Cooper, N. S. 2006. "Cultural 'Nature' and Biological Conservation." *Ludus Vitalis* 14 (25): 117–134.

Crifasi, R. R. 2005. "Reflections in a Stock Pond: Are Anthropogenically Derived Freshwater Ecosystems Natural, Artificial or Something Else?" *Environmental Management* 36 (5): 625–639.

Cronon, W. 1996. "The Trouble with Wilderness: Or, Getting Back to the Wrong Nature." In *Uncommon Ground: Rethinking the Human Place in Nature*, edited by William Cronon, 23–56. New York: W. W. Norton.

Cronon, W. 2003. "The Riddle of the Apostle Islands: How Do You Manage a Wilderness Full of Human Stories?" *Orion* 22 (3): 36–42.

Darling, F. F. 1955. *West Highland Survey: An Essay in Human Ecology*. Oxford: Oxford University Press.

Dudley, N. 2011. *Authenticity in Nature: Making Choices about the Naturalness of Ecosystems*. Oxon: Earthscan.

Featherstone, A. W. 2010. "Restoring Biodiversity in the Native Pinewoods of the Caledonian Forest." *Reforesting Scotland* 41: 17–21.

Feldman, J. 2011. *A Storied Wilderness: Rewilding the Apostle Islands*. Seattle: University of Washington Press.

Fisher, M., S. Carver, Z. Kun, R. McMorran, K. Arrell, and G. Mitchell. 2010. *Review of Status and Conservation of Wild Land in Europe*. Report commissioned by the Scottish Government.

Gustavsson, R., and A. Peterson. 2003. "Authenticity in Landscape Conservation and Management: The Importance of the Local Context." In *Landscape Interfaces: Cultural Heritage in Changing Landscapes*, edited by H. Palang and G. Fry. Dordrecht, Netherlands: Kluwer Academic.

Habron, D. 1998. "Visual Perception of Wild Land in Scotland." *Landscape and Urban Planning* 42: 45–56.

Hobbs, R. J. 2009. "Woodland Restoration in Scotland: Ecology, History, Culture, Economics, Politics and Change." *Journal of Environmental Management* 90 (9): 2857–2865.

Hobbs, R. J., D. N. Cole, L. Yung, E. Zavaleta, G. H. Aplet, F. S. Chapin III, P. B. Landres et al. 2010. "Guiding Concepts for Park and Wilderness Stewardship in an Era of Global Environmental Change." *Frontiers in Ecology and the Environment* 8 (9): 483–490.

Hull, R., D. Robertson, and A. Kendra. 2001. "Public Understandings of Nature: A Case Study of Local Knowledge about 'Natural' Forest Conditions." *Society and Natural Resources* 14 (4): 325–340.

Light, A. 2000. "Ecological Restoration and the Culture of Nature: A Pragmatic Perspective." In *Restoring Nature: Perspectives from the Social Sciences and Humanities*, edited by P. H. Gobster and R. B. Hull, 37–48. Washington, DC: Island Press.

Lister-Kaye, J. 1994. *Ill Fares the Land: A Sustainable Land Ethic for the Sporting Estates of the Highlands and Islands of Scotland*. Scottish Natural Heritage Occasional Paper no. 3. Perth, Scotland: Scottish Natural Heritage.

MacDonald, F. 1998. "Viewing Highland Scotland: Ideology, Representation, and the 'Natural Heritage'." *Area* 30 (3): 237–244.

Mackay, J. W. 1995. "People, Perceptions and Moorland" In *Heaths and Moorland: Cultural Landscapes*, edited by D. B. A. Thompson, A. J. Hester, and M. B. Usher, 102–111. Edinburgh: Her Majesty's Stationery Office (HMSO).

Mackenzie, A. F. D. 2004. "Re-Imagining the Land, North Sutherland, Scotland." *Journal of Rural Studies* 20: 273–287.

McMorran, R., M. F. Price, and C. R. Warren. 2008. "The Call of Different Wilds: The Importance of Definition and Perception in Protecting and Managing Scottish Wild Landscapes." *Journal of Environmental Planning and Management* 51 (2): 177–199.

Ridder, B. 2007. "The Naturalness versus Wildness Debate: Ambiguity, Inconsistency and Unattainable Objectivity." *Restoration Ecology* 15: 8–12.

Samuel, A. 2000. "Cultural Symbols and Landowner's Power: The Practice of Managing Scotland's Natural Resource." *Sociology* 34 (4): 691–706.

Sauer, C. 1925. *The Morphology of Landscape*. Berkeley: University of California Publications in Geography.

Scottish Natural Heritage. 2002. "Wildness in Scotland's Countryside: A Policy Statement." Scottish Natural Heritage, Inverness, Scotland.

Scottish Wild Land Group. 2012. "Scottish Wild Land Group." http://www.swlg.org.uk. Accessed 27 May 2015.

Smout, T. C. 1993. "The Highlands and the Roots of Green Consciousness, 1750–1990." Scottish Natural Heritage Occasional Paper no.1. Perth, Scotland: Scottish Natural Heritage.

Smout, T. C. 2000. *Nature Contested: Environmental History in Scotland and Northern England since 1600*. Edinburgh: Edinburgh University Press.

Summer, R. W., R. Proctor, M. Thorton, and G. Avey. 2004. "Habitat Selection and Diet of the Capercaillie Tetrao urogallus in Abernethy Forest, Strathspey, Scotland." *Bird Study* 51 (1): 58–68.

Thirgood, S., S. Redpath, I. Newton, and P. Hudson. 2000. "Raptors and Red Grouse Conservation Conflicts and Management Solutions." *Conservation Biology* 14 (1): 95–104.

Toogood, M. 2003. "Decolonizing Highland Conservation." In *Decolonising Nature: Strategies for Conservation in a Post-Colonial Era*, edited by W. M. Adams and M. Mulligan, 220–246. London: Earthscan.

Warren, C. R. 2007. "Perspectives on the 'Alien' versus 'Native' Species Debate: A Critique of Concepts, Language and Practice." *Progress in Human Geography* 31 (4): 427–446.

Warren, C. R. 2009. *Managing Scotland's Environment*. Edinburgh: Edinburgh University Press.

Wrightham, M., and N. Kempe. eds. 2007. *Hostile Habitats: Scotland's Mountain Environment*. Perth, Scotland: Scottish Mountaineering Trust.

CHAPTER 7 | # Environmental versus Natural Heritage Stewardship

Nova Scotia's Annapolis River and the Canadian Heritage River System

JENNIFER WELCHMAN

Introduction

The rapid transformation of built and natural environments since industrialization has resulted in the loss of iconic features of human environments. Wherever these losses have been perceived as threatening to eradicate surviving relicts of vanishing ways of life, heritage movements have proliferated in response. Artefacts, buildings, crafts, languages, and music, formerly seen as the property or practices of particular individuals upon which none but their immediate survivors could lay claim, are reconceptualized by heritage associations as the collective property of a whole community and thus the birthright of all its members. The reconceptualization of artefacts and practices as communal legacies has proved an effective means of generating public support for preservation of the artefacts and practices targeted by heritage initiatives. Environmental organizations have followed suit, routinely describing wild species and ecosystems as "natural heritage" assets, in the hopes of motivating public interest in their conservation or restoration. In this respect, the tactic of characterizing environmental stewardship as a special form of heritage stewardship has often been successful. Unfortunately, it has also encouraged an uncritical identification of environmental stewardship with natural heritage stewardship that is, at best, misleading and, at worst, liable to undermine both endeavors. Unless we appreciate the ways these two forms of stewardship diverge, strategies adopted to promote them may turn out to serve one at the expense of the other.

I take environmental stewardship to be the management of human activities that affect the natural environment, undertaken to protect the integrity of ecological systems, resources, and values for the sake of present and future generations (Welchman 2012). Environmental stewards study the past for insights into the impact of human activities on wild species, environmental assemblages, and ecosystem services, together with the values these elements support. If historical evidence suggests that human exploitation has diminished or is diminishing the integrity of the environmental systems future generations will inherit, environmental stewards will seek to re-engineer human activities to reverse those impacts. Heritage stewardship in all its forms likewise aims at maintaining the integrity of resources for future generations. But with heritage stewardship, the concern is focused on those resources, both cultural and natural, perceived as fostering the continuance of a particular community's identity and values through time. Consequently, while preserving or restoring a particular natural species or ecological system is sometimes of equal concern to both environmental and heritage stewards, their objectives, and consequently the means they will favor, can differ significantly. This is particularly likely when the species, systems, or assemblages occur in regions of cultural and environmental significance.

In what follows, I illustrate the problems that can arise when environmental and heritage stewardship are conflated by examining the failed campaign to win federal heritage status for Canada's Annapolis River. I begin by providing background on the Canadian Heritage River System (CHRS) program and then examine the campaign and its outcome. After reviewing the peculiar ways that heritage and environmental stewardship were conflated in the process by Parks Canada, the lead agency managing this federal government program, I conclude with a discussion of the relationship of environmental and heritage stewardship and their respective implications for restoration projects on landscapes with both environmental and human heritage value.

The Canadian Heritage Rivers System and the Annapolis River Campaign

The CHRS is a joint venture of provincial, territorial, and federal agencies, led by Parks Canada, providing national recognition to "important heritage rivers," so that "the opportunities they possess for recreation and heritage appreciation are realized by residents of and visitors to Canada" (Parks

Canada 1984, 3).[1] The program aims to protect the rivers of (i) outstanding heritage value, human or natural, or (ii) outstanding recreational value, by providing incentives for community-based management initiatives. The program is competitive. Communities must first organize to prepare proposals and development plans for submission to provincial officials. Only after provincial approval is received are rivers officially nominated to the CHRS board for consideration. The potential rewards are significant: the pride of possession of a national asset, federal assistance in developing a holistic ecological management plan, and the enhancement of local tourism and recreational industries. These are incentives for communities to pursue ecologically friendly forms of development over more damaging alternatives.

No community responded to the announcement of the program in 1984 with greater alacrity than did Nova Scotia's Annapolis Valley on behalf of the Annapolis River. As the Annapolis River watershed had been home to some of the earliest European settlements in Canada and was home to the indigenous Mi'kmaq for thousands of years, community leaders were confident their river would win recognition as an outstanding cultural heritage asset. They were motivated by more than simple pride or economic aspirations. Four hundred years of continuous European settlement had taken a toll on the watershed's environmental integrity. The Annapolis Valley Affiliated Boards of Trade were concerned by mounting evidence that their river's ecological health was in decline. The need to develop a comprehensive management plan was becoming urgent. Thus the CHRS program seemed to offer a timely solution to their problem. It took the Boards of Trade only a year to prepare and submit their proposal on behalf of the Annapolis River to the province's Ministry of Lands and Forests (Annapolis Valley Affiliated Boards of Trade 1987, 7; Legard 1986, 4).

The Annapolis River is neither unusually long nor fast moving by Canadian or provincial standards. For much of its length, it meanders through agricultural lands most noted for extensive apple orchards. The last third of the river becomes tidal as it approaches its mouth on the Annapolis Basin (a sub-basin of the Bay of Fundy). The river's tidal range in this section was once 7 to 9 meters (25 to 29 feet); unusual for rivers in other parts of Canada but not for those affected by the Bay of Fundy's extraordinary tides. In earlier periods, Fundy tide waters had supported extensive salt marshes along the river's lower banks. But through an ingenious system of dikes, French Acadian settlers and their successors had turned most of these into farmland, well before the end of the eighteenth century. By the mid-twentieth century, the costs of maintaining the dikes against rising tides and storm surges had grown prohibitive. So for flood control as well as transportation, a causeway was built just above the river's mouth to restrict normal tidal amplitude upstream to just 1 meter. A prototype tidal power generating station was added to the causeway in 1984 (Daborn et al. 1979).[2]

These modifications mitigated the threats to farms, homes, roads, rail lines, and other infrastructure near the river's banks, with the added benefit of supplying clean, renewable energy. However, there were indications that these modifications were also contributing to a decline in water quality and the loss of biodiversity. Studies of the causeway's impact on the river revealed significant unintended ecological effects. The restriction of tidal flows was restricting the mixing of saline and fresh water upriver of the causeway, with the result that subsurface oxygen levels were significantly depleted (Dadswell, Rulifson, and Daborn 1986). Reducing tidal flows was also reducing tidal flushing of pollutants entering the river from storm drains, farms, and outdated sewage-treatment systems, so pollutant levels were rising. Other modifications to the river's shorelines compounded the negative effects of the causeway and dam. Salt-marsh depletion and deforestation along the river and its tributaries were contributing to bankside erosion. Dams and poorly constructed culverts on tributaries were blocking fish passage to spawning areas. The tidal power station's turbines appeared to be adding to the problem, killing many of the fish attempting to swim upstream to spawn.[3] Local anglers were calling for action, fearing further declines in the shrinking fish stocks (Annapolis Valley Affiliated Boards of Trade 1987, 7). In response to these and related problems, the Boards of Trade had already sought a federal grant to conduct a cleanup and improve amenities along the river's upper reaches (Annapolis Valley Affiliated Boards of Trade 1985, 1). Nevertheless, the Boards of Trade did not expect the river's water-quality issues to be a serious threat to their campaign. In 1985 they released a new tourist guide, *Canoe Annapolis River*, inviting visitors to canoe, fish, and sail along "one of the most historic rivers in Canada" (Annapolis Valley Affiliated Boards of Trade 1985, 2).

Their hope of success did not seem not unreasonable, as the CHRS program guidelines permitted the nomination of rivers with "outstanding Canadian value" in any one of three categories: natural heritage value, human heritage value, or recreational potential (Parks Canada 1984, 13). Outstanding value in more than one category was not required. While the CHRS guidelines also required rivers to meet certain criteria for "ecological integrity," there was no requirement that rivers be "outstanding" in this respect.

To qualify on *natural heritage* grounds, a river had to possess "outstanding" representations of the major geological, fluvial, and/or other natural forces shaping the watershed or, alternatively, would have to support rare, unique, or outstanding natural phenomena and/or rare or endangered species. The Boards of Trade frankly acknowledged that "the river, though beautiful in many different ways, does not, to the best of our knowledge, possess natural features unique to the province of Nova Scotia" (Annapolis Valley Affiliated Boards of Trade 1986, 8). Neither the placid Annapolis nor its valley exhibited any remarkable geomorphic or other physical features. None of the river's flora and fauna were unique or of special importance for preserving biodiversity either in Nova Scotia, specifically, or in Atlantic Canada, more generally.

To qualify for *recreational* appeal, a river had to afford natural scenery that "would provide a capability for an outstanding recreational experience," experiences visitors could enjoy without detriment to the river's "natural, historical, or aesthetic values" (Parks Canada 1984, 15). Here again, the Annapolis failed to qualify. No striking or unusual landforms, rapids, waterfalls, or any other scenic features graced its course. All its recreational amenities were readily available elsewhere.

Therefore, the Boards of Trade campaign relied on the river's *human heritage value*. To qualify in this category, a river had to possess (1) outstanding importance in the historical development of Canada's "native people, settlement patterns and transportation"; (2) associations with persons, events, beliefs, or achievements of "Canadian significance"; and (3) historical sites "unique or rare or of great antiquity" and/or representative of "major themes" of Canadian history. In this respect, the river's claims seemed unassailable.

Port-Royal, Canada's first successful European settlement was established in 1605 near the river's mouth and later relocated to the site of present-day Annapolis Royal. From Port-Royal, settlements spread along the river. Port-Royal itself served as the capital of French Acadian Canada for over a century. Such was the town's strategic significance in this period that it was fought over more times than any other community in North America (Dunn 2004, viii). Earthworks constructed by a failed Scottish colony in 1629 are still visible at the site of present-day Fort Ann. Rebuilt and expanded by a succession of occupiers, Fort Ann was attacked by British, French, and Mi'kmaq forces, and even American privateers (Dunn

2004).[4] Though few original Acadian buildings survived the hostilities, many notable eighteenth- and nineteenth-century structures remain.

Moreover, the Annapolis Valley had been a focal point of Canadian heritage tourism since the mid-nineteenth century, thanks to the international success of Henry Wadsworth Longfellow's poem, *Evangeline: A Tale of Acadie* (Longfellow 2004). Longfellow's poem delighted readers with its romantic depiction of the lives of Acadian residents of the village of Grand Pré prior to their deportation in 1755. Soon after its publication in 1847, visitors began to arrive in Grand Pré hoping to immerse themselves in their imaginary heroine's environment—to look seaward, as Evangeline had done, over the Acadians' verdant fields, from the village's site at the edge of what Longfellow assured his readers had been, and still remained, "the forest primeval."

These visitors should have gone home disappointed. Like many Acadian communities, Grand Pré had been demolished by the British to discourage deportees from returning. Their holdings were redistributed to Anglophone colonists of British or American extraction, such as the New England Planters and, later, the Empire Loyalists (refugees from America's revolutionary war). There were few relicts of the eighteenth century: a stand of elderly French willows and a disused stone well, both of dubious connection to the Acadian colonists. One could indeed gaze over verdant fields from the site of the lost village; but thanks to Anglo-American redevelopment, these were not the fields Evangeline herself would have seen, had she ever existed. No "forest primeval" bordered those fields—not because of deforestation but simply because no forest of the type Longfellow described had ever existed in the region. Nevertheless, visitors routinely left the site entirely satisfied. The willows, the stone well, and the sprinkling of conifers around the site were sufficient for many to make the emotional connection they sought with the long-lost village and its inhabitants, real and imaginary. (To assist the less imaginative, the site was later embellished with a statue of Evangeline, a memorial church, a commemorative cross, and other amenities; McKay and Bates 2010).

Evangeline triggered a fascination with all things "Acadian" that sustained tourists' interest long after the poem's popularity faded. The Acadian diaspora began to return to visit the sites of pivotal events in their family histories. Descendants of later British and American settlers came to see where their ancestors had become Canadians. As more tourists came, new sites of heritage interest were uncovered, re-created, or commemorated throughout the Annapolis Valley. Fort Ann became a national historic site in 1917. A replica of the original Port-Royal settlement, the Habitation, was constructed at Annapolis Royal. Sites of former Acadian homesteads were located and marked along the Annapolis River, as well as sites associated with notable New England Planters, Empire Loyalists, and later settlers. Serious exploration of the heritage value of Annapolis River for the Mi'kmaq people and their diaspora began. In the 1980s, two significant archaeological sites were discovered along the river.

Since the Annapolis River's claim to outstanding Canadian human heritage value seemed assured, the only potential bar to success appeared to be the criteria for ecological integrity. Parks Canada had specified that the area of the river to be designated should be of "sufficient size and contain all or most" of the processes and properties of the river crucial for its outstanding value in the nominated category; that it should contain "ecosystem components required for continuity of the species, features or objects to be preserved;" and that the water quality should be sufficient to allow for the "continuity and/or improvement of the resources upon which 'value' to the system has been determined" (Parks Canada 1984, 16). As the Boards of Trade interpreted them, these criteria did not seem to present significant problems.

Some aquatic species and communities of life previously native to the river had been lost, and the water quality in certain stretches of the river was seriously impaired. But the CHRS criteria appeared to require only that existing "ecosystem components" and communities of life should be sufficiently robust to survive or recover with attentive management. As to water quality, the CHRS criteria seemed to require only that the river's existing water quality was or could be restored to levels adequate to support the features central to its claim to "outstanding" value. The Annapolis watershed's human heritage features were not at risk from existing impairments to the river's water quality. Nevertheless, the Boards of Trade were committed to improving the river's ecological and water quality with CHRS program support.

Thus community leaders were shocked and dismayed when two years later the proposal was rejected for insufficient environmental integrity. The Boards of Trade immediately requested a meeting with provincial officials to learn what had gone wrong. At this point, it became apparent that their campaign was up against two insurmountable obstacles. The first was Parks Canada's conflation of natural heritage and ecological values. As far as Parks Canada was concerned, these were one and the same thing. Rivers lacking one necessarily lacked the other. The second was that as Parks Canada and other federal agencies of the day understood "national heritage," the historical associations of the Annapolis River did not entail that it possessed national heritage value.

Juggling History, Heritage, and Environmental Values

As David Lowenthal argues in *The Heritage Crusade and the Spoils of History*, while "heritage" and "history" enterprises overlap, they differ in significant ways. History is (or aims to be) a form of empirical inquiry whose objective is the production of accurate accounts of past events. Historians' conclusions about the past are, of course, never wholly free from cultural or personal biases; nevertheless "testable truth" is the intended outcome. By contrast, Lowenthal points out, heritage enterprises are not attempts to construct "a testable or even a reasonably plausible account of some past, but a *declaration of faith*" in a narrative of the past that gives meaning and contributes to a community's continuing sense of its identity. Heritage narratives cannot float completely free of the known past, but they may—and routinely do—exercise considerable creative license regarding the historical facts on which they draw. The degree and scope of creative license taken is a function of the narrative's pedagogical goal, which is to educate present and future generations in how best to interpret a group's past history, not simply to recount it (Lowenthal 1998, 121).

Genuine historical relicts can be of great value for heritage appreciation as they facilitate feelings of direct connection with the persons, places, and events of special significance for a group's or nation's heritage. But reconstructions can be equally effective means for achieving imaginative engagement with the past, as the popularity of reconstructions such as the Shakespearean Globe Theatre in London and the Habitation in Annapolis Royal amply demonstrate. Furthermore, much of what is most central to any group's shared sense of its identity are intangibles, such as languages, myths, and cultural practices. To create or enhance emotional connection with these aspects of group heritage, it is sufficient to provide appropriately configured *performative spaces* in which they can be re-created and re-performed. Performative spaces can be provided by either authentic locales or restorations; for example, eighteenth-century blacksmithing can be re-enacted just as effectively in a twenty-first-century replica as in a carefully preserved antique structure. And because heritage is only tangentially related to actual historical events, fictional persons and events can become bearers of heritage value with which individuals and groups will seek to engage through suitable performative spaces. For example, thanks to the enduring influence of Conan Doyle's Sherlock Holmes stories on Britons' (and others') sense of British identity, values, and traditions, visitors flock annually to London's Sherlock Holmes Museum, at the fictional address 221b Baker Street, for the pleasure of immersing themselves in Holmes's environment, even though neither Holmes nor even the London of Conan Doyle's stories ever truly existed.

As heritage is always a matter of a group's subjective *appreciation* of its history, there are no objective measures to which rival parties can appeal when disputes arise about the heritage value to be assigned to particular objects, persons, practices, or landscapes. In societies composed of disparate groups with distinct heritage traditions, one and the same historical thing or event can bear different and even incompatible heritage values. When this is the case, neither the antiquity nor the authenticity of that historical relict can be relied upon to resolve the disputes, for such qualities are only contingently related to its heritage value. The real determinant is always the capacity of a given place or object to evoke a visceral connection with the past persons, events, or practices that a group's heritage tradition presents as significant contributors to its collective identity.

In the case of landscapes, such as the landscape through which the Annapolis flows, the heritage value arises not from historical facts about its discovery in 1603 by French explorers or its earlier history as a Mi'kmaq homeland. It depends entirely on the role it plays in individuals' subjective appreciation of that history. For descendants of the Mi'kmaq, French Acadian, Scots, British, and American immigrants who arrived before the nineteenth century, the pivotal role played by the Annapolis River watershed in their lives makes it the bearer of considerable heritage value. But for descendants of the immigrants who arrived on Canada's Pacific Coast, it may have little or none.

In young nations like Canada, whose populations have grown quickly through waves of immigration from many lands, governments are often tempted to try to kick-start the development of a common sense of national identity. Rather than wait the decades or even centuries that might pass before a shared Canadian identity would evolve naturally, Canadian governmental authorities decided to create a national heritage tradition that would inculcate the values they approved. For reasons noted earlier, a national heritage tradition could not be rooted in events or experiences with which many immigrants and their descendants would not be able to identify. The solution was to root it in the experience of immigration itself, or more specifically, in the experiences of exploration and adaption to Canada's vast territory that in some way or other all immigrants shared whenever and however they might have arrived. These became the officially endorsed bases for collective Canadian national identity from the 1930s through the 1980s: immigration and adaption to the vast Canadian landscape. The *voyageurs*, seventeenth- and eighteenth-century French, British, and Metis traders who established transcontinental trade routes from Canada's coasts through its wilderness interior, became the officially endorsed icons of Canadian's collective cultural ancestry.[5]

As Claire Campbell points out, this way of coping with the problem of creating a common national identity had many appealing features for the governmental agencies promulgating it:

> Nineteenth-century romanticism in both Europe and North America incorporated a strongly romantic attitude towards nature; by claiming a native landscape as part of its historical origins, a nation could make a stronger case for both its "natural" territory and its cultural distinctiveness . . . [T]his would of course appeal to a relatively young country perpetually insecure about the integrity of its identity and its borders (Campbell 2008, 11–12).

In this context, the symbolic value of the *voyageur*, paddling his canoe along wilderness rivers from settlement to settlement, French, English, and Aboriginal, was enormous because the *voyageur* transcended any one particular locality or ethnic identity, just as his transcontinental journeys transcended regional boundaries. As Campbell goes on to note, "Commemorating routes of exploration and trade implied a continental destiny of the future Canada, a justification for its existing borders . . . that these river routes predate provincial boundaries naturalized and privileged national cohesion over any provincial claims to distinctiveness" (2008, 13). Federal agencies promulgated Canada's *voyageur* heritage through public monuments, publications, and educational initiatives through the 1980s. Promulgation of the official "national" heritage narrative of the wilderness-traversing *voyageur* as Canadian's common cultural ancestor would become central to Parks Canada's mission. An early policy statement declared:

> In Canada we still have rivers that flow through essentially natural environments, their channels unobstructed and their waters relatively unpolluted. Such rivers are outstanding examples of our natural heritage. As well, some of these rivers provided a source of food and a means of transportation for native people and early settlers, thereby playing a significant role in the

exploration, trade, and settlement of our country. These rivers are important elements of Canada's natural and cultural heritage, which should be preserved in an unspoiled state for the benefit of present and future generations. (Parks Canada 1979, 65)

Parks Canada based its definition of heritage rivers on surveys of "wild rivers" in the Yukon and Pacific Northwest. Thus, heritage rivers were rivers "free of impoundments within designated sectors," having "shorelines essentially natural," waters free of "man-made pollutants," and courses "inaccessible by road except at occasional crossings" with flow rates sufficient for "low intensity recreational activities." Heritage rivers also provided visitors "with a natural experience by preserving the lands seen from the river surface and the shorelines as much as possible in an unaltered state" and ensuring "the ecological integrity of the river" (Parks Canada 1979, 65). That is, for Parks Canada, a heritage river was a river capable of providing authentic performative spaces in which visitors would be able to re-create the experience of actual historical voyageurs, or, alternately, a river sufficiently wild to serve as a substitute for the rivers actually traversed prior to later development that impaired their value.[6]

Significantly, there were no separate criteria for cultural and natural heritage value. The agency's position at the time was that "man and his environment cannot be separated" (Parks Canada 1979, 12). Natural heritage sites were simply a special category of human cultural heritage site, ones that recognized "that physiography and climate have been significant factors in Canada's development and history" (Parks Canada 1979, 12). The reasons the agency took this position are understandable. Since heritage value is always a matter of a group's subjective appreciation of past events, persons, or places, *all* heritage value is of fundamentally the same kind, differing only in the kinds of objects to which it attaches. This feature of heritage enterprises explains why debates about which "historical" baseline should be used to guide natural heritage preservation and restoration practices can never be settled by appeal to either scientific or historical fact. Heritage narratives, unlike historical accounts, do not aim to reveal truth of the past. Their purpose is to help us interpret and carry forward legacies we inherit from the past. Consequently, we can never determine the natural heritage value of any particular assemblage of natural species, entities, or processes by appeal to history. The historicity of a particular assemblage is only contingently related to that assemblage's natural heritage value.

Equally significant was the absence of any criteria for identifying a river's ecological integrity distinct from those provided for determining its heritage value. Parks Canada's mission in this period was first and foremost heritage preservation. The CHRS program was not a scheme for preserving or restoring the ecological integrity of Canadian rivers per se. It was a scheme for preserving and restoring the rivers that were most symbolic of an officially approved pedagogical narrative of Canadian origins and identity. Consequently, the necessity or importance of recognizing, let alone practicing, a form of stewardship of landscapes not directed to the preservation and interpretation of their heritage assets did not present itself to Parks Canada in this period.

Provincial and territorial officials pushed back against Parks Canada's initial proposal for the CHRS program. Restricting inclusion to rivers inaccessible to roads was not likely to help them promote riparian tourism and recreational industries. Moreover, few rivers in the Atlantic provinces of Nova Scotia, Prince Edward Island, or Newfoundland would qualify, as their long histories of human settlement ensured that adjacent lands were rarely "in an unaltered state" along all or most of their lengths. As a result, the official criteria for natural heritage values were substantially revised before the program was launched in 1984. Cultural heritage (rechristened as "human heritage") and recreational value were split off as separate but equal routes to heritage river status. Impoundments, human alterations to shore lines, accessibility by road, and specific references to the presence of man-made pollutants were no longer specified grounds for disqualification (Canadian Heritage Rivers Task Force 1981, 27–28).

But in practice nothing had changed. Parks Canada continued to identify the integrity of ecological resources it managed with the integrity of their natural heritage assets. When the CHRS program was implemented, Parks Canada, the CHRS board, and their provincial and territorial associates evaluated proposals in terms of the criteria for natural-heritage value specified in the original CHRS proposal, regardless of the category in which a given river was being nominated. Minutes of the meetings at which the ministerial response was discussed indicate that many of the officially excised criteria for natural heritage value had been reintroduced as unstated criteria for environmental "integrity."

For example, the section of the river below the "impoundment" created by the causeway was excluded from consideration. Even had the impoundment not provided an excuse to exclude the region around the river's mouth, it might well have been excluded anyway, since in this, the most heavily developed section of the river, neither the shores nor the adjacent lands retained a natural appearance. The evaluation of the river's water quality also employed Parks Canada's original criteria for natural heritage. The River Task Force was informed that river-bank erosion, the presence of man-made pollutants, and the extirpation of salmon made the Annapolis unacceptable as a heritage river. These were in fact indicators of significant decline in the watershed's environmental integrity relative to earlier periods. But as noted earlier, the 1984 CHRS integrity guidelines had only specifically required "continuity and/or improvement of the resources upon which 'value' to the system has been determined." They had not required the absence of man-made pollutants or of evidence of erosion. Nor had they required the continued existence of all or most of the species historically native to the watershed.

The officials adjudicating the Annapolis River proposal seem to have been as puzzled by the River Task Force's objections to the criteria they imposed as the River Task Force had been to their imposition. To the River Task Force, the imposition of hitherto unstated exclusions detrimental to their proposal seemed arbitrary and unfair, as did the refusal to include sections of the river impacted by impoundments. The latter was particularly prejudicial to their application, as the effect was to drop from consideration the section of the river retaining the greatest number of historic structures associated with the river; the seventeenth-century Scottish earthworks, the reconstructed Habitation, and historic eighteenth- and nineteenth-century buildings. To make matters worse, this also excluded the section where many of the most popular recreational activities were practiced, such as sailboat racing, surfboarding, and hydroplaning. For their part, the officials faced with the Boards of Trade's submission were flummoxed by the River Task Force's suggestion that a river lacking natural heritage values could still possess environmental values worth stewarding. They could not seriously believe that anyone would suppose ecological and natural heritage values were distinct. Campaigns on behalf of rivers like the Annapolis had not been anticipated. (Only after campaigns of this sort were rejected, to the discomfort of all concerned, did Parks Canada and the CHRS Board recognize the need to revise their program requirements.)

The River Task Force concluded, correctly, that meeting the CHRS requirements for ecological integrity was an impossible task. Even had it been feasible, returning the river to a pristine condition without visible human modifications along the shorelines had never been their goal. They did not share Parks Canada's restricted view of what constituted nationally significant heritage—specifically, redolence of the *voyageurs*.

They wanted to celebrate, not expunge, their riparian landscape's multiple layers of cultural development. Parks Canada had little interest in the watershed's historical associations because the Acadians and their successors had been farmers rather than *voyageurs* and because (thanks to the deportations) the Acadians had not, as a group, played any distinct or special role in the opening of Canada's wilderness interior. Though the officially endorsed heritage narrative of the *voyageur* was beginning to be contested, it retained official favor in Ottawa. And on that view, none of the heritage values of the Annapolis River were values warranting substantial investment.

Birth of the Clean Annapolis River Project

Disappointed, the Boards of Trade cut their losses and abandoned further pursuit of CHRS status. Instead, they conducted a series of workshops on the nomination debacle and on the environmental challenges that had been highlighted in the province's rejection of the proposal. As Diane Legard, the Boards of Trades executive manager would later remark, they found that the rejection had a "silver lining" of an unexpected kind:

> It crystallized for many local residents what the scientific community and public health officials already knew—the Annapolis River needed help . . . This realization has led to a wide spectrum of the community becoming concerned and involved. (Legard, undated, 2)

Whatever the faults of the process leading to rejection, the provincial officials had not exaggerated the river's water-quality issues. In the summers of 1988 and 1989, the Annapolis River had to be closed to all human and agricultural use because of *E. coli* (*Escherichia coli*) contamination. The losses to the region's agricultural, recreation, and heritage tourism industries were too significant to ignore.

Implementing the CHRS program's actual criteria for environmental integrity was never a serious option. Even if it had been financially feasible, it would never have received public support. Restoring the river and its shores to a "natural" appearance would have meant removing the causeway and tidal power plant at Annapolis Royal, as well as roads, homes, farms, businesses, and whole town sites along the river. It would also have meant relocating or demolishing sites of enormous heritage value for the thousands of people who visit the area annually, not to mention the

Annapolis Valley residents themselves. The quest to eliminate visible evidence of human intrusion along the river's course could even require the destruction of some of the region's most iconic scenery, its apple orchards.

The warning signs that human activity was overwhelming the river's capacity to supply ecosystem services and other resources on which area residents depended, reinforced by the river closures in 1988 and 1989, made stewardship of the river's ecological integrity the River Task Force's chief priority. Through their workshops, they educated the community about the environmental challenges the river faced and engaged community support for projects to restore the ecological values, functions, and services of greatest collective concern. This approach was highly successful, as it encouraged local communities to see themselves as equal stakeholders in the river's future, sharing common interests in protecting and enhancing its water quality, biodiversity, ecosystem services, and the values they represented. The sense of collective responsibility generated wide community support for initiatives the River Task Force proposed. It also prompted invitations from researchers at the Acadia Centre for Estuarine Studies to join in a series of partnerships intended to foster community-based approaches to watershed management, developing tools for educational outreach, and involving citizen-scientists in water-quality monitoring and other activities.[7] The Boards of Trade reconstituted the River Task Force as a separate body, the Clean Annapolis River Project (CARP) to better support these initiatives (Griffith 1990).

Setting achievable goals required gaining a more comprehensive understanding of the chief threats to the river's environmental systems and communities of life. These were identified as including unsustainable exploitation of the river as a freshwater resource, inadequate sewage treatment at many sites along the river's course, deforestation and removal of vegetation along the river's tributaries that encouraged river bank erosion and runoff of farm animal waste into the river, the loss of salt and fresh water marshes that had formerly buffered the river against these and other contaminants, and invasion by exotic species that compromised some local biotic communities.[8] With the help of members of the Acadia Centre for Estuarine Studies and other partners, CARP pursued provincial and federal government grants and partnered with municipal, provincial, and federal agencies and nongovernmental organizations, such as Ducks Unlimited, to develop means of restoring the river's water quality and the ecological services it provided.

The resources provided have allowed CARP to collaborate in the engineering of a 75-hectare freshwater marsh to serve Annapolis Royal as a tertiary sewage system. Working with thirty-seven local landowners, CARP has helped to restore 630,000 square meters of riparian habitat and has protected a further 570,000 square meters by installing bankside fencing to prevent livestock intrusions and planting trees, shrubs, and stakes to reduce bank erosion. To improve biodiversity of fish species, CARP has assessed culverts throughout the watershed, identifying obstructed or substandard culverts for remediation. It has also participated in the removal of a dam on an important tributary. Salt-marsh restoration projects are underway. A program to provide water-conservation assessments to community members has been launched. Other current projects are focused on protecting endangered turtles and managing invasive species. Because of its effectiveness as a grassroots organization, CARP has served as an influential model for community capacity building around the province. Headway against the Annapolis River's ecological problems is being made. Habitat for wetland species is being restored and some anadromous fish species are returning to the Annapolis River and its tributaries to spawn. While some contaminant levels remain high, the river's ecological integrity is no longer in decline and has in many respects significantly improved.[9]

At the same time that the River Task Force was contemplating its response to the nomination debacle, the CHRS board began to revise its integrity guidelines in light of the lessons it had learned from the program's initial rollout. Released the year after CARP was founded, the guidelines revised the criteria in each nomination category. The new criteria for human heritage no longer exclusively privileged associations with *voyageur* exploration as a qualification for national heritage significance. Thus rivers would no longer be disqualified automatically if they were no longer "wild" or influenced by human development. The appearance of continuity with earlier periods remained crucial; however, human infrastructure or modifications were allowable, so long as they were generally characteristic of the "historic period in which the waterway is ... of outstanding importance." The revised criteria for environmental integrity now clearly spelled out exclusions previously implicit. Only rivers or sections of rivers that were "unimpaired by impoundments and human land uses" could be considered. Moreover, the use of adjacent lands "must not seriously affect the historical experience offered by the river environment" (Canadian Heritage Rivers Board 1990, 28–29). Rivers had still to provide suitable performative spaces for visitors to engage in imaginative re-enactments of life in earlier periods, but now no particular period was prioritized.

Neither the Boards of Trade nor CARP ever seriously considered reviving their campaign to nominate the Annapolis to the CHRS. The revisions the CHRS adopted were not sufficient to markedly improve the campaign's chances of success. The causeway and tidal power generating station still constituted "impoundments" that were unacceptable to the CHRS board, as were other contemporary uses of adjacent lands.[10] Moreover, the requirement that rivers should exemplify a *single* historical period would have fractured the harmonious convergence of multiple overlapping heritage traditions in which the Annapolis River figured. Because there are no objective measures by which heritage narratives can be ranked or assessed, there would have been no objective basis on which the Boards of Trade could have defended a decision to privilege one over the others. Even the tidal generating station would have had its heritage proponents, as it is the first tidal power station ever built in North America.

But it is instructive to consider the difference it would have made to CARP's activities and initiatives had they chosen otherwise. A number of ecologically important projects that CARP has pursued in its quest to protect and enhance the river's ecological systems might never have been undertaken. For example, CARP might not have elected to invest its limited resources in efforts to increase the efficiency of residential or commercial water consumption, as the inefficiencies had no direct impact on the river's appearance. A later project to improve opportunities for fish passage up the river's tributaries by clearing blocked culverts might still have seemed worthwhile, for the sake of conserving or restoring the river's threatened and extirpated fish. But on reflection, an initiative like this one, which only re-engineers rather than removes human modifications to the adjacent landscape, might have been rejected. Other CARP initiatives might have suffered a similar fate. Installing fences along the banks of the river and its tributaries has proved an effective means of keeping livestock and their waste out of rivers and streams. At the same time, it tends to increase rather than decrease visible human intrusion along shore lines. Thus, a proposal to promote fencing along vulnerable stretches of shore line might well have been rejected. The freshwater marsh engineered as a tertiary sewage system for Annapolis is more "natural" looking than the brown site on which it was established, but is still less well suited to restoring "continuity" of ecological systems than restoration of the site's original salt marsh would have been. So, even though a restored salt marsh would not have been as practical a solution to the town's waste-water problems, preference would presumably have gone to restoring the lost salt marsh.

Instead of developing projects such as these, an organization dedicated to stewarding the watershed's natural heritage values would presumably have concentrated its efforts on the removal of visible impairments, starting with the causeway and tidal power generating station. Such efforts would almost certainly have been wasted. Due to natural coastal subsidence and rising sea levels, the causeway cannot be removed without potentially catastrophic consequences to the human infrastructure, including heritage sites, along the lower third of the river's course. The tidal power station could be removed from the causeway. But while the station disturbs the continuity of the river's appearance with its past, and while its turbines do kill fish, it is of considerable ecological benefit in other respects. Tidal power generation reduces coal usage and so also greenhouse gas and particle emissions. And as it turns out, the power station's turbines have other beneficial effects on fish and communities of life. Their activity contributes to water mixing above the causeway, counteracting, at least in part, the causeway's negative effects on the subsurface oxygen levels above it and so improving conditions for aquatic life upstream (Sharpe 2007).

Conclusion

The object of this case study has not been to argue that ecological stewardship of the sort practiced by CARP, focused on biodiversity and ecosystem services, is inherently superior to natural heritage stewardship. It has been to highlight the ways that environmental and heritage stewardship differ. Particular ecological assemblages of special rarity, uniqueness, beauty, or other significance to a community will often merit the stewardship practices peculiar to heritage stewardship. Sometimes focusing on natural heritage stewardship objectives will prove to be a win-win option, when these preserve particular assemblages and ecosystem services simultaneously. But we cannot assume that this will always be the case. When it is not, we may find too late that our efforts to preserve natural heritage values have had the unintended effect of diverting our attention from significant threats to ecosystem functionality.

We can avoid these kinds of unintended consequences by remembering that ecological stewardship and natural heritage stewardship are different kinds of enterprises, with distinct and different objectives. That they are sometimes complementary should not blind us to their distinctiveness or to the fact that choosing between them is sometimes unavoidable. At the same time, careful attention to their respective objectives can also help us to mitigate apparent conflicts between them. Heritage stewardship is more fundamentally committed to preservation than is environmental stewardship. Thus, when environmental stewardship goals require the removal of historical structures or the cessation of historical practices, they may seem incompatible with heritage stewardship. In such cases, it may help to remember that heritage preservation is the preservation of groups' subjective appreciation of their histories, not the preservation of antiques for their own sake. Antique objects and practices are helpful but not essential for enjoyment of heritage values. There *are* other ways of creating suitable performative spaces in which groups can imaginatively engage with significant events, persons, and places from the past. Re-creations, reconstructions, and memorial markers can and routinely do serve the objectives of heritage stewardship quite as well as historical relicts.

We should not forget that while environmental stewardship is informed by the past, it is not beholden to it. The goal of environmental stewardship is to manage human behavior in order to restore or maintain the integrity of environmental systems and their services to human and other communities of life. Protection and restoration of "antique" natural environmental systems, components, and processes are often effective means of maintaining the functionality of environmental systems. But they may not be the best or only means available. Sometimes the goals of environmental stewardship can be better served by introducing new elements into a landscape or system, for example, by relocating threatened species outside their historical range to maintain biodiversity, creating grass lands or forests where they did not previously exist to compensate for losses to environmental systems elsewhere, or engineering a freshwater marsh where a salt marsh once existed to improve water-quality management, as was done in Annapolis Royal. If we cannot guarantee that all conflicts between environmental and heritage stewardship goals for the same landscapes will be resolvable without significant loss to either, the flexible relationship of each practice to the landscape's historical past suggests that with thoughtful management, resolutions will be possible more often than not.

Acknowledgments

I am indebted to Dianne LeGard, former Executive Manager of the Annapolis Valley Affiliated Boards of Trade; Shea Griffith, former Chair of the Annapolis River Task Force; Stephen Hawboldt and Monik Richard, former Executive Directors of the Clean Annapolis River Project; and to Graham Daborn, former Director of the Acadia Centre for Estuarine Studies, without whose kind assistance in sharing advice and recollections and in locating unpublished presentations and reports, preparation of this case study would have been impossible.

Notes

1. Throughout this essay I shall concentrate on the CHRS's original 1984 program guidelines. The guidelines have since been reworked several times and now permit a much wider variety of rivers to qualify for heritage status.

2. By this time, hydroelectricity and flood-control dams had also been introduced to most major tributaries of the Annapolis River and Basin.

3. Later research confirmed early findings of high mortality rates for fish passing through the power stations' turbines. See Dadswell and Rulifson (1994).

4. The river was "discovered" by France in 1603, appearing as the Rivière du Dauphin on Samuel de Champlain's 1609 map of the area.

5. The Historical Sites and Monuments Board of Canada was dominated by adherents of the Laurentian School of historians, who credited traders and trading companies with opening the Canadian interior and thus laying the groundwork for Canada's transcontinental nationhood. Canadian's distinctive "nation character" was also held to be traceable to the pattern of life established through wilderness exploration. Parks Canada took advice from the Board. See Campbell (2008); Kaufmann (1998); and Mortimer-Sandilands (2009).

6. The final 1981 proposal for the CHRS program was even more specific about the most significant human heritage roles of Canada's rivers; provision of food and transport for aboriginal people and facilitation of European exploration and settlement "through the vast interior of the continent" as "with the establishment of the fur trade, these rivers became the country's major routes of commerce with trading posts and settlements established along their banks." (Canadian Heritage Rivers Task Force 1981, 7.)

7. The first invitation was to join the Atlantic Region Estuaries Program (AREP), which led to a further invitation to continue participate in the Atlantic Coastal Action Program (ACAP), the successor to the AREP.

8. Stephen Hawbolt, personal communication, June 12, 2013.

9. Reports by and information about CARP may be found on its home page. http://www.annapolisriver.ca/.

10. The same language appears in a draft revision of the guidelines currently under discussion. See http://www.chrs.ca/en/docs/PPOG_April2012.pdf.

References

Annapolis Valley Affiliated Boards of Trade. 1987. "Annapolis River News." *AVABT Action* 10 (1): 7.

Annapolis Valley Affiliated Boards of Trade. 1986. "The Annapolis River Nomination Document: Canadian Heritage Rivers System." Unpublished.

Annapolis Valley Affiliated Boards of Trade. 1985. *Canoe Annapolis River*. Annapolis and Kings Counties, Nova Scotia: Annapolis Valley Affiliated Boards of Trade.

Campbell, Claire. 2008. "'It Was Canadian, Then, Typically Canadian': Revisiting Wilderness at Historic Sites." *British Journal of Canadian Studies* 21:15–34.

Canadian Heritage Rivers Board. 1990. *Canadian Heritage Rivers System: Guidelines.* Ottawa, Ontario: Canadian Heritage River Board Secretariat.

Canadian Heritage Rivers Task Force. 1981. "A Canadian Heritage Rivers System: A Proposal Prepared by the Canadian Heritage Rivers Task Force/Final Report." Ottawa, Ontario: Parks Canada.

Daborn, Graham R., Robert G. Williams, J. Sherman Boates, and Peter S. Smith. 1979. "Limnology of the Annapolis River and Estuary: I. Physical and Chemical Features." *Proceedings of the Nova Scotian Institute of Science* 29 (2): 153–172.

Dadswell, Michael J., Roger A. Rulifson, and Graham R. Daborn. 1986. "Potential Impact of Large-Scale Tidal Power Developments in the Upper Bay of Fundy on Fisheries Resources of the Northwest Atlantic." *Fisheries* 11 (4): 26–35.

Dadswell, M. J., and R. A. Rulifson. 1994. "Macrotidal Estuaries: A Region of Collision between Migratory Marine Animals and Tidal Power Development." *Biological Journal of the Linnean Society* 51 (2): 93–113.

Dunn, Brenda. 2004. *A History of Port Royal, Annapolis Royal: 1605–1800.* Halifax, NS: Nimbus Publishing.

Griffith, Shea. 1990. "Proposal to the Annapolis County Council." Unpublished.

Kaufman, Eric. 1998. "'Naturalizing the Nation': The Rise of Naturalistic Nationalism in the United States and Canada." *Comparative Studies in Society and History* 40 (4): 666–695.

Legard, Dianne Hankinson. 1986. "The Annapolis River: A True Heritage River." Unpublished presentation.

Legard, Dianne Hankinson. Undated. Unpublished presentation.

Longfellow, Henry Wadsworth. 2004. *Evangeline: A Tale of Acadie.* Fredericton, New Brunswick: Goose Lane.

Lowenthal, David. 1998. *The Heritage Crusade and the Spoils of History.* Cambridge: Cambridge University Press.

McKay, Ian, and Robin Bates. 2010. *In the Province of History: The Making of the Public Past in Twentieth Century Nova Scotia.* Montreal and Kingston: McGill-Queen's University Press.

Mortimer-Sandilands, Catriona. 2009. "The Cultural Politics of Ecological Integrity: Nature and Nation in Canada's National Parks, 1885-2000." *International Journal of Canadian Studies* 39–40: 161–189.

Parks Canada. 1979. *Parks Canada Policy.* Ottawa, Ontario: Parks Canada.

Parks Canada. 1984. *Canadian Heritage Rivers System: Objectives, Principles and Procedures.* Ottawa, Ontario: Parks Canada.

Sharpe, Andy. 2007. "Report on the Investigation of Low Dissolved Oxygen Levels in the Annapolis River Estuary." Annapolis Royal, NS: Clean Annapolis River Project.

Welchman, Jennifer. 2012. "A Defense of Environmental Stewardship." *Environmental Values* 21: 297–316.

CHAPTER 8

"Get Lost in the Footnotes
of History"

*The Restorative Afterlife of Rocky
Flats, Colorado*

PETER COATES

Introduction

Environmental writer and activist Jenny Price has contrasted the suppos-
edly natureless City of Los Angeles (where she lives) with the ostensi-
bly closer-to-nature City of Boulder, Colorado (where she used to live).
Although Boulder presents itself as an "anti-L.A.," what Price sees is a
city in denial. "You can keep your air clean more easily when the factories that manufacture your SUVs and Gore-Tex jackets lie in distant cities. . . . It is too easy to call your town the Great Right Place," she claims,
"when you live with far fewer of the problems you create" (Price 2005). In
fact, Boulder is far from divorced from the real world of "fallen" nature.
For sixty years, its residents have lived in the shadow of an environmental hazard—a "hidden factory" virtually invisible from public highways
(Iversen 2012)—equal to anything Los Angelenos face.

Eleven miles south of Boulder, at an elevation of 6,000 feet, lies Rocky
Flats (RF), a former nuclear weapons components plant that Price over-
looks in her comparison. Between 1952 and its closure in 1989, this is where
the Atomic Energy Commission (AEC) and its successors (US Energy
Research and Development Administration [ERDA] and Department
of Energy [DOE]) assembled the fissionable plutonium trigger (pit) for
every weapon in the US nuclear arsenal. In its heyday, Rocky Flats was
Colorado's seventh largest employer; the productive facility occupied an

area half the size of Manhattan, and it housed sufficient bombs to make Colorado the world's fourth-largest nuclear power (Morson 1999).

In 2007, after one of the largest remediation operations in American history, which took place from 1996 to 2005, jurisdiction over 4,000 acres of buffer zone was gifted to the US Fish and Wildlife Service (USFWS). Seven years later, though, the Rocky Flats National Wildlife Refuge exists only in name. As the home page of the refuge's website points out, as of May 2014, there was still no public access to the site, "due to a lack of appropriations for refuge management operations" (USFWS 2014). This chapter explores the site's strange "postnuclear" career of renaturalization and restoration, specifically, how this hotspot of contamination—a cornerstone of the "Dead West" (Davis 1999)—metamorphosed from hazard to habitat, and liability to asset.

The title of a book about the earlier cleanup of a toxic sister site, the Rocky Mountain Arsenal, on the other side of Denver, *When Nature Heals: The Greening of Rocky Mountain Arsenal* (Shattil et al. 1990), implied that nature itself took the initiative in the "weapons to wildlife" (W2W) conversion (see *Backpacker Magazine* 1992; Obmascik 1995; Havlick 2006; and Havlick, chap. 9 this volume). Yet the W2W conversion at Rocky Flats is not the automatic outcome of the disarming of the "Gunbelt" (the primary geographical locale of the so-called US military-industrial complex that emerged in the 1950s). Before it can dispose of property to a private interest, the Department of Defense (DOD) must grant fellow federal agencies the right of first refusal (Lewis 1994). Between 1988, when the Base Realignment and Closure (BRAC) process was initiated, and 2004, DOD transferred twenty-one military bases representing 1.1 million acres to the USFWS (Dycus 1996; Williams 1999; Havlick 2006). However rich the biotic resources that many of these facilities unwittingly harbored, this acreage represents just 5 percent of the area occupied by approximately 400 military installations that have been decommissioned to date. Multiple reuse is the most likely future they face.

This chapter concerns a postindustrial brownfield site that is broadly comparable to others in the United States, such as those at Rocky Mountain Arsenal and the Upper Clark Fork River (Montana), as well as those in Germany at the derelict steel plant that is now Landscape Park Duisburg North and defunct coal mining areas near Leipzig in the former German Democratic Republic (see chapters 9, 12, 3, and 5, respectively, this volume). Yet Rocky Flats is also different from these other examples, owing to its uniquely nuclear nature. The chapter examines distinct phases in the recent history of what some have called the "Rocky horror show"

(Lemonick 1993)—closure, cleanup, transition to wildlife refuge, and management planning—with reference to these themes: the acquisition and formal protection of biodiversity value; the debate among interest groups over the "end state" of the decommissioned and decontaminated plant/site (Rocky Flats Coalition of Local Governments 1999); the remembering and representing of the layered site's past; and the options for the restoration and management of a refuge in an arrested state of development.

Shielding Wildlife with Weapons: Militarized Island of Biodiversity

Located fifteen miles northwest of downtown (and upwind of) Denver, Rocky Flats was just one of the area's militarized sites. A second was the Rocky Mountain Arsenal, eight miles northeast of the city, where the US military produced a bevy of chemical weapons between 1942 and 1982 (private companies also leased areas to manufacture pesticides). In 2004, the USFWS inherited a chunk of the 17,000-acre buffer zone for Rocky Mountain Arsenal National Wildlife Refuge. Journalists loved the irony, penning headlines such as "toxic deathtrap becomes a wildlife haven" (Stein 2003). The unanticipated ecological value of sites such as the Arsenal and the Flats, explained Mark Udall, the Democratic congressman for Boulder who sponsored the Rocky Flats refuge bill in the House of Representatives, was a "hidden reward for having closed off these areas" (Rosner 2005).[1]

In *The World Without Us*, in which he tries to imagine what would be left of the world we have made if our species suddenly disappeared, Alan Weisman (2007) refers to the "alchemy" of the Arsenal's and Rocky Flats's transmutation into wildlife refuges. This sense of a quasi-magical metamorphosis also informs the announcement of Wayne Allard (Republican, Colorado), Senate cosponsor of refuge legislation, that he wanted to convert Rocky Flats from an "active" weapons manufacturing site into an "active refuge" for wildlife (United States Congress 2000). Yet, like the buffer zones of other US military installations (Butt 1994), Rocky Flats was already far from inactive as a wildlife sanctuary, if in a de facto capacity.

The size of the original Rocky Flats withdrawal in 1942 was 2,520 acres, of which plant facilities consumed 384 acres. The rest remained "undeveloped" save for firebreaks, holding ponds, effluent monitoring stations and gravel pits (figure 8.1). Rocky Flats was expanded to 7,660

FIGURE 8.1 Aerial view (looking northeast) of the Rocky Flats site, Golden, Jefferson County, Colorado (undated). Credit: Historic American Engineering Record, Prints and Photographs Division, Library of Congress, Washington, DC.

acres in 1975, creating a 6,000-acre buffer zone. The federal government seized large swathes of ranch land to maximize security and secrecy, but to protect the Industrial Area against private property encroachment as well. Site expansion also provided an extra margin of safety for the burgeoning Denver area, whose population leapt by 29 percent between 1940 and 1950 (from 322,000 to 416,000) and by almost as much over the next decade (to 494,000 in 1960).

When health and safety concerns surfaced in the late 1960s and a critical mass of protestors coalesced, activists wondered why the military had chosen a site so close to a growing metropolitan area. Yet, in addition to the "strategic invulnerability" a heartland location conferred, Pentagon planners (to the near-universal acclaim of local politicians, community officials, and business interests) chose Rocky Flats precisely because of the adjacent workforce and infrastructure (Abas 1989; Markusen et al. 1991; Ackland 1999). The area's vigorous population expansion continued, prompting the concern that "the [plant] will not enjoy rural isolation much longer" (ERDA 1976).

Each time another undeveloped acre was consumed (not least by sub-urban developments such as the one in Arvada where Kristen Iversen, author of the recent acclaimed personal history of Rocky Flats *Full Body Burden* grew up), the ecological value of Rocky Flats's buffer zone lands crept up a notch. Two important biomes—the Rocky Mountains and the high Great Plains—meet and overlap here, producing a mosaic of sagebrush, "upland" wetland, tall upland shrubland (perhaps unique within North America), and dry (xeric) tallgrass grassland (the latter one of North America's largest remnants) that support 600 species of flora.[2] The site also houses around 1,300 species, of which about 250 are mammals, birds, fish, reptiles, and amphibians. The mammals and birds include mule deer, whitetail deer, porcupine, striped skunk, coyote, American badger, bald eagle, prairie falcon, great-horned owl and Swainson's hawk; mountain lion, American elk, and black bear occasionally visit on their descent from the foothills (USFWS 2005). Nonetheless, the most illustrious of the species inadvertently protected for a half century within a "self-contained" militarized "island" of bio-diversity (Leslie et al. 1996) is Preble's meadow jumping mouse. This example of charismatic minifauna is endemic to the Front Range of Colorado and southeast Wyoming, where its preferred habitat is damp streamside meadow. Since the 1950s, though, agricultural, residential, and commercial developments have gobbled up 90 percent of its dwell-ing space (Edgerton, Germeshausen, and Grier 1992). The marginalized mouse's status in federal wildlife law (since 1998) is "threatened," the category below endangered.

The buffer zone's role was not confined, though, to passive protection for a preexisting wealth of biodiversity. Military appropriation triggered a process of environmental improvement. The quality of vegetation on the rangelands surrounding the core had progressively deteriorated since ranch-ing's late nineteenth-century arrival. Heavy grazing on rocky ground subject to uneven rainfall and harsh, dry winds had encouraged the spread of prickly pear, Spanish bayonet (yucca), and Russian thistle, as well as cheatgrass and other invasive plants. Cattle removal after 1952 initiated floral recovery. By the mid-1970s, native grasses had reestablished their hegemony in the buffer zone. In turn, a host of beleaguered wild herbivores and associated preda-tors returned. ERDA acknowledged increased levels of plutonium in certain species, but insisted that health was unimpaired: "The presence of numerous and varied animals ... suggests that operations ... are having no adverse effect ... the restricted, undeveloped areas ... are [a factor] in an improving, ecological environment at Rocky Flats" (ERDA 1976).

For much of its American history, the cause of wildlife preservation has been spearheaded by citizen groups such as the American Bison Society, Audubon Society, and National Wildlife Federation, working with the USFWS (and its predecessors). The conversion of the first US military reservation into a wildlife sanctuary, for instance, was the brainchild of a president who was an enthusiastic wildlife conservationist. Theodore Roosevelt's executive order in 1912 established 19,131-acre Fort Niobrara, a frontier garrison in Nebraska from 1879 to 1911, as a "preserve and breeding ground for native birds" (a remit quickly expanded to include bison and elk conservation).

However, the recent additions of the Rocky Mountain Arsenal and the Rocky Flats to the national wildlife refuge system bucked the trend. Wildlife managers and environmentalists did not take the initiative. That the main critics were not the forces of commerce that traditionally chafed against "lock up" of extractive resources in wildlife refuges and parks also ran against the grain. Local boosters supported extension of formal protection to informal reserves. They saw the potential of Rocky Flats's buffer zone to remove the stigma of the local "death factory" by serving as urban amenity and visitor attraction.

Cleaning Up the Mess

Production at Rocky Flats was suspended following Operation Desert Glow, a raid in June 1989 by FBI agents acting on reports of multiple violations of health and safety and environmental regulations by its operator, Rockwell International. The following summer, FBI agents raided the plant again, along with Environmental Protection Agency (EPA) officials (Zaffos 2004).[3] Just weeks after the dissolution of the Soviet Union in December 1991, in 1992 the DOE announced that production would not resume.

As the plant's mission shifted to remediation, Rocky Flats was in good company: the EPA's Superfund Program of the National Priorities List, first drawn up in 1982, embraces toxic legacies on nonmilitarized and non-federal lands (such as Montana's former copper mining sites on Clark Fork) as well as "formerly used defense sites." Yet the DOD owned 81 percent of the federal facilities on the initial list (such as the Rocky Mountain Arsenal and Fort Devens–Sudbury Training Annex; Shulman 1992; Wegman and Bailey1994; Durant 2007; see also Havlick, chap. 9 this volume).[4] At the same time, the scale of the task was unprecedented. In

1995, the DOE estimated that remediation at the renamed (in 1994) Rocky Flats Environmental Technology Site would take fifty years and cost $36.6 billion. A few months later, in October 1995, Kaiser-Hill (an environmental engineering company that had recently assumed charge) announced an accelerated operation lasting just seven years and costing only $6 billion. Visiting the site in early August 1997, energy secretary Federico Peña, former mayor of Denver, revised these estimates upward—but not by much. The job would be done by 2006 and would cost $7 billion (Eddy 1998a, 1998b; Kaiser-Hill 2005). In the event, Kaiser-Hill finished over a year ahead of schedule in October 2005 (Clark et al. 2006).[5]

According to the established rule of toxic remediation, if the envisaged future use is residential, then the standard will be more exacting than for an industrial end state. In its final report, the Industrial Area Transition Task Force recommended cleanup within the core area to a level suitable for an industrial park. It also noted that dedication as open space would set the least demanding target (Rocky Flats Stewardship Council 2008). Rocky Flats cleanup legislation stipulated that the person to be protected was the "maximally exposed individual," who, according to the yardstick adopted by the DOE, the EPA, and Colorado's Department of Public Health and Environment, was the "putative wildlife refuge" worker. This person "will not eat local food. He will not bring his children to the site, so they will not be exposed to the soil. He will drink little, if any, of the local water. His time exposed to plutonium left in the soil will be a fraction of that of a permanent resident." If he was protected, then so too, by default, would be all potentially exposed others (Makhijani and Gopal 2001).

The Institute for Energy and Environmental Research (IEER) disputed this approach. Regulators' criteria required treating soil materials registering up to 50 picocuries per gram of soil (a picocurie measures the level of radioactivity). But as the IEER reported (2001) to the Boulder-based Rocky Mountain Peace and Justice Center, this effectively confined cleanup to the surface layer down to 3 feet. Between 3 and 6 feet below surface, concentrations of up to 1,000 picocuries per gram would be tolerated, while the soil below six feet would be essentially ignored. The IEER posited an alternative "maximally exposed individual." The subsistence (a.k.a backyard) farmer scenario involved "a hypothetical person who lives on the land, consumes local water and eats only locally produced food" (Makhijani and Moore 2001; Makhijani, 2001). In all previous instances of wildlife refuge creation, the refuge has been regarded as a permanent end-state. But the IEER and the Rocky Mountain Peace and Justice Center did not regard this condition as inalienable—especially in an area where, by 1994, over two million people lived within fifty miles (Reed, Lemak, and Hesser 1997): "If a law can create a wildlife refuge out of a plutonium contaminated site in a few months' time, a reversal of such a decision can also be made. The pressures of development make such a reversal plausible, if not likely" (Makhijani and Gopal 2001). The Peace and Justice Center's cofounder, LeRoy Moore, was less circumspect: "[W]e should assume that eventually people will live on the site … cleaning … only to the refuge worker level provides poor protection for unsuspecting future residents" (Moore 2001).

Winning a Wildlife Refuge: Whose Victory?

Discussion of Rocky Flats's future began while production was still going strong. In 1975, the Lamm-Wirth Task Force on Rocky Flats recommended phasing out weapons manufacture and relocating plant functions.[6] As for reuse, the task force urged retooling to a "less hazardous energy-related industry," such as solar energy research (Lamm-Wirth Task Force 1975; Moore 1979). The following year, the ERDA announced that "the land could be returned, essentially to its original condition, for long-term agricultural, industrial, or residential use provided adequate resources were committed" (ERDA 1976). Nor was a wildlife refuge among the options contemplated under the rallying cry, "Convert Rocky Flats" (Rocky Flats Action Group 1979).

Neither was a refuge in the cards when reuse planning began in earnest. Visiting in June 1992, energy secretary James Watkins envisaged the cleansed site as a magnet for manufacturing and business (Roberts 1992). In February 1998, the Rocky Flats Local Impacts Initiative, a panel of community and government leaders preparing for the economic impact of conversion, disclosed six options. Four had been previously aired: a conventional industrial estate/office park; a more innovative eco-industry park; a renewable energy research facility; and an environmental remediation research facility. But the fifth and sixth options were making a fresh appearance: a Cold War museum and open space (Industrial Area Transition Task Force 1998).

The open space option had been floated in 1995 by the Citizens Advisory Board, established to advise the DOE on closure and cleanup (Rocky Flats Citizens Advisory Board 1991; Future Site Use Working Group 1995). However, understandings of "open space" varied enormously during the postproduction planning phase (one planner suggested a golf course). One of the earliest calls for reuse as refuge was issued by Tim Heaton, the Local Impacts Initiative's director, who told a journalist that "the place where the wildlife gather is pristine enough to give serious thought to a wildlife refuge." Noting that owls roosted in the rafters of an old ranch house and elk wandered in and out of the buffer zone, the reporter pointed out that prairie grassland "unfettered by plows or horses" was a "rare commodity" locally (Scanlon 1992).

In May 1999, speaking at a lectern against the backdrop of Lindsay Ranch (built in 1949 to house a caretaker by the Lindsay family, who had acquired the ranch site in 1941 but lived in Denver), Energy secretary Bill Richardson announced the creation of Rock Creek Reserve. He referred to this 800-acre wildlife sanctuary in the buffer zone, which hosts species like Preble's mouse, as "a unique habitat untouched by human development for 25 years" (Eddy 1999). A few months later (also speaking at the site), Udall and Allard announced their intention to introduce full refuge legislation,[7] which noted that the site had largely "remained undisturbed" since 1952 (Rocky Flats National Wildlife Refuge Act 2001; RFCAB 2002). In a cooperative initiative with Colorado's other senator, Allard introduced the bill to transform Rocky Flats from "producing weapons to protecting wildlife" (United States Congress 2000).

When President George W. Bush signed the bill on December 28, 2001, Allard hailed it as a "victory for our wildlife" (Stein 2001). But which human groups also claimed victory? W2W is often regarded as a win-win scenario. The DOD offloads surplus lands and the USFWS expands its holdings (Havlick 2007). And yet, just as W2W is not base closure's most likely outcome, neither is it necessarily a source of delight for wildlife managers and environmentalists. US military lands contain more biodiversity per acre than any other category of federal lands. But they are also the most heavily contaminated of these lands—which is as important a trigger for reinvention as wondrous biodiversity.

According to the Rocky Flats Citizens Advisory Board, refuge creation enjoyed extensive local support (Rocky Flats Citizens Advisory Board 2002). Yet this support was resigned as well as enthusiastic. And others were openly critical. For many locals, whose efforts to close the plant had spanned decades, opposition to the refuge was inseparable from criticism of the cleanup. As cleanup wound down, Moore (who had campaigned against the plant since 1979) contended that if the site's intended future use had been residential, farmland, or public park, the operation would have been more rigorous: refuge status was an "excuse for a cheaper cleanup" (Moore 2005).

Critics of "dirty closure" also queried the neat distinction between a small, contaminated core and a large and clean buffer zone. For wind and fire and the movement of soil and water (ground and surface) dispersed particles. Bioturbation also assisted contaminant spread. The City of Boulder pointed out that black-tailed prairie dogs could burrow to fifteen feet and, moving between core and buffer, create new frontiers of contamination (USFWS 2004). Nor were critics impressed by the apparently healthy condition of buffer zone wildlife (USFWS 2004). The Alliance for Nuclear Accountability (a nationwide network of organizations representing communities downwind and downstream of nuclear plants and waste-disposal sites) warned that, though individual specimens might appear largely unaffected, plutonium exposure's longer-term evolutionary and genetic effects (known as "body burden") were poorly understood (Makhijani and Gopal 2001; USFWS 2004).

Local politicians' concern revolved around public safety. "When you or I take our kids out in open space and walk on trails and observe wildlife and ride our bikes," objected Broomfield city councilman, Hank Stovall, "we don't expect to be breathing high levels of plutonium" (quoted in Morson 1999). Refuge sponsors Udall and Allard denied that it was a cheap ploy to justify a minimalist cleanup. They opposed detoxification to residential use standard as this would encourage the view that a more demanding cleanup "should result in a commensurate return on this investment . . . through development" (Udall and Allard 1999).

Most environmentalists disagreed that a cleaner cleanup potentially jeopardized ecological values (Morson 2004). Whistleblowers were equally suspicious of the refuge. Wes McKinley, foreman of the federal grand jury that conducted a three-year investigation of Rockwell International and the DOE officials, regarded it as a calculated attempt to erase awareness of past misdeeds and their persisting legacy. In a coauthored book about the alleged cover-up, McKinley (2004) asked, "Why speak out now?" Because "a decade later [after the grand jury investigation], unaware of what really happened at Rocky Flats, officials have announced that the former nuclear weapons plant can be partially cleaned up, turned into a wildlife refuge, and opened for recreation" (McKinley and Balkany 2004; McGuire 2005).

The Citizens Advisory Board noted that "a former nuclear weapons facility is not a typical addition to the refuge system, and careful precautions must be taken to ensure a successful transfer" (Rocky Flats Citizens Advisory Board 2002). USFWS staff are mostly biologists with little toxic hazard expertise, let alone radiological knowledge. Moreover, the agency is notoriously underfunded, receiving fewer dollars per acre than any other federal land management agency (at Rocky Flats, it cannot even afford to tackle the invasive plants ("noxious weeds"), such as Canada thistle and Dalmatian toadflax, that threaten the biodiversity the refuge is supposed to protect; Hooper 2011). Unsurprisingly, some staff regard decommissioned lands as burdensome (Havlick 2010, 2011).

Managing the Risky Refuge

At other postindustrial brownfield sites around the world, the challenge is one of restoration and renaturalization rather than the preservation of the elements of the natural world that have somehow survived. At Rocky Flats, however, it has been just as much a case of formalizing and consolidating the preservation of the rich biodiversity in the buffer zone that was intimately connected to the weapons production function at the site's core. The shift from informal to formal protection through refuge establishment awaited the EPA's verification of cleanup completion to a satisfactory standard. In June 2007, EPA removed the so-called offsite areas at Rocky Flats from the Superfund list, to which the entire site had been added in 1989. This act of partial site deletion covered more than 25,000 acres of surface and subsurface media (including groundwater) in the buffer zone (Federal Register 2007a, 2007b; EPA 2007). But planning by the new owners was already underway. On February 19, 2004, the USFWS issued a draft combined Comprehensive Conservation Plan and Environmental Impact Statement for the refuge's first fifteen years. Public meetings in local communities supplemented the forty-five-day public comment period. Feedback was invited on four potential "use options." Alternative A was a "no action" plan. "Alternative B—Wildlife, Habitat & Public Use," the plan the USFWS backed, proposed management for a combination of wildlife/habitat conservation with compatible public uses such as (limited) hunting, off-road driving, cycling, walking, and horseback riding. Alternative C was ecological restoration to "replicate presettlement conditions," with provision for limited public use and minimal facilities. Alternative D offered various more intensive public uses, including educational programs for schoolchildren, consonant with the refuge's "wildlife-first" mandate (USFWS 2004; Bunch 2004).

More than 5,000 comments were received in the form of public-hearing testimony, letters, petitions, and e-mails. Boulder County's Board of

County Commissioners was among the 63 percent of commentators who backed the refuge proposal as the "highest and best use of these lands," but its members cautioned against haste and were unhappy about the level of public access that Alternatives B and D envisaged. The commissioners' support for Alternative A, grounded in public safety concerns, was dramatically restated by the Alliance for Nuclear Accountability. Arguing that the entire Rocky Flats site was more or less contaminated, and that recreational activity could stir up and re-suspend radioactive particles—and concerned about the setting of a precedent for other contaminated DOE sites[8]—the Alliance recommended public closure for at least two centuries. Colorado's Division of Wildlife, the City of Arvada, the City and County of Broomfield, and the City of Westminster supported the official recommendation (B). And without endorsing a particular option, the Rocky Flats Coalition of Local Governments reiterated its general support for the refuge and the principle of continuing federal ownership (USFWS 2004).

Alternative C, focused on ecological restoration, also precipitated extensive commentary (just 15 percent of respondents chose this as their preferred alternative). Boulder's Board of County Commissioners selected ecological restoration as the next best way to protect the public and the site's wildlife populations. Other respondents probed deeper into the meaning of ecological restoration (though *rewilding* is a term absent from discussions of future scenarios for Rocky Flats). Replying to a request for clarification from the Jefferson County Board of Commissioners (the bulk of the site is located in Jefferson County) regarding "presettlement" conditions, the USFWS explained that "conceptual goals for habitat restoration [were] based on ecological conditions that existed prior to ranching and modern use and disturbance of the site." In other words, the historical baseline adopted here, as was the norm elsewhere in North America, was "pre-Columbian": the era of settlement did not include the centuries when Native peoples were in sole occupancy. Insofar as possible, therefore, presettlement species and ecological processes would be reinstated and all Euro-American influences and landscape layers removed (USFWS 2004).

"Predisturbance" is another central—and contested—notion within the discourse of restoration, given that the concept of ecological dynamism has now largely superseded the notions of "ecological balance" and "state of nature." In the context of frequent descriptions of the Rocky Flats site as "(relatively) undisturbed" for fifty years, the meaning of "disturbance" also generated considerable comment. Disturbance is often synonymous with disturbance by humans, but, as Boulder's Open Space and Mountain Parks Department emphasized, various forms of natural disturbance essential to healthy ecosystem functioning, such as grassland fire and grazing, were suppressed during the plant's operation. Given a half century's worth of fire prevention in the buffer zone, it was misleading to refer to militarization's total conservation of a presettlement environment, and the attempt to peel back the layers imposed by Euro-American activities to reveal the original core was regarded as a dubious enterprise. The even longer absence of wild bovines had also left its mark on the buffer zone ecosystems. To replicate the bison's presettlement grazing regime, the USFWS proposed "flash grazing" by cattle, with goats deployed to control the postsettlement spread of invasive weeds. The service also suggested prescribed burning and mowing as ways to mimic a "more natural" disturbance regime (both management tools were included in the Final Comprehensive Conservation Plan) (USFWS 2004, 2005).

Remembering Rocky Flats: The Danger of Erasure

Reservations about the feasibility of ecological restoration and concerns for public safety were supplemented by criticism of a wholly different sort. A vocal local constituency felt that refuge creation endangered the memory of the site's multiple layers of identity as ranchland, weapons factory, place of work, and rallying point for antinuclear protest.[9] Critics identified two competing narratives: an uplifting environmental story and a human history that the former obscured, whether deliberately or inadvertently. Human geographer J. S. Davis has captured this concern in the notion of double erasure—of both premilitary social history and the military era—formulated with reference to a Puerto Rican example of W2W (a former US Navy artillery range that is now the Caribbean's biggest wildlife refuge; Davis 2007a, 2007b). A wildlife refuge, in short, is regarded as a weapon against the (unpalatable) past.

The potential for friction between the objectives of cultural landscape preservation and those of environmental remediation/restoration is undeniable. At Rocky Flats, however, to date at least, the notion of double erasure is not so clearly applicable.[10] In "Rocky Flats unilateral mushroom transplant serenade," a poem delivered in July 1978 at a protest poetry reading on the rail tracks entering the industrial area, Michael Brownstein challenged the plant:

Roll up your cancer carpet
. . . And get lost in the footnotes of history

With your enemies
Your fear
And your hourglass boss
And gimme back my future. (Godfrey et al. 1979)

The stance of plant protesters is more complex, however, than this sentiment suggests. Critics indubitably wanted to relegate the plant to history's footnotes. Yet they did not want to see its nefarious memory cleansed. Plant critics felt that the new environmental narrative with its happy ending in a wildlife refuge directly competed with the unsavory Cold War story Brownstein addressed. Public memory of the toxic-tragic history of these shadowed and tainted grounds was in danger of erasure because "it would be unreasonable to assume long-term site control or that site use will not be changed in the future due to loss of institutional control and institutional memory" (Makhijani and Gopal 2001). As Nature trumps History, so to speak, in the agenda of rehabilitation and restoration, they were concerned that tales of secrecy and subterfuge, of the subordination of safety and the democratic process to national security and profit, would be rubbed out.

Len Ackland (1999), author of the authoritative history of the working plant, has created an interactive online virtual museum about a fire at the plant in 1969 (its worst). "There is an effort to normalize Rocky Flats and hide its history," he observed, but "if the story isn't told, the place where Rocky Flats existed is going to vanish and merge with the rest of the Front Range" (Lozano 2006; Long 2002).[11] The radiological half-life of a radioactive substance is the time it takes for half the original quantity of radioactivity to decay; for uranium and plutonium residues, this begins at 24,000 years. The other half-life, the biological half-life, is much shorter. And those who seek to commemorate the plant's history fear that the half-life of human memory may be even briefer: "Rocky Flats' contested history is now invisible to the naked eye" (Nordhaus 2009). The refuge website, noted Jon Wiener in 2012, "doesn't report that Rocky Flats manufactured plutonium triggers for hydrogen bombs from 1952 to 1989 . . . It doesn't report that . . . they were burying radioactive materials with half-lives of 24,000 years upstream of Denver" (Wiener 2012).

Yet there is no inherent conflict between fidelity to the site's human elements and histories and showing due regard for its nonhuman stories and components. In 1997, the National Park Service placed Rocky Flats on the National Register of Historic Places. And the provision to establish a museum as a "tribute to the Cold War and those who worked at Rocky

Flats" was squarely part of refuge legislation and a central feature of the "public use, education and interpretation" management objective (USFWS 2004, 2005). Friends of the Rocky Flats Cold War Museum received its initial operating grant in 2001 from Kaiser-Hill (supplemented by a congressional appropriation that Allard secured). The Friends' mission is to "document the historical, social, environmental and scientific aspects of Rocky Flats, and to educate the public about Rocky Flats, the Cold War, and their legacies through preservation of key artefacts and development of interpretive and educational programs." The museum website gives eight reasons to donate. The first is the imperative, now the buildings are gone and "memories are fading fast," to preserve the site's stories and material relics. Yet sharing information about the refuge's wildlife and ecology is also stipulated as a reason to support the cause (Friends of the Rocky Flats Cold War Museum 2012).

Initially, the board and members were mainly drawn from the ranks of long-serving retired plant workers. Representation has since diversified. Moore joined the board in 2001, and membership now encompasses former peace activists, as well as environmentalists and local community figures. And so, among the artefacts already donated to the future museum are not just glove boxes, protective suits, and radiation measuring equipment, but also banners wielded at anti-plant demonstrations and the tepee erected across the rail tracks (in 1979) to disrupt the flow of radioactive materials. Former antagonists—workers and protesters separated by barbed wire (Daniel and Pope 1979)—agree on the imperative to preserve the prerefuge past. The museum lobby's major accomplishment to date, in the bid to forestall memory loss, is ninety videotaped interviews with plant workers, regulators, local citizens, and community activists (Friends of the Rocky Flats Cold War Museum 2007; Wiener 2012).[12]

Since January 2007, the Friends have published a regular newsletter entitled "Weapons to Wildlife" (though the refuge itself rarely features in it). The search for a museum site led to a lease being taken in 2011 on the former post office in Arvada. The anticipated opening date of September 2012 was delayed, but the since renamed Rocky Flats Institute and Museum opened on another temporary site in Arvada in September 2013 (Friends of the Rocky Flats Cold War Museum 2011, 2012b; *Arvada News* September 3, 2013; Petrak 2013; Rocky Flats Institute and Museum 2014).[13]

In the meantime, persisting concern over memory loss was reflected in the debate about future signage at the refuge. Should signs simply inform? Or also warn? The section on interpretative facilities in the Final

Comprehensive Conservation Plan stipulates signs at all trailheads and other public access points that carry information about the site's history (including early settlement) and cleanup. The text finally agreed to for the future signs—now posted on the refuge website, along with twenty-seven pages of responses to the consultation exercise—consists of two sections: "What Happened Here?" and "Is there Residual Contamination?" The former explains that "for nearly four decades, thousands of women and men worked here, building nuclear components for the United States' deterrent weapons," and adds that the work was "dangerous and secret" and acknowledges that "there were accidents," some of which (along with waste-handling practices "of the early decades") led to "releases of plutonium and other contaminants into the environment."

The second section emphasizes that "levels of contamination on refuge lands are low, meet conservative state and federal cleanup standards and are similar to adjacent lands," and that the health risks for visitors are much lower than they are for refuge workers (the latter having a "maximum life-time increased cancer risk of about 2 in a million due to residual contaminants"). Finally (with breathtaking flippancy, condescension and trivialization, according to some commentators), the text also reminds visitors that "there are hazards involved in any form of wildland recreation"—including "the potential for trips, slips and falls; poisonous snakes; and unreasonable or illegal acts by other persons" (USFWS 2007; see also: Hourdequin and Havlick 2013; Hourdequin, chap. 2, this volume).[14]

With regard to heritage value, USFWS is just as sensitive as the local Jefferson County Historical Society to the importance of the Lindsay Ranch as a cultural resource, which every refuge management report acknowledges (adoption of Alternative C—ecological restoration—would have required its removal). The USFWS is not averse to restoring and interpreting this eminently picturesque site, redolent of the "Old West" with its dilapidated fences and farm buildings, which has gained recognition as the best surviving material evidence in rapidly developing Jefferson County of the earlier twentieth-century cattle ranching era (there are no remnants of original structures from when the area was first homesteaded in 1868; see figure 8.2). But it lacks the resources. Rocky Flats has not been entirely released from grubby but honest history and elevated to a pure and somehow deceitful realm of nature. On the basis of the evidence currently available, the applicability to Rocky Flats of a dehistoricizing and renaturalizing narrative that is reinventing the site as a floral and

FIGURE 8.2 Looking beyond the historic Lindsay Ranch to residential developments bordering the Rocky Flats site (October 2008). Credit: Peter Coates.

faunal wonderland that buries deep the less palatable historical layer of weapons manufacture (as well as the premilitary past) can be questioned.

Rocky Flats Today

Many of the problems refuge managers at Rocky Flats confront are the same as those faced at more conventional wildlife refuges. Others, pertaining to public access (wildlife refuges are mandated to provide opportunities for scientific research, education, and recreation), are more specific to W2W refuges. The attentive visitor to Rocky Flats's sister site, the Rocky Mountain Arsenal National Wildlife Refuge, which has admitted the public since 1997, can spot species such as black-tailed prairie dogs, coyotes, and Swainson's hawk. The biggest animal draw at the Arsenal, however, is the bison, whose reintroduction reflects a shift from preservation by default to active conservation management: to restore the bulk of the site to a condition akin to that encountered by the first Euro-Americans. The Arsenal also hosts "nature and educational activities." In October 2012, a nine-mile Wildlife Drive opened up the refuge's main habitats (though it steers well clear of the most contaminated areas and landfills). And for a number of years, attractions unrelated to wildlife, publicized in *Wild News*, the Arsenal's regular newsletter, also became an established part of the refuge's rhythm. Old West Day, held in October was billed as "a free family celebration of the American West and National Wildlife Refuge Week." Visitors could take a hayride and fortify themselves with a chuckwagon meal. Musical entertainment was provided by Ron Ball, the Singing Cowboy.

To raise the stakes of objection at Rocky Flats, McKinley insisted that its "radioactive fields" were also intended for recreation, including horseback riding and hiking, but especially as a destination for school trips (McKinley and Balkany 2004). In common with whistleblowers and various community outfits, environmental groups have warned against activities such as education tours since the late 1990s (Gerhardt 1997; Lowrie and Greenberg 1998). The Comprehensive Conservation Plan and Environmental Impact Statement that the USFWS released in April 2005 envisaged increasing public use over the next fifteen years, as financial and human resources became available. Projected facilities consist of 3.8 miles of hiking trails and 12.8 miles of multiuse trails (mountain biking and horse riding as well as hiking), converted, mostly, from existing dirt roads; a seasonally staffed visitor station; trailhead parking lots and outlook points. Limited hunting is also contemplated. So are environmental classes for high school and college students (McGuire 2004; USFWS 2005).

As the Denver-Boulder metropolitan area's population continues to grow, readily accessible open space carries an ever higher premium. In 2009, 3.5 million people lived within fifty miles of Rocky Flats; 300,000 reside within the site's watershed. Yet, access restrictions during and after the site's working life are precisely why wildlife has flourished at Rocky Flats. It is perhaps better, for the sake of biodiversity—not to mention human health (concerned citizens recently located plutonium they claim is breathable in soil samples near the site; Environment News Service 2010)—to keep the refuge off-limits for plutonium's radiological half-life (at least), which, for plutonium isotope Pu-239, is 24,000 years.

Conclusion

This chapter has examined one example of the paradox that some of the most contaminated sites in the United States are adjacent to—indeed, inseparable from—some of its richest natural environments (Greenberg et al. 1997). Humanities research on the geography of nuclear contamination has mainly focused on the legacy of unmitigated environmental ruin inflicted by testing and weapons production that dominates the "landscape of national sacrifice" in the "ugly" and poisoned American West (Kuletz 1998; Davis 1999; Riebsame 1997; Beck 2009). Increasingly, though, following Rebecca Solnit's lead, scholarly attention has shifted to the "unofficial" nature surviving surprisingly at former nuclear and other militarized places that compares favorably with the "official" nature formally protected within flagship national parks such as Yosemite and Yellowstone (Solnit 1994; Wills 2001; Coates et al. 2011; Coates 2014). This case study of Rocky Flats ponders the adaptability of nonhuman nature rather than restates the conventional narrative of ecological fragility and vulnerability. Are cases of nature's survival at hybrid, layered sites such as Rocky Flats as shocking as examples of the other-than-human world's demise elsewhere?

And yet, it is hard to predict how long this unusually high level of biodiversity will survive. Natural systems rarely stay still, even in the absence of direct human intervention. The inspector general of the Department of Interior, which houses the USFWS, recently noted that, since site remediation, "while the Refuge sat idle, invasive weeds displaced native species and increased the potential risk for migration of nuclear contaminants to surface water" (Ashe 2011). In a borderless world in which the global movement of species is a constant feature, and in the absence of funding for robust management, the security of floral and faunal resources cannot be guaranteed even within a refuge closed to the public for the foreseeable future.

This exploration of the afterlife of a particular nuclear-weapons manufacturing complex also engages with larger issues concerning environmental contamination, postindustrial uses, the coexistence of toxicity and biodiversity, and the mingling of human and ecological histories—despite the absence of physical traces of the human past, recent and more distant—at obsolete industrial sites. Scholars such as Havlick are rightly critical of the motivations that often propel W2W conversions. But the story of Rocky Flats suggests that we should also acknowledge their incontrovertible ecological assets. This case study also queries J. S. Davis's belief that "the labelling of any environment as 'natural' necessarily involves the erasure of the social history of the landscape" (Davis 2007a) and S. R. Krupar's view that the "refuge overlay" obscures "the historical production of the landscape" (Krupar 2011; see also Krupar

2012, 2013). The unexpected biodiversity value of disused nuclear sites was the mushroom cloud's silver lining, and there is no necessary conflict between awareness of Rocky Flats's "natural" assets and recognition of its recent human past.

At other former nuclear sites, recognition of intertwined human and natural histories is also more evident than erasure (provided, that is, that erasure is defined as a deliberate act rather than a more incremental, passive, and unintentional form, more akin to forgetting). The most recent example is the addition in August 2010 of the Bikini Atoll Nuclear Test Site (where the United States conducted twenty-three nuclear and thermonuclear weapons tests between 1946 and 1958) to the list of World Heritage Sites by UNESCO (United Nations Educational, Scientific and Cultural Organization). This monument and memorial to the nuclear era and the superpowers' arms race is also replete with biodiversity and harbors ecological systems considered to be in a state of recovery—though nobody is allowed to live there because the soil contains the radioactive isotope cesium-137, which would be taken up by any crop residents might plant (Niedenthal 2001, 2009; UNESCO 2010; Gwynne 2012). In fact, the value of the renaturing process is acknowledged by the UNESCO listing, which emphasizes that the "degradation of the human artifacts by the natural elements," far from being antithetical, "forms part of the cultural process illustrated by the property" (UNESCO 2010).

Building on research by human geographers, such as David Havlick and J. S. Davis, and studies by other humanities scholars such as Kuletz and Solnit, this chapter contributes the perspective of an environmental historian working with the concept of the socionatural site and the notion of socioecological hybridity, and operating with a local case study, site visits, and written records in an effort to advance our understanding of the remediation, redeployment and remembering of contaminated militarized landscapes. At the same time, it questions the validity of the customary dichotomy within the restoration discourse between the desire to preserve the historical elements within multistoreyed (and storied) landscapes and the prioritization of fidelity to their ecological elements. For there is such a thing as natural heritage as well as cultural heritage (cf. Welchman, chap. 7, this volume), and the restoration of nature is all about restoring a sense of history as well. In fact, the deep time scale that ecological restoration involves—whether the main aim is to release a set of natural processes or return to a particular point in time—is arguably capable of communicating a far more profound sense of history and the depth of the past than can the shallower elements of (merely) human time scales.

Acknowledgments

The author thanks Bruce Hastings (USFWS) for setting aside the best part of a day to show him around the Rocky Flats National Wildlife Refuge and the Rocky Mountains Arsenal National Wildlife Refuge in October 2008; the staff at the Western History Collection, Denver Public Library, and at the Special Collections Department, University Libraries, University of Colorado at Boulder; and David Havlick for his insights, updates, and rigorous fact-checking.

Funding

The United Kingdom's Arts and Humanities Research Council funded this research through its Landscape and Environment Programme award, "Militarized Landscapes in Twentieth-Century Britain, France and the United States" (2007–2010).

Notes

1. Rocky Flats National Wildlife Refuge is managed as part of the Rocky Mountain Arsenal National Wildlife Refuge Complex. A Complex is an administrative grouping of two or more refuges that occupy a similar ecological area and have comparable purposes and management needs. The third refuge in this particular complex is the much smaller Two Ponds National Wildlife Refuge, also located in the Denver metropolitan area.

2. According to the Colorado Natural Heritage Program, Rocky Flats's xeric tall-grass grassland community is the largest surviving extent in Colorado and perhaps even in North America as a whole (USFWS 2005).

3. In 1992, federal grand jury prosecutors and Rockwell agreed to a plea bargain. Rockwell was fined $18.5 million but the most serious charges (and the indictments of individuals) were dropped. In addition, the grand jury report was sealed, and jurors who broke secrecy faced prosecution.

4. "Superfund" is shorthand for the Comprehensive Environmental Response, Compensation, and Liability Act (1980), which authorized EPA to compile a National Priorities List of sites eligible for funding for long-term remedial action.

5. For a glowing account by business/management studies researchers of cleanup as mission accomplished against all odds ("lessons from the cleanup of America's most dangerous nuclear weapons plant"), see Cameron and Lavine (2006).

6. Richard Lamm, governor of Colorado, and congressman Timothy Wirth, were Democrats elected in November 1974 with trade union, environmentalist, and peace activist support.

7. Allard had recently been appointed chairman of the Strategic Subcommittee of the Senate Armed Services Subcommittee, which had direct oversight of former DOE weapons facilities.

8. In its response, the USFWS pointed out that the first conversion was in fact Saddle Mountain National Wildlife Refuge, carved from the Hanford buffer zone in Washington state in 1971 and incorporated into Hanford Reach National Monument in 2000.

9. For the diversity of narratives and multiple meanings of place attached to Rocky Flats, see Iversen (2012).

10. At Rocky Mountain Arsenal's visitor center (a new one opened in May 2011), the weapons manufacturing phase is also formally acknowledged, embedded within a narrative of environmental change that begins with the indigenous occupants: "Agriculture altered the plant and animal communities and changed the landscape. Military and industrial production left soil and water contaminated with chemical waste. Today, the cleanup continues to shape this site, guiding it to a future as a home for wildlife and as a natural resource and learning place for the community." A plaque outside the visitor center honors the Arsenal employees, "who worked to heal and restore this land as a legacy for future generations." Whether this embeds this incarnation of the Arsenal—and earlier ones—or the notion of the local landscape as a palimpsest within the consciousness of visitors is another matter.

11. At http://www.colorado.edu/journalism/cej/exhibit/index.html.

12. Available online through the Maria Rogers Oral History Program, Carnegie Branch for Local History, Boulder Public Library, http://boulderlibrary.org/carnegie/collections/mrohp.html.

13. The new name reflects the institution's expanded mission to include not just historic preservation but "dialogue about today's nuclear challenges, using the lessons of Rocky Flats as a guide."

14. Since being elected to the state legislature in 2005, Wes McKinley, supported by environmentalists, had tried to pass a bill requiring refuge managers to post signs informing visitors about what happened there once upon a time and the environmental legacy. Local politicians, however, have been concerned about negative publicity, specifically, the impact on real estate values and the area's appeal to potential residents (Nordhaus 2009).

References

Abas, B. 1989. "Rocky Flats: A Big Mistake From Day One." *Bulletin of the Atomic Scientists* 45 (10): 18–24.

Ackland, L. 1999. *Making a Real Killing: Rocky Flats and the Nuclear West.* Albuquerque: University of New Mexico Press.

Ashe, D. M. 2011. Memorandum to K. Elmore, "Inspection of the Rocky Flats National Wildlife Refuge." Report No. C-18-FWS-0017-2010, July 11.

Ashton, J. 1978. "Scientists Blast Flats at Protest Trial." *Rocky Mountain News,* November 18.

Backpacker Magazine. 1992. "Weapons to Wildlife." *Backpacker* 20 (117):12.

Beck, J. 2009. *Dirty Wars: Landscape, Power, and Waste in Western American Literature.* Lincoln: University of Nebraska Press.

Bunch J. 2004. "Seeing into Rocky Flats' Future." *Denver Post,* March 11.

Butt, K. H. 1994. "Why the Military is Good for the Environment." In *Green Security or Militarized Environment,* edited by J. Käkönen, 83–109. Brookfield, VT: Dartmouth Publishing.

Cameron, K. S. and M. Lavine. 2006. *Making the Impossible Possible: Leading Extraordinary Performance—The Rocky Flats Story.* San Francisco: Berrett-Koehler.

Clark, D. L., D. R. Janecky, and L. J. Lane. 2006. "Science-based Cleanup of Rocky Flats." *Physics Today,* September, p. 34.

Coates, P. A. 2014. "Borderland, No-man's Land, Nature's Wonderland: Troubled Humanity and Untroubled Earth." *Environment and History* 20: 499–516.

Coates, P. A., T. Cole, M. Dudley, and C. Pearson. 2011. "Defending Nation, Defending Nature?: Militarized Landscapes and Military Environmentalism in Britain, France, and the United States." *Environmental History* 16: 456–491.

Daniel, J., and K. Pope. 1979. *Year of Disobedience.* Boulder: Daniel Productions.

Davis, J. S. 2007a. "Military Natures: Militarism and the Environment." *Geojournal* 69: 131–134.

Davis, J. S. et al. 2007b. "Military Pollution and Natural Purity: Seeing Nature and Knowing Contamination in Vieques, Puerto Rico." *Geojournal* 69: 165–179.

Davis, M. 1999. "Dead West: Ecocide in Marlboro Country." In *Over the Edge: Remapping the American West,* edited by Valerie J. Matsumoto and Blake Allmendinger, 339–354. Berkeley: University of California Press.

Durant, R. F. 2007. *The Greening of the U.S. Military: Environmental Policy, National Security, and Organizational Change.* Washington, DC: Georgetown University Press, 77.

Dycus, S. 1996. *National Defense and the Environment.* Hannover: University Press of New England.

Eddy, M. 1998a. "Figuring out Flats' Future." *Denver Post,* February 25.

Eddy, M. 1998b. "Pena Affirms Promise: Flats Closure by 2006." *Denver Post,* June 6.

Eddy, M. 1999. "Habitat Saved at Flats." *Denver Post,* May 18.

Edgerton, Germeshausen and Grier/DOE. 1992. *Rocky Flats Environmental Restoration Update (a Periodic Update on RF Cleanup),* October/November: 3.

Environment News Service. 2010. "Rocky Flats Nuclear Site Too Hot for Public to Handle, Citizens Warn." August 5. http://www.ens-newswire.com/ens/aug2010/2010-08-05-01.html.

EPA (US Environmental Protection Agency). 2007. "NPL Partial Site Deletion Narrative." http://www.epa.gov/superfund/sites/npl/pdel/pnar865.htm.

ERDA (US Energy Research and Development Administration). 1976. "Omnibus Environmental Assessment for the Rocky Flats Plant (draft, May)." Box 2, folder 9, Rocky Flats Project, Rocky Flats Monitoring Committee, General Material, American Friends Service Committee (Colorado Branch), Archives, University of Colorado at Boulder.

Federal Register. 2007a. "Environmental Protection Agency: National Oil and Hazardous Substances Pollution Contingency Plan; National Priorities List." March 13, 72/48: 11313–11319.

Federal Register. 2007b. "Environmental Protection Agency: National Oil and Hazardous Substances Pollution Contingency Plan; National Priorities List." May 25, 72/101: 29276–29277.

Friends of the Rocky Flats Cold War Museum. 2007. "90 Rocky Flats Oral Histories Completed & Online." *Weapons to Wildlife*, April/May, 1/3: 1.

Friends of the Rocky Flats Cold War Museum. 2011. "Board Approves Lease of Old Arvada Post Office for Rocky Flats Museum." *Weapons to Wildlife*, April, 5/1: 1.

Friends of the Rocky Flats Cold War Museum. 2012. Rocky Flats Institute and Museum. http://www.rockyflatscoldwarmuseum.org/.

Gerhardt, G, 1997. "Rocky Flats 'Refuge' Opens for Visitors: Auto Tours Show Off Remarkable Slice of Tall-grass Ecosystem." *Rocky Mountain News*, March 23.

Godfrey, R. J., G. Dorskind, and A. Santoli. 1979. *Clean Energy Verse: Poetry from the Tracks at Rocky Flats*. Woodstock, NY: Safe Earth Press.

Greenberg, M., K. Lowrie, D. Krueckeberg, H. Mayer, and D. Simon. 1997. "Bombs and Butterflies: A Case Study of the Challenges of Post Cold War Environmental Planning and Management for the US Nuclear Weapons Sites." *Journal of Environmental Planning and Management* 40: 739–750.

Gwynne, S. C. 2012. "Paradise with an Asterisk." *Outside Magazine*, October 17. http://www.outsideonline.com/outdoor-adventure/nature/Paradise-With-An-Asterisk.html?page=all.

Havlick, D. G. 2006. "Bombs Away: New Geographies of Military-to-Wildlife Conversions in the United States." PhD diss., University of North Carolina-Chapel Hill.

Havlick, D. G. 2007. "Logics of Change for Military-to-Wildlife Conversion in the United States." *Geojournal* 69: 151–64.

Havlick, D. G. 2010. "Militarization, Conservation and US Base Transformations." *Militarized Landscapes: From Gettysburg to Salisbury Plain*, edited by C. Pearson, P. Coates, and T. Cole, 113–134. London: Continuum.

Havlick, D. G. 2011. "Disarming Nature: Converting Military Lands to Wildlife Conservation." *Geographical Review* 101: 183–200.

Hooper, T. 2011. "Invasive Weeds Raise Nuclear Concerns at Rocky Flats." *Colorado Independent*, August 4.

Hourdequin, M., and D. G. Havlick 2013. "Restoration and Authenticity Revisited." *Environmental Ethics* 35 (1): 79–93.

Industrial Area Transition Task Force, Rocky Flats Local Impact Initiative. 1998. "From Swords to Plowshares: A Plan for the Reuse of the Industrial Area of the Rocky Flats Environmental Technology Site—Final Report." Arvada, CO. September 10.

Institute for Energy and Environmental Research. 2001. "Cleanup of Nuclear Weapons Sites May Leave High Levels of Plutonium in Soil." December 11.

Iversen, K. 2012. *Full Body Burden: Growing Up in the Nuclear Shadow of Rocky Flats*. New York: Crown.

Kaiser-Hill/DOE. 2005. *Rocky Flats: A Proud Legacy, A New Beginning: The Story of the World's Largest and Most Complex Environmental Cleanup Project*.

Krupar, S. R. 2011. "Alien Still Life: Distilling the Toxic Logics of the Rocky Flats National Wildlife Refuge." *Environment and Planning D: Society and Space* 29: 268–290.

Krupar, S. R. 2012. "Transnatural Ethics: Revisiting the Nuclear Cleanup of Rocky Flats, Colorado, through the Queer Ecology of Nuclia Waste." *Cultural Geographies* 19: 303–327.

Krupar, S. R. 2013. *Hot Spotter's Report: Military Fables of Toxic Waste*. St. Paul: University of Minnesota Press.

Kuletz, V. L. 1998. *The Tainted Desert: Environmental and Social Ruin in the American West*. New York: Routledge.

Lamm-Wirth Task Force. 1975. *Documentary Report on Rocky Flats*. August 15. University of Colorado at Denver. Unpublished Report. Available online at: http://www.lm.doe.gov/land/sites/co/rocky_flats/closure/references/150-Lamm-Wirth%20Task%20Force%20on%20RF.pdf.

Lemonick, M. D. 1993. "Rocky Horror Show." *Time*, November 27, pp. 69–70.

Leslie M., G. K. Meffe, L. Jeffrey, J. L. Hardesty, and D. L. Adams. 1996. *Conserving Biodiversity on Military Lands: A Handbook for Natural Resources Managers*. Arlington, VA: The Nature Conservancy.

Lewis, R. K. 1994. "When 'Army Surplus' Is Real Estate: Fort Belvoir Plan Illustrates Larger Issues. *Washington Post*, March 5.

Long, M. E. 2002. "Half-Life: The Lethal Legacy of America's Nuclear Waste." *National Geographic*. http://ngm.nationalgeographic.com/ngm/0207/feature1/fulltext.html.

Lowrie, K., and M. Greenberg. 1998. "Cleaning It up and Closing It Down: Land Use Issues at Rocky Flats." *Federal Facilities Environmental Journal* 10 (October): 769–797.

Lozano, V. 2006. "Virtual Museum Recounts Rocky Flats Disaster." *Inside*, February 14. http://www.colorado.edu/insidecu/editions/2006/2-14/story3.html.

Makhijani, A. 2001. Press Conference. National Press Club, December 11. Washington, DC.

Makhijani, A., and S. Gopal. 2001. "Setting Cleanup Standards to Protect Future Generations: The Scientific Basis of Subsistence Farmer Scenario and its Application to the Estimation of Radionuclide Soil Action Levels (RSALs) for Rocky Flats." Report for the Rocky Mountain Peace and Justice Center. December. Washington, DC: Institute for Energy and Environmental Research.

Makhijani, A., and L. Moore. 2001. "Fed Plan is Weak: Subsistence Farmer Scenario the Way to Go." *Denver Post*, August 12.

Markusen, A., P. Hall, S. Campbell, and S. Deitrick. 1991. *The Rise of the Gunbelt: The Military Remapping of Industrial America*. New York: Oxford University Press.

McGuire, K. 2004. "Flats Refuge Proposal Jells." *Denver Post*, December 3.

McGuire, K. 2005. "Ex-FBI Agent Accuses Feds of Rocky Flats Cover Up." *Denver Post*, January 6.

McKinley, W., and C. Balkany. 2004. *The Ambushed Jury: How the Justice Department Covered Up Government Nuclear Crimes and How We Caught Them Red Handed*. New York: Apex Press.

Moore, L. 1979. "Rocky Flats: Skirmish, or Struggle for the Soul of Society?" *Rocky Mountain News*, September 26.

Moore, L. 2001. Statement, Press Conference, December 11. National Press Club, Washington, DC.

Moore, L. 2005. "The Bait-and-Switch Cleanup." *Bulletin of the Atomic Scientists* 61 (January/February): 50–57.

Morson, B. 1999. "Flats is on Track: Company Disputes Congressional Report Saying Cleanup Unlikely to be Finished by 2006." *Rocky Mountain News*, May 30.

Morson, B. 2004. "Keep Rocky Flats Closed, Activists Tell U.S. Agency." *Rocky Mountain News*, March 12.

Niedenthal, J. 2001. *For the Good of Mankind: A History of the People of Bikini and their Islands*. Majuro, Marshall Islands: Bravo Publishers.

Niedenthal, J. 2009. "The World's Debt to Bikini." *Bulletin of the Atomic Scientists*, March 11. http://www.thebulletin.org/web-edition/op-eds/the-worlds-debt-to-bikini.

Nordhaus, H. 2009. "The Half-Life of Memory: The Struggle to Remember the Nuclear West." *High Country News*, February 16, p. 41. http://www.hcn.org/issues/41.3/the-half-life-of-memory.

Obmascik, M. 1995. "Arsenal Cleanup Tab Loaded with Frills." *Denver Post*, January 15.

Petrak, N. 2013. "Rocky Flats Museum Exhibit Honors Nuclear Workers—And Reveals Their Double Lives." *Denver Westword* (blog), October 30. http://blogs.westword.com/latestword/2013/10/rocky_flats_museum_national_day_of_remembrance.php.

Price, J. 2005. "Thirteen Ways of Seeing Nature in LA." In *Land of Sunshine: An Environmental History of Metropolitan Los Angeles*, edited by W. Deverell and G. Hise, 220–244. Pittsburgh: University of Pittsburgh Press.

Reed R., D. J. Lemak, and W. A. Hesser. 1997. "Cleaning Up after the Cold War: Management and Social Issues." *Academy of Management Review* 22: 614–642.

Riebsame, W. 1997. *Atlas of the New West: Portrait of a Changing Region*. New York: Norton, 132–137.

Roberts, J. A. 1992. "Watkins: Plant's Future Looks Bright." *Denver Post*, June 13.

Rocky Flats Action Group. 1979. *Action: The Voice of Nuclear Criticism and Education in Colorado*, August, 3.

Rocky Flats Citizen Advisory Board. 1991 (October). *A Vision for the Cleanup of Rocky Flats*, 11.

Rocky Flats Citizen Advisory Board. 2002. "From Weapons to Wildlife." *The Advisor: A Publication of the Rocky Flats Citizens Advisory Board*. Spring, pp. 1–5.

Rocky Flats Coalition of Local Governments. 1999. Board Meeting Minutes (Final Draft). May 6. http://www.rockyflatssc.org/rfclog_meetingminutes/1999/rfclog_minutes_5_6_99.pdf, p. 1.

Rocky Flats Institute and Museum. 2014. "Past, Present, and Future." http://www.rocky-flatscoldwarmuseum.org/about-rfim/history/.

Rocky Flats National Wildlife Refuge Act. 2001. S.1438, 107th Congress, 1st Session, House and Senate.

Rocky Flats Stewardship Council. 2008. "Rocky Flats History: Timeline of Key Events." http://www.rockyflatssc.org/RFSC_fact_sheets/RF_timeline_final_5-08.pdf.

Rosner, H. 2005. "At the Foot of the Rockies, Cleaning a Radioactive Wasteland." *New York Times*, June 7.

Scanlon, B. 1992. "Rocky Flats: A Future Environmental Mecca?" *Rocky Mountain News*, November 18.

Shattil, W., B. Rozinski, and C. Madson. 1990. *When Nature Heals: The Greening of Rocky Mountain Arsenal*. Boulder: Roberts Rinehart/National Fish and Wildlife Foundation.

Shulman, S. 1992. *The Threat at Home: Confronting the Toxic Legacy of the US Military*. Boston: Beacon Press.

Solnit, R. 1994. *Savage Dreams: A Journey into the Landscape Wars of the American West*. New York: Vintage.

Stein, T. 2001. "Flats Refuge Bill Hailed as 'Victory' for Wildlife." *Denver Post*, December 18.

Stein, T. 2003. "Arsenal Cleanup to Pass Milestone." *Denver Post*, February 29.

Udall, M., and W. Allard. 1999. "Coming Clean at Rocky Flats: Wildlife Refuge Does Not Short Change Cleanup." *Denver Post*, August 12.

UNESCO. 2010. Bikini Atoll Nuclear Test Site. http://whc.unesco.org/en/list/1339.

United States Congress. 2000. *Congressional Record-Senate*, September 21: 18930-32.

USFWS (U.S. Fish and Wildlife Service). 2004. "Rocky Flats National Wildlife Refuge: Comments and Responses on the Draft Environmental Impact Statement; Appendix H to the Final Comprehensive Conservation Plan and Environmental Impact Statement." September.

USFWS. 2005. "Rocky Flats National Wildlife Refuge: Final Comprehensive Conservation Plan." Commerce City, CO. April 19.

USFWS. 2007. Rocky Flats National Wildlife Refuge, Final Rocky Flats Signage. Last updated 12 December 2011. http://www.fws.gov/rockyflats/Signage/Sign.htm.

USFWS. 2014. "About the Refuge," http://www.fws.gov/refuge/Rocky_Flats/about. html. Last updated September 22, 2013.

Wegman, R. A., and H. G. Bailey. 1994. "The Challenge of Cleaning Up Military Wastes When US Bases are Closed." *Ecology Law Quarterly* 21: 865–945.

Weisman, A. 2007. *The World Without Us*. New York: Picador.

Wiener, J. 2012. *How We Forgot the Cold War: A Historical Journey across America*. Berkeley: University of California Press.

Williams, T. N. 1999. Pave It or Save It: Wildlife Protection Planning under the Base Closure and Realignment Acts. PhD diss., University of Colorado-Denver.

Wills, J. 2001. "Welcome to the Atomic Park: American Nuclear Landscapes and the 'Unnaturally Natural.'" *Environment and History* 7: 449–472.

Zaffos, J. 2004. "Toxic Waste, Tainted Justice." *High Country News*, December 6. http://www.hcn.org/issues/288/15168/print_view.

CHAPTER 9 | Restoration, History, and Values
at Transitioning Military Sites
in the United States

DAVID G. HAVLICK

Introduction

In November 2005, I drove thirty minutes west from Boston, Massachusetts, to visit Assabet River National Wildlife Refuge for the first time. A boarded up guard shack stood near a US Fish and Wildlife Service sign and a gravel parking lot at the refuge entrance. It was a crisp day, autumn had fully fallen, and the refuge trails were nearly deserted. But the trails were also unusual, with peculiar names: Trail A, Trail B, Trail C, and the longest of the batch, Patrol Road. Weathered asphalt showed in patches beneath a layer of fallen leaves, and in places overgrown road signs marked the trail routes: speed limit 15, sharp left turn ahead. A cluster of abandoned houses peeked through the forest in places. Later, hiking around a bend, I came upon the first of dozens of massive concrete bunkers.

This was clearly not only a wildlife refuge, or at least, it had not always been simply a refuge. The site's former life as a US Army ammunition storage depot still showed in a variety of ways, mixing and blending throughout my day's hike: a barred owl winking at me from a wooded perch; a large steel container at the edge of a field ("Warning: Vent Must Be Open for Aircraft Transport"); wetlands and ponds flooded by beavers, spilling over trails and roads; rusted steel gates opening onto a grassy meadow; the ubiquitous bunkers, some nearly invisible beneath a cover of soil, leaves, shrubs, and saplings.

On this first visit, the Assabet River refuge had been open to the public for less than one month following sixty-three years of military use and closure. The complexity of its history, its layers of use, meaning, and change were hard to avoid. Even for the most casual of visitors, ample evidence showed that something was different here. The structures, signs, and bunkers had clearly not always been the principal domain of browsing deer, roosting bats, or reclusive spiders.

Today's visitors to Assabet River National Wildlife Refuge find a place somewhat changed since 2005. A new visitor center welcomes the public and provides an engaging overview of the site's wildlife and habitat, its human history, and its military use. The guard shack is gone, as are the other vacant buildings, old roads have been largely converted to trails, and refuge maps reveal new trail names that resonate with the site's new orientation: Fisher Loop, Sweet Fern Trail, Towhee Trail, Kingfisher Trail, Mink Link, and Otter Alley (Patrol Road is still there, too). There are also new signs posted around the refuge, many just guiding visitors through the maze of trails, but a few loaded with historical detail, describing the site's early transition "from nature to farmland" and "to wartime and a return to nature" (Friends of Assabet River 2013). These signs include maps of early family homesteads, describe the evictions and condemnations that cleared the land for the Army's use in 1942, highlight the location of all fifty bunkers (more properly called "igloos") that pepper the site, and reach back to Native American uses of the area long before European colonization. Visitors can now more easily enjoy a day walking, biking, birdwatching, or canoeing on the refuge, but they likely will still do so with a distinct awareness that this is a place with a particular set of histories, and that the current emphasis on wildlife and habitat protection is relatively new.

Though unique in its particulars, Assabet River National Wildlife Refuge is not alone. Since 1988, nearly two dozen former military sites in the United States have undergone similar conversions to turn aging US Department of Defense installations over to the US Fish and Wildlife Service to become national wildlife refuges (figure 9.1) ([NWRs]; Havlick 2007, 2011).

In this chapter, I turn to two of these sites—Assabet River NWR in eastern Massachusetts, and the Rocky Mountain Arsenal NWR in Colorado—to consider how the perceptions of the visiting public and refuge managers relate to the ecological and cultural attributes of the sites. I contend that the historical activities, refuge policies, physical characteristics, and changes made in the effort to restore and protect refuge resources generate a complex mix that can challenge traditional objectives of ecological restoration. Recognizing more fully the socioecological layers of these and other sites with complex histories ought to be part of the core embrace of ecological

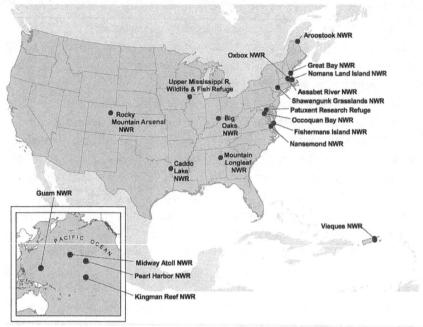

FIGURE 9.1 National Wildlife Refuges designated on former military sites in the United States since 1988. Courtesy of Bill Haskins, Big Sky Conservation Institute.

restoration efforts moving forward. This research is based on document analysis, interviews, site visits, and visitor surveys conducted at the specific wildlife refuges between 2010 and 2012, as well as fieldwork conducted at these and more than a dozen similar sites dating back to 2004.

Two Sites

The conditions found at Assabet River and Rocky Mountain Arsenal National Wildlife Refuges vary dramatically, as do the specific contexts of their military-to-wildlife transitions. At the broadest level, the military installations in question closed and transitioned as a result of shifting strategic considerations and geopolitics that emerged in the 1980s. These included global efforts to halt chemical weapons production and storage, the break up of the Soviet Union, and a series of efforts by the United States to streamline and modernize its military. Each military-to-wildlife (M2W) refuge varies in its degree of cleanup, the types of military residuals that remain, and how prior military uses continue to influence contemporary wildlife management objectives. At some sites the explosive hazards scattered across a broad area have never been meticulously inventoried and were not systematically removed or treated by the military before the transition to national wildlife refuge status. At Big Oaks NWR in Indiana, for example, Army explosives experts respond as needed to munitions reported along roadways or other surface features of the refuge.

Although past or present hazards at most M2W sites are made quite apparent to all refuge visitors, described in pamphlets or brochures, visitor center displays, websites, or safety videos, as a physical presence on the landscape, they are often mostly invisible. (This is also true at former DOE sites-turned-refuge, such as Rocky Flats in Colorado; see Hourdequin, chap. 2, and Coates, chap. 8, this volume.) The public use areas of these refuges are typically outside the zone where weapons testing, storage, or manufacturing occurred, and visitors are not permitted to stray from designated routes or areas. Even as the landscape conditions that draw visitors to these sites are very much the product of military activities—without decades of military command these areas would no doubt look much like the surrounding cities, farmlands, fields, or forests—this role has now subsided into a backstory that today's visitors almost never encounter directly.

At the Rocky Mountain Arsenal NWR, located immediately north of Denver, Colorado (figure 9.2), this is largely true thanks to a multibillion

FIGURE 9.2 Rocky Mountain Arsenal National Wildlife Refuge looking southwest toward Denver, Colorado. Photo by the author.

dollar cleanup effort spurred by lawsuits from federal and state regulators. From 1942 to 1982, the Arsenal operated as a chemical manufacturing facility, for weapons such as white phosphorus, sarin, and VX nerve gas, along with rocket fuel, napalm, and other incendiaries, and commercial pesticides and herbicides. Portions of the site were leased to private-sector chemical manufacturers as early as 1947; these lessees were eventually consolidated to the Shell Chemical Corporation (later Shell Oil Corporation; Rocky Mountain Arsenal FFA 1989; Hoffecker 2001; see also Hourdequin, chap. 2; Coates, chap. 8; Drenthen, chap. 13, this volume). When chemical manufacturing ceased at the Rocky Mountain Arsenal in 1982, the site included more than 400 structures concentrated on several hundred acres near the center of the facility's twenty-seven square miles (Explanation of Significant Differences n/d [ca. 2005]).

By that time, the Rocky Mountain Arsenal had earned a lurid reputation in the Denver area for contaminating groundwater supplies, generating noxious fumes, and even triggering a series of earthquakes after the Army injected toxic sludge into a 12,000-foot deep storage well (Deep Injection Well 2001). In one surface depression, known as Basin F, the Army stored a brew of chemicals so toxic that it was later described as "the most contaminated square mile on Earth" (Westing 2008, 80).

After two decades of intensive (and expensive) remediation, funded primarily by the two main operators at the site, the US Army and the Shell Oil Corporation, the Rocky Mountain Arsenal has altered not just its name, but its physical characteristics as well. The chemical manufacturing infrastructure has been demolished, contaminated sites have been cleaned and consolidated into state-of-the-art landfills, and in their stead the US Fish and Wildlife Service has undertaken an ambitious restoration of native shortgrass and mixed-grass prairie. The casual visitor to the Rocky Mountain Arsenal NWR today is far more likely to see grazing bison, mule deer, or prairie dogs than any sign of the chemical production or contamination that kept this land outside the reach of Denver's sprawling suburban and commercial development. Rather paradoxically, the restored prairie that today appears to be so well preserved is in some respects a direct outgrowth of the poisons that were produced at the site.

The military impacts take a different and much more accessible form at Assabet River NWR. Here, some of the military remains are not only quite visible, but actually feature as a set of historical attractions that draw visitors specifically for tours. From 1942 to 2000, the US Army

FIGURE 9.3 Ammunition igloo, or "bunker," along a visitor path at Assabet River National Wildlife Refuge, Massachusetts. Photo by the author.

managed more 2,200 acres of this site as an ammunition storage and troop training facility called the Fort Devens Sudbury Training Annex. Army munitions were stored in fifty large concrete igloos (most visitors refer to these as "bunkers") that connected by rail lines to munitions factories farther west and to coastal arsenals to the east (figure 9.3). Although ammunition was removed from the site before the Army transferred the land to Fish and Wildlife Service management in 2000, the massive igloos remain stationed along the former railroad lines that now serve as recreational trails for refuge visitors. To unsuspecting visitors who come upon these concrete monoliths, the igloos may be the first indication of the site's layered histories, but these military remains also serve as a particular attraction for busloads of visitors who join "bunker tours" led by local historians.

As a site used predominantly by the military for ammunition storage, Assabet River NWR also differs from Rocky Mountain Arsenal and a number of other M2W sites in the scope of its military contamination. Several areas on site suffered from chemical contamination in soils and groundwater, including PCBs, solvents, and residues from pesticides, but after the Army removed approximately 160 tons of PCB-laced soil, 1,110 cubic yards of soil from a former fire-training area, and several under-ground storage tanks, the US Environmental Protection Agency deemed the cleanup complete and removed the site from its National Priorities List for Superfund cleanup (Fort Devens-Sudbury Training Annex 2013). At the Rocky Mountain Arsenal, by comparison, more than 27 billion gallons of contaminated groundwater have been treated thus far in an ongoing effort, and 3.5 million cubic yards of contaminated soil have been removed (Balzer 2011).

One other aspect of Assabet River NWR worth noting is the extended time frame for European and Colonial settlement here. A Massachusetts Bay Colony formed in the area in the 1620s, and by the late 1700s, the region was well established as an epicenter of early American colonial activity. A granite post still present on the refuge marks the site of Rice's Tavern, an inn where General George Washington reportedly once stopped for a drink (Herland 2011). The area surrounding the site of the Rocky Mountain Arsenal, by contrast, was still characterized by indigenous use and occupancy prior to 1800, and as late as the 1860s, the South Platte River near the site was still seeing significant use by the native Arapaho and Cheyenne.[1]

Public Expectations and Management Goals

To evaluate how the visiting public views these M2W refuges, and what expectations and interests they have when visiting, my colleagues and I developed a visitor survey to administer directly at both Rocky Mountain Arsenal and Assabet River NWRs. Questions began with basic demo-graphic information and details about visitors' experiences at the refuge, then asked visitors for their opinions about how certain features of the site ought to be represented, which cultural and ecological attributes of the site they most valued, and open-ended queries about the qualities they now associated with these national wildlife refuges (Havlick et al. 2014). We also completed in-depth semistructured interviews with key personnel and outside constituencies (e.g., refuge Friends groups, volunteers, and local history organizations) at the refuges to develop a fuller sense of how land managers and others who are dedicated to these sites identify their duties and restoration and management goals. Some of the results reported here also include information from interviews conducted at other M2W ref-uges; these help establish a broader context for the phenomena we found at Assabet River and Rocky Mountain Arsenal NWRs.

The mission of the National Wildlife Refuge System is "to administer a national network of lands and waters for the conservation, management, and where appropriate, restoration of the fish, wildlife, and plant resources and their habitats within the United States for the benefit of present and future generations of Americans" (Public Law 105-57, sec. 4). For national wildlife refuge managers, this statement provides clear, if also very broad, guidance that directs policy toward ecological priorities. The same 1997 law that established this mission also provides for "compatible wildlife-dependent recreational uses" of refuges, as well as environmental education and interpretation (Public Law 105-57, secs. 2(7) and 5). This mission statement, and the language of the National Wildlife Refuge System Improvement Act of 1997 more generally, has been hailed for establishing the strongest conservation mandate of any US federal land system (e.g., Fischman 2003).

The clear conservation directive for the refuges provides necessary structure and focus for refuge managers, but it can also serve to limit the breadth of activities that refuge officials are willing or able to undertake. Historic preservation or management efforts designed to maintain cultural features of refuges are commonly disregarded by citing the refuge system's "wildlife first" mission. Significantly, the Fish and Wildlife Service also suffers from severe shortfalls in federal funding, which creates chronic difficulties for managers to conduct even the activities that fall directly within their mission. On more than one occasion, managers interviewed as part of this research pointed out that allocating resources to maintain or restore cultural features was difficult to justify given their agency's mission and funding. As a manager at one eastern US refuge noted, "Our job is to manage for wildlife, not to keep a coat of paint on a concrete bunker." Or as a visitor services manager elsewhere put it, "Congress has turned this into a national wildlife refuge now. It's not for buildings, it's not for relics of the past. It's for wildlife now."

The cleanup and restoration activities contributing to the conversion of the Rocky Mountain Arsenal into a national wildlife refuge very much reflect this orientation. Initial work focused on demolishing all the chemical manufacturing infrastructure on site, and subsequent efforts have restored thousands of acres of native shortgrass and mixed-grass prairie communities to the refuge, including a herd of bison. Refuge officials are aware of the importance of cultural features at the site, and they acknowledge the value of interpretation in advancing visitors' understanding of the site's history, but they also recognize the policy, financial, and practical constraints they face in bringing history to the fore. As one Rocky Mountain Arsenal refuge official commented, "Let's face it, if you're coming to a national wildlife refuge, do you want to hear about our restoration efforts, or all about the bison, or about bald eagles, or the burrowing owls?"

The Rocky Mountain Arsenal NWR visitor center does include a number of vivid displays portraying the chemical production era at the site, the displacement of the agricultural families that preceded the Army's takeover of the area, and the efforts to consolidate and contain the site's contamination problems. On the grounds of the refuge itself, however, very little visibly remains of these earlier layers of activity. Considering how little physical evidence of the Rocky Mountain Arsenal's prior history and uses persists (at least to casual visitors), it seems worth asking how much visitors today value or know about the site as it existed prior to refuge designation in 1992.

Visitor Surveys

We conducted refuge surveys in person, generally approaching refuge visitors in the area around the visitor centers as they concluded their activities for the day. Within the constraints of using a convenience sampling method, we tried to approach every available adult visitor and recruit the broadest possible participation in the survey. Surveys were conducted at the Rocky Mountain Arsenal NWR on seven days in July, August, and October 2010; at Assabet River NWR surveys were conducted on four days in June 2011 and July 2012.

In one survey question we asked visitors to rate the importance of including different attributes of the site in visitor-center exhibits. At both refuges, more than 90 percent of the respondents rated "plants and wildlife" as *very important* or the next highest category (i.e., important). This was the highest rated category at each location, suggesting that the "wildlife first" mission of the national wildlife refuges is matched by what visitors consider important in visitor-center exhibits (see table 9.1). This might be expected considering that most visitors come specifically to visit a destination known as (or at least named) a national wildlife refuge.

Table 9.1 also shows that there is substantial agreement by visitors to Rocky Mountain Arsenal NWR that the story of contamination ought to be told. A considerably higher percentage (83 percent) of visitors to the Colorado refuge compared to visitors to Assabet River (66 percent) indicated that the history of contamination, base closure and environmental cleanup was important or very important to include in visitor center

TABLE 9.1 Comparison of visitor answers to the question, "Which aspects of this site do you think are important to include in visitor-center exhibits?" at the Rocky Mountain Arsenal and Assabet River NWRs.

	1 & 2 COMBINED (NOT IMPORTANT)	3 (NEUTRAL)	4 & 5 COMBINED (IMPORTANT)
Plants and wildlife			
Rocky Mountain Arsenal NWR	0.0	9.1	90.9
Assabet River NWR	2.6	5.3	92.1
National wildlife refuge mission and policies			
Rocky Mountain Arsenal NWR	1.8	9.0	89.2
Assabet River NWR	7.1	21.1	72.4
Contamination/base closure and environmental cleanup			
Rocky Mountain Arsenal NWR	7.2	9.8	83.1
Assabet River NWR	12.2	21.6	66.2
Native American History			
Rocky Mountain Arsenal NWR	8.1	15.3	76.5
Assabet River NWR	6.5	21.1	72.4
Homestead and farming/colonial history			
Rocky Mountain Arsenal NWR	11.8	22.7	65.4
Assabet River NWR	4.1	28.4	67.6
Chemical production/military history			
Rocky Mountain Arsenal NWR	10.0	20.9	69.1
Assabet River NWR	17.3	24.0	58.6

NOTE: (1 = not at all important, 5 = very important). Answers are expressed as percentage of all respondents. RMA n = 110; Assabet n = 74.

exhibits. This suggests that even as the management of plants and wildlife at the refuges may hold a privileged position for visitors, this position is not exclusive. Visitors do not appear to be blind to the significance of some of the cultural layers of the sites, especially the Rocky Mountain Arsenal, even as they orient strongly toward the restored environmental (or seemingly *natural*) attributes found there.

The source of the difference in responses between sites is open to interpretation, but as noted earlier the legacy of contamination at Rocky Mountain Arsenal vastly surpasses that of Assabet River, or almost any other M2W refuge. Groundwater contamination dramatically impacted the communities adjacent to the site for decades, and groundwater intercept and filtration systems are still operating at down-gradient boundaries of the refuge. Throughout metropolitan Denver, which traditionally has been the source of most visitors to the refuge, the Arsenal was long known as a site of severe environmental degradation. This reputation likely persists to some degree, even as the physical features of the place have changed dramatically as a result of the past twenty years of remediation, redevelopment, and ecological restoration.

In fact, given the Arsenal's history, the greater surprise may be that visitors rate the past military chemical production of the site as less important to represent in visitor-center exhibits than most of the other categories surveyed. Visitors rated the Native American history of the Arsenal site, for example, and the national wildlife refuge mission and policies as more worth including than the military chemical production history.

Perhaps more telling are the results from a separate, open-ended question we asked in the survey. We simply asked respondents to list three words "you would use to describe this place." To analyze these responses we grouped words in clusters with similar connotations. The top three clusters we found were, "peaceful/quiet," "wild/ natural," and "beautiful." Each of these appeared in 25 percent or more of the visitor responses. The most common response that potentially included some distinct association with military or chemical production at the site was the ambiguous "interesting," which we found in 15 percent of responses. Only 4 percent of responses made an explicit reference to cleanup efforts at the site—and this at a time when active remediation was still occurring and visitors' public use was much more restricted than it is now that the cleanup is considered complete.

This same open-ended question at Assabet River NWR elicited a similar suite of responses, with "beautiful" appearing the most often (48 percent), followed by "peaceful/quiet" (36 percent), and "wild/natural" (23 percent). References to the history of the site or the military use (including the bunkers) each appeared in only 3 percent of the responses.

These open-ended responses from both refuges are marked by their generality. Visitors seem to associate the refuges with generic qualities of beauty, naturalness, and quiet rather than site-specific attributes or prior uses. Bunkers, cleanup activities, and chemical contamination each appear only infrequently in the open-ended responses. Even activities relating directly to the core mission of the refuge, such as wildlife and habitat protection, resource conservation, environmental education, and wildlife-compatible recreation, are not evoked strongly by visitors despite the explicit efforts the Fish and Wildlife Service makes to orient toward these.

When we asked survey questions that guided visitors more directly to site-specific issues and management activities, these more constrained responses still weighted the natural or environmental qualities of the site above its cultural or historical qualities. A rank ordering question on the survey asked visitors to evaluate the importance of various management goals for the site. Visitors at the Rocky Mountain Arsenal NWR responded that *protection of plants and wildlife* was the most important goal for the refuge, followed by restoration and revegetation of damaged areas, and environmental education. Rounding out the list of responses in order of priority were the more cultural/historical aspects of public safety and the monitoring of remaining contaminants, education about cultural and historical resources, and public use and recreation (figure 9.4).

Assabet River NWR visitors also ranked protection of plants and wildlife as the most important goal for the refuge, but put public use and recreation and environmental education as second most important, ahead of restoration and revegetation of damaged areas. These priorities plausibly reflect the fact that recreational activities such as bicycling, jogging, hiking, and canoeing are already becoming popular at Assabet River NWR, and the fact that the contamination problems there were not nearly as widespread, severe, or well-known as those at Rocky Mountain Arsenal. Perhaps more revealing of visitors emphasizing natural features over cultural features is the preference they express for environmental education above education about the cultural and historical resources at Assabet River NWR. This is somewhat surprising in light of the strong visitor interest in bunker tours and the site's local history described by refuge staff and volunteers. In this

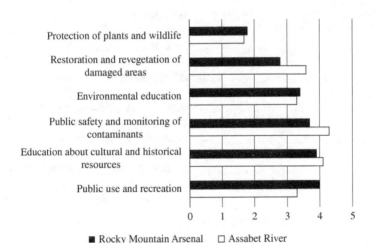

FIGURE 9.4 When asked to rank, in order of importance, six different refuge management goals for the respective wildlife refuges, visitors to the Rocky Mountain Arsenal and Assabet River NWRs ranked the protection of plants and wildlife first, restoration of damaged areas second, and culturally oriented goals as less important (1 = most important 6 = least important).

respect, there appears to be a mismatch between visitor attitudes expressed in our survey responses and those perceived by refuge managers and volunteers. One refuge official commented, "I would consider them [bunkers] an attraction. They're more popular than anything else [at Assabet River NWR] . . . more so than the birds." One of the local historians who leads the bunker tours also noted that a lot of people, perhaps most, want to visit the refuge primarily because of its cultural history.

One additional survey question asked specifically about restoration and protection efforts at each refuge to try to discern if cultural or ecological objectives were valued differently in the context of the Fish and Wildlife Service mission statement. Here, we asked visitors to rank order the importance of protecting or restoring: plants and animals that existed at the site prior to human disturbance; plants, animals, and fish that people enjoy; evidence of past military use; evidence of past farming and homesteading; Native American history; and a healthy environment for people. In response to this question, visitors at both refuges weighted their answers toward the protection and restoration of predisturbance conditions, that is, the conditions existing at the sites before the substantial influence of human activity. This has been a traditional focus of ecological restoration and suggests a willingness to accommodate restoration goals that are unfettered by cultural associations (figure 9.5).

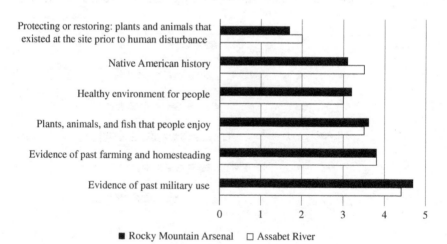

FIGURE 9.5 When asked to rank, in order of importance, which aspects of the respective wildlife refuges should be protected or restored, visitors to the Rocky Mountain Arsenal and Assabet River NWRs ranked the protection or restoration of plants and animals that existed prior to human disturbance above all others (rating of 1 = most important, 6 = least important). Maintaining evidence of past military use at these sites was ranked as the least important goal.

On this question, both sites returned very similar visitor responses: restoration of predisturbance plants and animals came through as the clear priority in each case. In conjunction with this, the most notable result may be the apparent lack of support for restoring evidence of the prior military use. In general, the historically older human uses received more visitor support for restoration than more recent uses. That is, visitors expressed more interest in protecting or restoring Native American history at the sites than they did in the homesteading or colonial uses, which, in turn, ranked ahead of the recent military use. The clear privileging of native plants and animals (existing prior to human disturbance) above plants and animals simply there for human enjoyment also seems to support the idea that visitors consider and value these refuges first and foremost as *natural* places.

Refuge Planning and Local Constituencies

The most recent tourist draw to the Rocky Mountain Arsenal NWR, a nine-mile-long, self-guided automobile tour that opened in 2013, will likely further reduce the opportunities for Fish and Wildlife Service exhibits or interpretation to moderate the visiting public's focus on ecological features at the site. The driving tour is a boon to the refuge in many respects as for the first time it opens portions of the interior beyond the visitor center and offers the public the opportunity to travel a designated route without the restrictions of a guided bus tour. Some refuge officials believe that visitation has increased more than tenfold as a result of the new driving tour.[2] Many of these motorists, however, no longer even check in at the visitor center, which in the past was virtually the only destination possible by private automobile, and they see only the bison and prairie elements of the refuge with no additional interpretation or exposure to cultural exhibits (the visitor center is also closed on Mondays and Tuesdays). What visitors find on the physical grounds of the refuge—primarily wildlife, wetlands, and prairie—provides a single lasting impression of the site as a natural or ecological landscape.

In 2013 the Rocky Mountain Arsenal NWR launched the planning process for its Comprehensive Conservation Plan (CCP), the critical document that sets site-specific management direction for the refuge for the next fifteen years.[3] In its formal public notice of the CCP process, the Fish and Wildlife Service highlighted four specific areas for which it was particularly interested in receiving public input: suggestions for managing wildlife and habitat in the face of climate change; ideas regarding wildlife-dependent public uses on the refuge; changes desired in the ongoing management of the site; and any concerns relating to the management of bison, prairie dogs, or a proposed reintroduction of black-footed ferrets. The prior history of the site and decades of chemical manufacturing were not mentioned (Federal Register 2013).

In addition to these questions of emphasis, the conservation planning process conducted thus far at Rocky Mountain Arsenal NWR also highlights how difficult it can be to engage the local constituencies most proximate to or most affected by these M2W transitions. In August 2013, I attended one of the three initial public scoping meetings designed to introduce the CCP process to local communities and to solicit public comment. The meeting was well-organized, featured graphic displays of the refuge planning process, and included two simultaneous information sessions, one conducted in Spanish and one in English. At least ten Fish and Wildlife Service officials were available to provide information, field questions, and engage the public, but only three other members of the public turned out for the event. Refuge personnel described similarly low turnout at their first meeting. The second meeting attracted close to two dozen people, most of whom came to express their concern about a single issue: the lethal control of prairie dogs on refuge grounds (Hastings 2013).

Poor attendance at these meetings notwithstanding, there are a number of people and groups who are very interested in what is happening at transitioning military sites. Refuges such as the Rocky Mountain Arsenal and Assabet River often have "friends" groups that help to sponsor and coordinate activities, volunteer at visitor centers, and support Fish and Wildlife Service staff in a variety of ways. These groups are often composed of a small but dedicated number of individuals, many of whom have a personal connection to the site as former employees or due to a particular wildlife interest. More generally, though, M2W sites seem to struggle to develop local constituencies. This may be because they have been off-limits for decades as Department of Defense facilities, and in many cases were known as dangerous or heavily guarded places. Often, even after transitioning to new Fish and Wildlife Service management, they retain quietly imposing military infrastructures including gates, guard stations, and high-security fencing. As federal facilities staffed by federal employees, they can appear to be somewhat isolated from local communities, even as programs offered by the refuge staff actively try to invite community members and students to visit the site. In most cases, today's M2W refuges were set aside as military installations in the 1940s using the federal government's power of eminent domain, and this may also foster a lingering sense of local alienation in long-time residents and neighboring communities.

At the Rocky Mountain Arsenal NWR, nearby residents have formed a group that effectively dedicates itself to preserving the history of the site as it existed before it became a wildlife refuge. As noted earlier, the refuge opened a new visitor center in 2011, but the primary push for commemorating and preserving the site's history comes from an independent off-site group, the Commerce City Historical Society. The society has worked to secure a location for a museum that would include exhibits and information about the farming families displaced by the creation of the Arsenal in 1942, as well as displays about the chemical production and contamination that ensued. The group is actively concerned about the loss of historical artifacts from the refuge site, including the dismantling, in 2012, of the south entrance gate and guardhouse. During one meeting I attended members also emphasized a desire to have the stories of individuals and their community represented more fully in refuge materials. As one of them noted, "I think the fact that there were people that lived there [at the site of today's refuge], that were raising their families there—it was a whole community, it wasn't just a couple houses up—was a big thing. And if we're going to say that we want to preserve the history of Commerce City and the area, then that's got to be a big thing for us."

As our survey and interview data suggest, the prospective historical erasure of military activity at M2W sites is not a moot point. Despite the continuing presence of the word "arsenal" in the name of the refuge and the very well-done exhibits in the visitor center, some visitors to the Rocky Mountain Arsenal already express surprise when discovering the site's history. On one of the first refuge tours I joined in 2004, when the tour guide began describing the chemical weapons production that occurred there, a woman in front of me on the bus exclaimed, "I didn't know this had been an Army base!" Erasure of prior histories in this case is not an intentional process—to the contrary, the Fish and Wildlife Service makes a clear effort to represent what happened at the site—but seems to happen more passively or indirectly as the area becomes naturalized as a wildlife refuge.

The fact remains that people come to this and similar sites to see wildlife—bison are featured front and center in the Rocky Mountain Arsenal visitor center (taxidermic specimens as well as live viewing through spotting scopes), and in the visitor brochure. The growing bison herd is also a key attraction, generating interest for the new driving tour. Understandably, bison, bald eagles, burrowing owls, prairie dogs, mule deer, even the catch-and-release pike, bass, and bluegill fishery in refuge lakes are highlighted more prominently than the military or chemical weapons history in order to attract visitors. This makes perfect sense, but it also bypasses some of the important lasting lessons that the Rocky Mountain Arsenal NWR and other M2W sites could convey. Ultimately, we need to ask what is at risk if we lose sight of the decades of chemical production and contamination at Rocky Mountain Arsenal on the edge of Denver, or the weapons storage and training that occurred just outside Boston, Massachusetts at Assabet River. What lasting legacy ought we preserve of the agricultural periods that existed prior to military use of many of these sites, or the land condemnations required to clear the areas in the name of national security? What about other significant uses at these and similar sites, dating back to Native Americans and North American prehistory? Which activities or meanings should we maintain or restore in light of these various layers and prior uses?

Restoration, History, and Values

In some respects, history and ecological restoration have long had a fraught relationship. Restoration, after all, is predicated on the idea that by erasing prior human impacts we can bring a site or an ecosystem to a better, more natural (and thus, less human) condition. As Hourdequin points out elsewhere in this volume, despite this tendency toward historical erasure, restoration ecology has also long valued historical fidelity as a guide for setting restoration goals and determining the success of restoration efforts (see also, more generally, Hall 2009). In layered landscapes such as M2W refuges, however, the hybridity of natural and cultural features may actually serve to provide new ways through what in other contexts might seem intractable. The confusion described by one refuge official at Assabet River NWR over how wetlands came to exist—was the initial flooding caused by poorly engineered Army culverts beneath roads or much earlier by beaver dams?—becomes an opportunity for new interpretation and values rather than a burdensome quandary. At M2W sites, the fact that many of the wildlife and habitat conditions we now value *as nature* are the direct or indirect result of military activities and impacts can press us to move beyond conceptions of nature as something largely distinct from human culture. In other words, these places might encourage us to think productively about the integration of natural and cultural landscapes.

More specifically, how we move forward to restore and manage conditions at M2W refuges can provide examples of how we negotiate these challenging categories of nature and culture in other contexts. A first step might be to embrace rather than to work to obliterate tangible examples of socioecological hybridity. This has been done only to a limited extent at the Rocky Mountain Arsenal NWR, and somewhat more explicitly at the Assabet River NWR. The restoration treatments at the Rocky Mountain Arsenal NWR actually differ from one part of the refuge to another depending on their prior uses. In the northern and central portions of the site, where Army infrastructure and impacts were most concentrated, ecological restoration goals orient to pre-settlement shortgrass prairie and the eradication of human impacts of chemical production and agricultural periods. (The center of the refuge also includes significant, lasting human impacts in the form of two large landfills, where contaminants from across the site have been consolidated and, hopefully, contained.) The southern tier of the refuge includes areas of prairie restoration as well, but managers have integrated the restoration efforts here with historical irrigation canals, lakes and ponds, windbreaks, and trees and shrubs left behind by earlier settlers and subsequent uses. These historical elements are often quite subtle—few visitors are likely to notice a rosebush that lingers as the sole marker of the site of a former elementary school, or a row of cottonwoods lining a worn-out canal—but managers recognize these and utilize them as habitat amenities that add diversity to the mix available on the refuge.

At Assabet River NWR, as well as other sites, such as the Aroostook NWR in northern Maine and the Great Bay NWR in New Hampshire, Fish and Wildlife Service officials are experimenting with concrete igloos and modifying them to serve as bat hibernacula. At the Big Oaks NWR, former ammunition-spotting bunkers have been converted to what one former Army official half-jokingly described as "the world's largest birdhouses." The adaptation of large military structures to serve new purposes as wildlife habitat create vivid, tangible examples of how hybrid spaces can function in productive, instructive ways that erode nature-society dichotomies.

Of course, managers at M2W refuges also face a number of challenges. Simply adhering to a wildlife-first mission in the context of lands with complex prior histories and potentially conflicting contemporary uses can be trying. At Assabet River NWR, refuge officials view recreational activities, such as bicycling and jogging, as a distraction from the refuge's main purpose, but these also represent some of the most common uses that bring visitors to the refuge and may then lead over time to heightened interest in and support for core refuge activities (many national wildlife refuges prohibit jogging or bicycling entirely). The igloos scattered across the refuge present an unusual but valued attraction that can be difficult to align with the primary purpose of the refuge. To their credit, Assabet officials have tried to turn these military leftovers into an asset by working with volunteers and a local historian to draw people in for tours that then include information on the military and colonial history of the area as well as its new mission to protect wildlife and habitat. In this way, the prior uses and layers of the site are kept visible and present, but without compromising the new mission.

This strikes a balance hinted at by one official working on restoration at the Rocky Mountain Arsenal NWR:

> You know, I think the full story ought to be told. I think it ought to be—I think that's the great story out here, is how it was such a contaminated place and what it's changed into ... I think we're wrestling with a choice. We're trying to bring people onto the refuge to get them to experience it, but those people don't want to come if they have this perception that there was chemical contamination out here. So we're kind of wrestling with how much do we tell the story. How much do we delve into what was out here? What's the right way to present that, essentially, so we get the visitation that we want, but we're not necessarily hiding the fact that we have—that this was a Superfund site, with how contaminated it was out here.

Every M2W refuge, every layered landscape, has a different set of histories and a different set of stories that could be told. Where prior contamination or hazards were more severe, agencies can scarcely be faulted for prioritizing remediation and restoration at the expense of the preservation of cultural landscapes, but even in these settings there are surely ways to accommodate the latter. As Drenthen and Ingram highlight elsewhere in this volume, the links between art, restoration, and commemoration can be much more fully explored than they have been to date. Former militarized sites along the Iron Curtain borderlands of central Europe, including the Berlin Wall, offer a number of intriguing examples of this. At many of these sites there is a M2W trajectory very similar to that found in the refuges highlighted here, but along the Iron Curtain the memories of separation, violence, and transition are maintained through a combination of open-air museums, remnants of the wall or wire or guard towers that have been left in place, information kiosks, and a variety of sculptures and other artistic representations that symbolize—sometimes quite obtusely—previous layers and uses of these lands. These conspire to ensure that the thousands of miles of death strips and barriers that loomed for decades are now mostly lost but not entirely forgotten (see Havlick 2014).

It certainly is possible, and often quite tempting, simply to read M2W transitions affirmatively as a statement about the resiliency of nature. Even where there have been intensive human efforts to clean sites and restore them to a "natural" condition, such actions are now largely invisible. We can visit these places and feel assured that, in a redemptive sense, nature bats last. But in the deeper layers of what took place here, we should also recognize that not just nature, but also a host of human communities were compelled to submit to the single-mindedness and hostility of military priorities. This speaks to the ambiguity and power of layered landscapes. They will send us a message, they carry meaning, but we are often left with the responsibility of interpretation (see Hourdequin and Havlick 2011, 2013). Restoration based exclusively on ecological principles may well guide this meaning to one of human ability and mastery—we can rebuild nature, no matter how great the insult—whereas a more deliberately integrative approach can bring us into a *conversation* with nature, to encourage us to take responsibility for our impacts over the long arc of these sites' histories. In this, it remains important to remember that these layered sites are not only natural spaces, but also very much cultural landscapes that have and should continue to carry meaning rich with human history as well as the more recent flourishing of nature.

Notes

1. Spanish exploration throughout the region started in the sixteenth century, and French and Spanish territorial claims covered the region until the 1803 Louisiana Purchase; but through the early 1800s the nearest large colonial settlement was more than 300 miles south in Santa Fe, New Mexico. Native Americans frequented portions of today's refuge mostly on a seasonal basis.

2. There is widespread consensus among refuge officials that visitation has dramatically increased as a result of the driving tour, but at the time of this writing the FWS has not counted visitors directly. Estimates of 2013 visitation range from 100,000 to 300,000. This represents a significant increase over officials' 2012 (and prior) estimate of 25,000 to 30,000 annual visitors. New signage along the busy Interstate-70 highway corridor is also likely contributing to the 2013 rise in visitation.

3. The Draft CCP was released for public comment in May 2015.

References

Balzer, John R. 2011. "Development of a World Class Safety Program at Rocky Mountain Arsenal (RMA), a Complex Environmental Remediation Site." Presentation available online at: http://coloradoasse.org/wp-content/uploads/2011/09/WorldClassSafetyProgram.pdf. Accessed August 26, 2013.

Deep Injection Well. "Fact Sheet." 2001. Rocky Mountain Arsenal Remediation Venture Office. Available online at: http://www.co.adams.co.us/DocumentCenter/Home/View/822. Accessed May 26, 2015.

Explanation of Significant Differences for North Plants Soil Remediation of the Rocky Mountain Arsenal Federal Facility Site. n/d [ca. 2005]. Fact sheet available online at: http://www.rma.army.mil/files/7714/1038/0030/Explanation_of_Significant_Differences_for_the_North_Plants_Soil_Volume.pdf. Accessed May 26, 2015.

Federal Register Notices. 2013. Department of the Interior. Fish and Wildlife Service. Rocky Mountain Arsenal National Wildlife Refuge. Commerce City, CO; Comprehensive Conservation Plan and Environmental Impact Statement. Vol. 78, No. 152: 48183–48185. August 7.

Fort Devens-Sudbury Training Annex. "Waste Cleanup and Reuse in New England. US Environmental Protection Agency." 2013. Available online at: http://yosemite.epa.gov/R1/npl_pad.nsf/31c4fec03a0762d285256bb80076489c/a4350eb2d816bcd68525691f0063f6ca!OpenDocument. Accessed August 26, 2013.

Fischman, Robert L. 2003. *The National Wildlife Refuges: Coordinating a Conservation System through Law*. Washington, DC: Island Press.

Friends of Assabet River National Wildlife Refuge. 2013. "History of the Assabet River NWR." http://www.farnwr.org/refuge1.html. Accessed 27 October 2013.

Hall, Marcus, ed. 2009. *Restoration and History: The Search for a Usable Environmental Past*. New York: Routledge.

Hastings, Bruce. Deputy Refuge Manager, Rocky Mountain Arsenal National Wildlife Refuge. Interview, August 5, 2013.

Havlick, David G. 2007. "Logics of Change for Military-to-Wildlife Conversions in the United States." *GeoJournal* 69: 151–164.

Havlick, David G. 2011. "Disarming Nature: Converting Military Lands to Wildlife Conservation." *Geographical Review* 101 (2): 183–200.

Havlick, David G., Marion Hourdequin, and Matthew John. 2014. "Examining Restoration Goals at a Former Military Site." *Nature and Culture* 9 (3): 288–315.

Havlick, David G. 2014. "The Iron Curtain Trail's Landscapes of Memory, Meaning, and Recovery." *Focus on Geography* 57 (2): 126–133.

Herland, Elizabeth. Refuge Complex Leader, Assabet River National Wildlife Refuge, MA. Personal comm. June 22, 2011.

Hoffecker, John F. 2001. *Twenty-Seven Square Miles*. Denver, Colorado: US Fish and Wildlife Service, Rocky Mountain Arsenal National Wildlife Refuge.

Hourdequin, Marion, and David G. Havlick. 2011. "Ecological Restoration in Context: Ethics and the Naturalization of Former Military Lands." *Ethics, Policy, and Environment* 14 (1): 69–89.

Hourdequin, Marion, and David G. Havlick. 2013. "Restoration and Authenticity Revisited." *Environmental Ethics* 35 (1): 79–93.

Public Law 105-57. 9 October 1997. US Congress.

Rocky Mountain Arsenal Federal Facilities Agreement. 1989. Foster Wheeler Environmental Corporation. February.

Westing, Arthur H. 2008. "The Impact of War on the Environment." In *War and Public Health*, 2nd ed., edited by Barry S. Levy and Victor W. Sidel, 69–86. Oxford, UK: Oxford University Press.

PART III | Representation and
Interpretation of Layered
Landscapes

CHAPTER 10 | Slavery, Freedom, and the Cultural Landscape

Restoration and Interpretation of Monocacy National Battlefield

JOHN H. SPIERS

THIS CHAPTER EXAMINES THE interpretation of preserved and restored landscapes through a case study of Monocacy National Battlefield, a 1,647-acre site administered by the US National Park Service (NPS) on the edge of the Washington, DC metropolitan area in Frederick County, Maryland. Official interpretation and popular memory of the site have long been tied to themes of patriotic commemoration and national reunification following the Civil War. Cultural landscape studies and archeological investigations undertaken under the aegis of the NPS since the mid-1990s, however, have broadened knowledge about the site's history to span three hundred years of intensive human activity, including the operation of a slave plantation, local farming, and a past and present piedmont and riparian ecosystem. Because of the site's location in a rapidly developing metropolitan area, however, erosion, flooding, and air and water pollution have increasingly presented challenges for preserving, restoring, and interpreting it.

Although the historical record for the Monocacy battlefield supports a broad interpretation of its intertwined cultural and natural histories, official activities at the site remain selectively focused on its Civil War heritage. This difference between history and heritage is crucial. Drawing on the work of David Lowenthal (1998), Jennifer Welchman explains (see chap. 7 of this volume) that history and heritage have quite different objectives. While the former is concerned with producing accurate, verifiable accounts of the past in their full complexity and controversy, heritage adopts a highly selective approach to presenting the past that often elides multiple perspectives and controversy in favor of a triumphant narrative of progress over time. The NPS's tendency to preserve, restore, and interpret the Monocacy landscape in light of a specific moment in time reflects a commitment to heritage over history that has two major drawbacks. The first is that focusing on some "authentic" past requires relying on assumptions that are hard to verify with the historical record. The second is that restoring a landscape to a specific past can obscure or even commit violence to its surviving elements. Historical "authenticity" cannot be found in these efforts because a landscape's conditions, particularly its ecological resources, are dynamic and change over time; whereas new research can broaden and deepen understanding of the site's history (Jordan and Lubick 2011; Clewell and Aronson 2007).

This chapter advocates taking a more inclusive and balanced approach in the preservation, restoration, and interpretation of layered landscapes. What is challenging for a site like Monocacy National Battlefield is that it fosters two conflicting impulses—a preservationist aim to resist change in the built environment with the need to accommodate and restore dynamic ecological conditions (Welchman, chap. 7, and Havlick, chap. 9, this volume; Longstreth 2008; Clewell and Aronson 2007). Given this challenge, this chapter argues that protecting Monocacy National Battlefield's integrity and enhancing the public's understanding of it in all its complexity requires showcasing its extant natural and cultural features as well as ensuring its ecological stability and functioning over the long term. Finding support in Marion Hourdequin's concept of "plurivocal narratives" and "thick description" in chapter 2 of the present volume, this chapter insists that a more faithful model of stewardship and public interpretation would move away from the prevailing Civil War–centric narrative of the Monocacy landscape to a more comprehensive and inclusive narrative that spans the histories of slavery and civil war, local rural life, and the ongoing ecological concerns associated with exurban sprawl from the Washington metropolitan area. The chapter concludes by providing just such a model for interpretation.

Historical Context and Protection of the Site

Monocacy National Battlefield was the site of a Civil War battle fought in 1864. As part of his Shenandoah Valley campaign to break the Union's stranglehold on Confederate supply bases and attack its capital in Washington, DC, Confederate Lieutenant General Jubal Early moved his troops across the Potomac River from Virginia into Maryland on July 5, where, four days later, he encountered a Union force led by Major General Lew Wallace. The area, near the town of Frederick, Maryland, was the nexus of several transportation routes, including the Georgetown Pike, the Baltimore and Ohio Railroad, and the Monocacy River. The natural features of the site, including its ridges, valleys, and riverbanks, directed troops and supplies along particular routes at the Battle of Monocacy, which was fought on July 9. Wallace's forces were defeated, and thereafter the Confederate forces hastened to Washington. However, the battle had delayed the Confederates just long enough to allow General Ulysses Grant to send reinforcements north from Petersburg, Virginia, to defend the Union capital, leading Early to call off his attempted siege. The significance of the delay led Wallace to memorialize Union soldiers at the Battle of Monocacy: "These men died to save the National capital, and they did save it" (Cooling 1997; Thornberry-Ehrlich 2008).

Public memory of the Civil War and early efforts to preserve Monocacy battlefield as it appeared on the eve of conflict were motivated by patriotic commemoration of the combatants and a narrative of national reunification following the war that lent symbolic recognition to the landscapes where its conflicts were waged. By the mid-1930s, Monocacy had seen the installation of four regimental monuments; publication of *Fighting for Time*, a book by a local author that reinforced the battle's "national" significance; and designation by Congress as a national military park, albeit without money for land acquisition (National Park Service n.d., Interpretive File; Worthington 1932). At a centennial celebration at the battlefield in 1964, state officials dedicated the first memorial recognizing Maryland's involvement in the Civil War, reinforcing traditional themes of commemoration and patriotism for a state that joined the Union cause (*Frederick News* 1964). These activities, however, obscured the state's own legacy of slavery at the outset of the war and the existence of slavery at the site, a chronic shortcoming of traditional memory and the heritage of Civil War battlefields (Linenthal 1991; Blight 2001, 2002; Trail 2005).

Despite some intermittent bursts of interest, the Monocacy battlefield received little support from the public or the government for preservation efforts until growth pressures from the Washington metropolitan area threatened the site (*Frederick News* 1964; Lichtenstein 1963). In the 1950s, the State of Maryland built what became Interstate 270 from Frederick to Rockville. The highway bisected the battlefield and attracted development that crept closer to it over the next half century, threatening its cultural and natural resources (*Frederick Post* 1951; Stern 1956; Raver

1973; Frederick County Planning and Zoning Commission 1970,1991). By the early 1970s, this had catalyzed support for federal land acquisition to preserve the site, an effort led by Maryland congressman Goodloe Byron. While recognizing the battlefield's Civil War heritage, Byron highlighted the park's prospects as a tourist destination given that its historical resources were relatively intact and its open fields offered valuable green space and outdoor recreational opportunities on the edge of a rapidly growing metropolitan region (Haley 1971). In 1973, the battlefield was designated a National Historic Landmark. With Byron's support, Congress, in 1976, authorized $3.5 million to the Park Service to acquire 850 acres of land through outright purchase or scenic easements that would protect the views of the site (Public Law 94-578 1976). By 1980, Congress had expanded the boundaries to 1,671 acres and appropriated more funds for land acquisition and public facilities (National Parks and Recreation Act of 1978; *Washington Post* 1978; Public Law 96-607 1980).

In 1981, the NPS re-dedicated Monocacy National Battlefield, although the site remained closed to the public. During the 1980s, the NPS purchased land and scenic easements on almost half of the site, enabling it to open the battlefield to regular public access beginning on July 13, 1991 (Hankin 1991). Over the next decade, growth from the Washington metropolitan area surrounded the site, reinvigorating local interest in its preservation and leading Congress to authorize another $20 million for land acquisition (Meyer 1994; *Frederick Post* 1992; Cooling 1992; *Frederick News* 1992; Public Law 102-202 1991; Civil War Sites Advisory Commission 1993).[1] In 2001, the Park Service purchased the last property for the battlefield, and in 2007 it opened a new visitors center (Associated Press 1992; Burns 1993; Tallman 2001; *Frederick Post* 2001).[2] At present, Monocacy National Battlefield is 1,647 acres, with over fifty eighteenth- and nineteenth-century historic structures as well as many other natural and cultural resources (see figure 10.1).

Changing Understandings of the Monocacy Landscape

Over the past thirty years, the Park Service's approach to preservation, restoration, and interpretation of Civil War battlefields, including Monocacy, has changed significantly. Historically, interpretation has focused on providing a detailed discussion of the battle, with references to features of the site that existed at the time of the battle; the battle itself was situated within a narrative of national progress and reconciliation that saw the end of racial

Monocacy National Battlefield

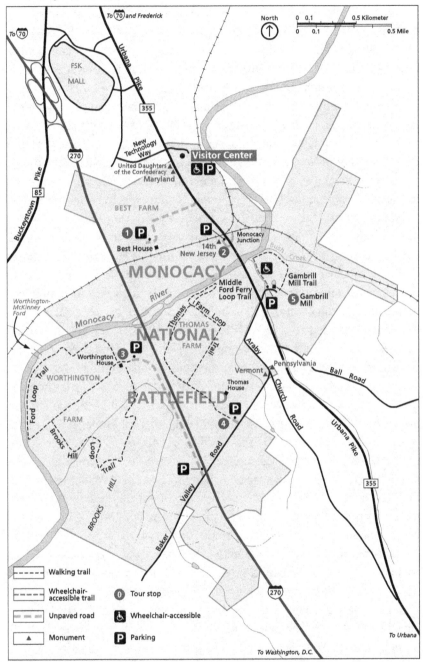

FIGURE 10.1 Monocacy National Battlefield. Source: National Park Service (2009).

slavery by the end of the war (Watt 2001; Meringolo 2012). An example of this focus on preserving and interpreting heritage can be found in a 1983 draft of the NPS's Land Protection Plan for Monocacy, which noted that "[t]he natural aspects of this historic site are perhaps as valuable as the physical remains . . . [T]his important natural setting forms a scene that is similar to that which comprised the battlefield in 1864" (4). This mode of interpretation, however, reflected serious tensions between preserving the built environment in an unaltered form and the reality that the natural environment is dynamic and changing (Longstreth 2008). While preservation can effectively protect historic structures, managing the site's ecological resources based on their aesthetic fidelity to the past undermines the need to ensure the present and future functioning of the natural environment.

Administrative changes at the national level during the 1990s recast the Park Service's management of Monocacy and other battlefields. In 1992, *The Secretary of the Interior's Standards for Historic Preservation Projects*, which governs entities listed on or eligible for the National Register, was revised to apply to all historic resource types (e.g. architectural, cultural, and natural) and to include a range of preservation options. These revisions led to a new NPS policy in 1994, which integrated the Park Service's traditional focus on preserving the natural environment with more robust consideration of the cultural history of its landscapes (Birnbaum 1994). For Monocacy, this opened the door to a series of studies that expanded and deepened historical understanding of the site. In the early 1990s, a cultural landscape study of one Monocacy site, the Araby tract, found an intact pre–Civil War mill, the bluffs overlooking the Monocacy River and Bush Creek, tracks for the Baltimore and Ohio Railroad, a local road, and a mansion built in 1872 (EDAW Inc. 1993). The findings led the author of the study to support expanding the chronology for the battlefield from 1830, when the mill was built, to 1901, when the Gambrill family terminated its operations and sold the property.[3] The first cultural-resources study of the entire battlefield was conducted in 1999 by Paula Stoner Reed, who assessed historical developments from over three centuries of continuous human habitation before and after the Civil War. Her study uncovered several artifacts on part of the site, including a late eighteenth-century manor house and secondary house, miscellaneous farming houses and sheds, and road traces. Later investigations found other structural remains, personal effects, and evidence of a tavern from the 1750s (Beasley 2007; *Historic American Buildings Survey* 2009).

The most notable investigations have occurred at Best Farm (Reed 2004; Temkin 2000; Beasley, Gwaltney, and Temkin 2001). Written records had previously documented that the Vincendiere family, who had migrated to the United States from Saint Domingue during the Haitian Revolution, established a slave plantation known as *L'Hermitage* in 1795 after purchasing 457 acres of land (later adding 291 acres). The family's nineteen-year-old daughter Victoire, surprisingly and for reasons unknown, owned the plantation. Having brought an initial twelve slaves to the planation, by 1800 she owned ninety slaves, a large population for Maryland. Victoire owned *L'Hermitage* until 1827, when she sold it and moved to the town of Frederick. Following the sale, the farm was divided in half. The Trail family acquired the southern portion, which it held until 1993. During the family's ownership, two other families worked as tenants: the Bests (1850–1910) and the Wiles (1928–1999).

While written records indicated the existence of a slave plantation, it was not until the early 2000s that archeological work confirmed its location. In 2005, Joy Beasley, the cultural-resources program manager for Monocacy National Battlefield, inventoried the resources of Best Farm, which previous research had found included the Vincendiere's manor house, a log secondary dwelling, and a stone crop barn, built in a hybrid of French Caribbean and local German and Scots-Irish vernacular architecture. Although it was intended to support the battlefield's interpretation as a Civil War site, Beasley's (2005) investigation uncovered structural remains and domestic objects that were consistent with the Vincendiere plantation. In 2010, she and a team of students uncovered the foundations of several slave dwelling houses and artifacts, revealing the largest known slave habitation site in the Mid-Atlantic (National Park Service 2010; Stern 2010; Ruane 2010). Their findings confirmed a slave population about ten times the number expected for a plantation of its size and type. The position of the slave cabins, which were lined up in front of the plantation house rather than behind it, was unusual, as was the discovery of remains of whips and stocks, which suggested the re-creation of a large-scale and brutal slave system like that found in St. Domingue at the time. Historical research undertaken by Beasley and her team to complement their archeological work found that members of the Vincendiere family had been charged in nine state court cases with cruelty against slaves, although these charges were dismissed. These archeological discoveries have expanded both the historical understanding of the Monocacy battlefield and the NPS efforts to preserve the site's cultural resources. Yet, the impact of exurban development has necessitated more active concern about the health and integrity of the site's ecological resources.

Ecological Management

The management of a complex historical landscape such as Monocacy National Battlefield is compounded by the threat that adjoining exurban development poses to its ecological resources. The site is a piedmont plateau landscape near the Blue Ridge Mountains, a part of the Appalachian Mountain system. It features several different natural habitats, including deciduous forests, temperate grasslands, and riparian environments, created by the Monocacy River and its three tributaries, as well as agricultural land for crops and pastures. This mixture of habitats supports a diverse array of wildlife, including eighty species of birds; amphibians such as salamanders and American toads; reptiles such as the copperhead and other snakes, turtles, and lizards; three dozen types of freshwater fish; and a mixture of mostly small, but also medium and large, mammals that includes squirrels, foxes, raccoons, black bear, and white-tailed deer. Although the wildlife species found at Monocacy National Battlefield are not considered rare, their diversity and population is notable given the site's location in a major metropolitan area. There are over 250 species of plant life including deciduous trees, grasses, seasonal wildflowers, and agricultural crops. The two most significant collections of plants are several species that are considered threatened in the state of Maryland or are on watch lists, as well as several "witness trees" that were present at the time of the Battle of Monocacy. The witness trees serve a number of functions. Given their history, they serve as tangible natural artifacts, which is especially valuable in light of the loss of several built structures since the nineteenth century. The trees also help depict the landscape's appearance on the eve of battle and in 150 years since, while also serving as a habitat for wildlife and a buffer zone between the Monocacy River, its tributaries, and the land. The Park Service monitors the health of the trees regularly (Thomas et al. 2011; National Park Service n.d.; "Nature & Science").

The Monocacy National Battlefield site has two major ecological issues that impair preservation, restoration, and interpretation. The first includes nearby development associated with the Washington metropolitan area. One of the most significant problems is the interstate highway that bisects the battlefield. Not only does it create a major barrier to the territorial integrity of the site, but its impervious surface and the development it attracts generate air pollution from automobiles and traffic congestion, soil erosion, and the runoff of road salts and residential chemicals, particularly on the northern edge of the battlefield. The runoff from exurban sprawl is a particular problem for wetland and waterway habits, producing acidification, low oxygenation, and high nutrient loads (Thornberry-Ehrlich 2008; Weeks et al. 2007).

The second major threat to the ecological health of Monocacy National Battlefield is invasive or nonnative species. Historically, the Park Service has marginalized ecological restoration for its historical properties, seeking to freeze the natural environment in time at a specific moment. But, over the past twenty years, the NPS has taken more interest in the issue, seeking to eliminate nonnative species where feasible and to control them otherwise (Jordan and Lubick 2011, 53–60; Clewell and Aronson 2007, 59–62; Dombeck, Wood, and Williams 2003; Stone and Loope 1996, 132–158). Thomas et. al (2011) found that insect pests, such as the gypsy moth, and fungal agents posed significant threats to plant species at the Monocacy battlefield. It also revealed that two of the six most abundant plant species at the battlefield are nonnative, which can impair the ability of native species to function properly. One particular issue of concern has been the Tree of Heaven (*Ailanthus altissima*), an invasive species that releases harmful chemicals that keep other trees from growing nearby (National Park Service n.d., "Nature and Science"). The most significant wildlife issue is the presence of very high populations of whitetail deer, which have limited the diversity and capability of plant species to regenerate because of trampling and overgrazing (Thomas et al. 2011). The loss of vegetation near waterways has exacerbated the issue of runoff associated with the exurban development near the site. This, in concert with the relatively wet climate of the eastern United States and the presence of substantial storms during the warmer months, has resulted in structural and electrical damage to facilities and harm to crops in the nearby fields during the Monocacy River's seasonal floods (Thornberry-Ehrlich 2008).

One ecological restoration strategy that the Park Service plans to deploy is to create fifteen acres of meadows (National Park Service n.d., "Nature and Science"). The environmental goals of this initiative are to develop better riparian buffers, reduce the impact of invasive species on the quality of the grasslands in the park, and increase the abundance of ground nesting birds and small mammals. Because the Monocacy battlefield has an especially broad and deep cultural history, particularly given its connections to racial slavery and the Civil War, there are important questions to consider about the impact the restoration might have on the site's historical integrity. Several of the contributors to the present volume underscore the importance of not neglecting or damaging cultural histories and meanings when restoring the ecological components and functions of a site. For the Monocacy battlefield, the ecological damage associated with metropolitan development, particularly the issues with runoff and the influx of invasive species, have already impaired the site's historical integrity. Adding meadows then would be a useful corrective to protecting the site's extant natural and cultural features while also ensuring its ecological stability and functioning over the long-term.

The landscape of ownership for Monocacy National Battlefield plays a significant role in efforts to preserve, restore, and interpret it. According to Thomas and colleagues (2011), 80 percent of the land is federally owned, and the balance has scenic easements or is under private ownership. About half of the site includes agricultural land, for which special-use permits are issued for five-year periods that establish conditions for use as well as govern nutrient management, chemical and pesticide usage, and the maintenance of riparian buffers. The presence of agriculture is unusual for sites managed by the Park Service; recreation is the most common "active use." To evaluate the site's ecological resources, Thomas and his colleagues (2011) divided the battlefield into two categories: habitats managed for natural resource values and those managed for agriculture. It then established threshold conditions for what represented a desirable state of the ecosystem based on current use and what would be a significant impairment of the system, with specific evaluations for air and climate, water resources, biological integrity, and landscape dynamics.

Thomas et al. (2011) made several significant discoveries about the site's ecological health. Overall, it concluded that the site's habitats were in good condition, with 61 percent attainment of the threshold conditions. Interestingly, resources managed for natural resource values had lower levels of attainment of ecological goals (45 percent) than those managed in agriculture (71 percent). Although the reasons for the difference are not entirely clear, one explanation is that it is easier to attain threshold conditions for agricultural land, given the Park Service's leasing regulations, than it is for "open space," where more delicate ecosystems exist that are more susceptible to the negative effects of nearby exurban sprawl.

Current best practices in ecological restoration show that making a damaged ecosystem self-sustaining over the long term requires active efforts to reestablish its structure and function (Jordan and Lubick 2011; Clewell and Aronson 2007). This recognition of the need for adaptation to improve the health of the natural environment, however, contrasts with the Park Service's general approach to interpreting its cultural landscapes, which attempts to freeze history in time (Wiens, et al., 2012; Dombeck, Wood, and Williams 2003, 124–134). Given how far knowledge of the history of the Monocacy National Battlefield has come in the past twenty years, the

Park Service should consider applying its approach to ecological restoration to re-envisioning how it might interpret this site to be more inclusive of its layered history.

Interpretation

In 1989, two years before Monocacy National Battlefield was open to the public, the NPS hosted a battle reenactment featuring over 2,000 participants and more than 10,000 visitors, capping a high point of popular interest in a traditional interpretation of the landscape's significance (Riechmann 1989; *Frederick Post* 1989). Historical understanding of the site since has transcended the Civil War and a traditional narrative of patriotic commemoration and national reunification. The archeological discoveries at the Vincendiere family's slave plantation in particular have created a valuable opportunity to discuss the history of slavery and its central role in the Civil War, something that has long been marginalized at Civil War battlefields (Seibert 2011, 67–84; Pitcaithley 2008; Blight 2002). As NPS archeologist Joy Beasley explained in 2004, before the discovery of slave dwellings, "The Vincendieres' slaves are almost invisible in the historical record. Archeology is the only way their story can ever be told" (quoted in Baker 2004, 23). Unfortunately, archeological discoveries at Civil War battlefields have generally been used to reinforce existing narratives (Heard 2006; Schackel 2002, 157–166). Although it is too early to tell whether this will be true for Monocacy because the analysis and interpretation of what was found has yet to be completed, the existing interpretive plan for the site suggests the NPS has much more work to do to enhance its interpretation of slavery in relation to the Civil War.

Despite an increase in knowledge about the complex history and current ecology of the Monocacy battlefield, official interpretation has lagged behind. The NPS *Long Range Interpretive Plan* (2009), released just before the archeological discovery of the slave plantation, identified eight major themes to guide its interpretive activities. Most of the themes focus on recounting the Battle of Monocacy, weaving in stories about the families, structures, and land mostly as they relate to the site's Civil War era history, and some references to pre- and postwar circumstances. While the interpretive plan was developed just before the archeological discoveries of *L'Hermitage*, written records documenting the slave plantation were available but were not adequately incorporated into the plan. There are, however, a few references within the third theme to the existence of slavery in Maryland, including Maryland's liminal status as a slave state that joined the Union, albeit with a larger free black population. Moreover, since the discoveries at *L'Hermitage*, the Park Service has incorporated a more robust discussion of slavery at Monocacy National Battlefield in its interpretation and, for those who are unable to visit the site, on its website (National Park Service n.d., "Slavery at Monocacy"). The site focuses primarily on *L'Hermitage* but also makes references to other tenants who owned slaves. More critically, one of the Plan's eight themes essentially dismissed the site's history following the Civil War, brusquely noting: "Civil War ended; segregation/issues continued." The wording of this theme, and the lack of elaboration, underscores the limited interpretation that the NPS offers of the Civil War's consequences in terms of the persistence and changing contours of racial discrimination, even though, in the interpretive plan, it recognizes that Civil War commemorations did not create national unity. The Plan also elides the site's local postwar history.

Environmental issues factor more significantly in the "Long Range Interpretive Plan." Interpretive themes two and three explore how the location of Monocacy as a "crossroads" of several transportation routes positioned it as a site for battle, how the environmental features of the site at the time of battle shaped the conflict, what the environmental impact of the battle was, and how the environmental features of the landscape at the time of the battle compare with those existing today. These themes suggest the NPS has made significant strides in addressing the environmental history of the battlefield, although the site's use and environmental history after the Civil War remain only marginally discussed. A final theme, more fully developed than some of the others in the Plan, underscored the importance of understanding, engaging, and promoting environmental stewardship within and outside park boundaries. A survey of "desired visitor experiences" that was incorporated into the interpretive plan includes such visitor outcomes as: "experience the beauty and solitude of Monocacy National Battlefield and . . . understand the importance of preserving our national Parks" and to "touch, feel, learn and appreciate Monocacy National Battlefield in ways that encourage them to become responsible stewards" (7). While the former outcome is a long-standing mission for NPS sites, the latter marks a significant advance in the Park Service's interpretive goals, underscoring the present ecological challenges that impact the site. But, this goal does not offer any real ways in which people can act as environmental stewards other than not littering or causing other direct harm.

Thanks to the extensive historical and archeological research undertaken for Monocacy National Battlefield over the past two decades, we know far more about the landscape's blended cultural and natural histories as well as its current ecological functioning. Yet, this knowledge has not had a substantial impact on the Park Service's interpretation of the site to the public, perpetuating a gap between its work and that of the history profession. In the mid-1990s, the NPS signed an agreement with the Organization of American Historians (OAH) to help the Park Service draw on the expertise and resources of the most prominent American history professionals. While that collaboration has yielded some successes, there continue to be major shortcomings in the NPS's historical interpretation at its Civil War battlefields and other sites, for a number of reasons. These include "the agency's weak support for its history workforce, by agency structures that confine history in isolated silos, by longstanding funding deficiencies, by often narrow and static conceptions of history's scope, and by timid interpretation" (Whisnant et al. 2011, 1). In light of the creative and critical work undertaken by history professionals, one Park Service employee argued that history at the NPS was "poised for transformation from the archaic, static, single-themed interpretive presentations of the mid-twentieth century to a new, vibrant, multiple perspective, interactive entity for the future—but only if the NPS brings to the table vision, money, and openness to new ways of doing business" (Whisnant et al. 2011, 26). This chapter cannot necessarily offer solutions for the structural and financial issues impairing the Park Service's activities, including the need to complete the analysis of the archeological investigations of *L'Hermitage* to more fully incorporate discussions of slavery into the public interpretation. Instead, it offers an alternative interpretation of the site to promote historic preservation, ecological restoration, and public interpretation that is more inclusive of the site's layered history while also attuned to the needs for ensuring its long-term ecological functioning.

Such an interpretation might go something like this: Before the Civil War, the land on either side of the Monocacy River in Frederick County, Maryland, on which the Battle of Monocacy would be waged, witnessed nearly a century of intensive human settlement. After the end of the French and Indian War, the hilly and wooded terrain near the Monocacy River proved quite fertile for agriculture, leading to the establishment of half a dozen farms by 1800. The property owners, including the Vincendiere family, owned slaves who cultivated wheat and corn, while the county's proximity to Pennsylvania, which abolished slavery in the early nineteenth century, led it to experience an increase in the number of free blacks during the antebellum period. Although Frederick County became the "breadbasket" of Maryland, culminating in the opening of a mill on the Monocacy site in 1830, industrialization and the presence of a railroad to ship raw materials to Baltimore prompted a decline in its economic fortunes. In 1864, this rural landscape, like many others in the mid-Atlantic and the South that had histories of slavery, became the site of a battle during a civil war that inscribed a broader historical significance onto that landscape when the war ended and slavery was abolished.

Once the Civil War ended, Americans came together to rebuild a nation. Although many commemorated the sacrifices of those who fought, racial discrimination persisted for African Americans, while poorer whites in the Monocacy area struggled to survive as they exchanged wheat production for work in the dairy, fruit, and vegetable industries. By 1900, tenant farming had divided the larger prewar farms on the landscape where the Battle of Monocacy had been fought. Despite public commemoration of the Battle of Monocacy, the portion of the battlefield land not used for farming remained unkempt except for a handful of monuments. As exurban development made its way to the area by the early 1970s, local residents, congressional funds, and Park Service officials worked to preserve the battlefield's heritage, rural way of life, and open space. Into the present day, this preserved landscape is interpreted for the public, continues to offer a living for farmers, and exists as a source of open space in a rapidly developing area, although it faces serious ecological challenges from exurban sprawl.

What this interpretation does—and what the official interpretation does not do—is to broaden and deepen public understanding of the layered natural and cultural history of Monocacy National Battlefield as well as its present conditions. First, it broadens the chronology of interpretation beyond the Civil War to include over three centuries of continuous human use of the site. Second, it blends natural and cultural histories together in a more dynamic and interconnected way, rather than using the natural environment as a "backdrop" for the Battle of Monocacy. Third, it offers a way to examine the site's uses after the Civil War while highlighting the threats to the natural and cultural history that exurban development poses. This mode of interpretation may be more complex for visitors, but it is also more faithful to the layered nature of the landscape and its extant features than an imagined past that cannot be fully re-created.

Conclusion

Historically, the Park Service had managed national battlefields with an eye to "freezing" them in time. By the mid-1990s, however, it began to embrace a broader approach to these landscapes that produced a more comprehensive understanding of their historical significance and greater attention to ecological restoration (Watt 2001). A major part of the impetus and justification for this broadened management approach has to do with the greater threats to the site associated with exurban sprawl over the past few years. In addition, archeological investigations culminating in the discovery of *L'Hermitage* slave plantation in recent years have revealed aspects of historical and cultural significance that, even today, have yet to be fully appreciated.

This chapter maintains that the most "authentic" approach to preservation, restoration, and interpretation would focus on managing the extant landscape to protect its intertwined cultural and natural histories and ensure its long-term ecological functioning. Historical authenticity cannot be found in freezing a landscape, because its conditions are dynamic and change over time, while new research can broaden and deepen understanding of the site's history. The interpretive approach recommended here is admittedly more difficult than remaining selectively focused on promoting the site's Civil War heritage. But the historical record for the battlefield warrants a broad and inclusive interpretation of the landscape in all of its complexity, while the ecological threats require immediate attention to avoid further destruction of the site's cultural and natural resources.

By creating a broader and more inclusive narrative for Monocacy National Battlefield, the Park Service could also appeal to different audiences for the site. To enhance its success in improving the ecological health of the landscape, it might also consider doing two things. The first is to become more involved in the local community (Jarvis 2000). Given the exurban development that surrounds the battlefield, the NPS has a vested interest in ensuring that new or existing development does not harm the park. Promoting the "green space" of Monocacy would also appeal to local residents, who can see open space disappearing as the sprawl encroaches. The second thing, which the Park Services to some extent already does by leasing agricultural lands at Monocacy battlefield, is to create a community-based constituency to promote stewardship (Jordan and Lubick 2011). Creating a more collaborative decision-making model would increase the public's stake in the battlefield and potentially yield new resources for preservation, restoration, and interpretation. Ultimately, a more inclusive approach to preserving, restoring, and interpreting Monocacy National Battlefield is not only more historically "authentic" but also more capable of ensuring the long-term ecological health of the site.

Notes

1. In the early 1990s, similar conversations about preserving battlefields unfolded throughout the United States. In 1991, Congress established a commission to assess battlefield preservation, which grouped battlefields into four priority categories based on the significance of the battle to the war. Monocacy was ranked in the second highest category, but was included as having a "high" threat of potential development.

2. The Civil War Trust, a private land trust, contributed $36,000 toward the purchase of the final property.

3. The Gambrill mansion was later renovated to serve as the home of the NPS Preservation Training Center beginning in 2006.

References

Associated Press. 1992. "Trust Buys Option to Save Monocacy Farm." *Frederick Post*, May 22.

Baker, Joe. 2004. "L'Hermitage Plantation: Investigating a Landscape of Pain at Monocacy Battlefield." *Common Ground* 9 (4) (Winter): 14–25.

Beasley, Joy, ed. 2005. "Archeological overview and assessment and identification and evaluation study of the Best Farm, Monocacy National Battlefield, Frederick, Maryland." Occasional Report no. 18. Washington, DC: National Park Service.

Beasley, Joy. 2007. "The Middle Ford Ferry Tavern Project, Monocacy, NB." National Park Service website. Archeology Program. Accessed May 14, 2011. http://www.nps.gov/archeology/sites/npsites/monocacyTavern.htm.

Beasley, Joy, Tom Gwaltney, and Martha Temkin. 2002. "Gaining New Perspectives on the Past: An Application of GIS at the Best Farm. *Maryland Archeology* 37 (September): 22–37.

Birnbaum, Charles A. 1994. "Protecting Cultural Landscapes: Planning, Treatment and Management of Historic Landscapes." Preservation Brief 36. Washington, DC: National Park Service. Accessed May 27, 2015. http://www.nps.gov/tps/how-to-preserve/briefs/36-cultural-landscapes.htm.

Blight, David. W. 2001. *Race and Reunion: The Civil War in American Memory*. Cambridge, MA: Belknap Press of Harvard University Press.

Blight, David W. 2002. "Healing and History: Battlefields and the Problem of Civil War Memory." In *Beyond the Battlefield: Race, Memory and the American Civil War*, 170–190. Amherst: University of Massachusetts Press.

Bodnar, John. 1993. *Remaking America: Public Memory, Commemoration, and Patriotism in the Twentieth Century*. Princeton, NJ: Princeton University Press.

Burns, Dan. 1993. "Funding to Buy More Land for Monocacy Battlefield Denied." *Frederick News-Post*, June 17.

Civil War Sites Advisory Commission. 1993. *Report on the Nation's Civil War Battlefields*. Washington, DC: National Park Service. Accessed May 10, 2011. http://www.cr.nps.gov/hps/abpp/cwsac/cws0-1.html.

Clewell, Andre F., and James Aronson. 2007. *Ecological Restoration: Principles, Values, and Structure of an Emerging Profession*. Washington, DC: Island Press.

Cooling, B. Franklin. 1992. "A National Treasure in Frederick's Back Yard." *Frederick News-Post*, July 1.

Cooling, B. Franklin. 1997. *Monocacy: The Battle That Saved Washington*. Shippensburg, PA: White Mane Publishing Company.

Dombeck, Michael P., Christopher A. Wood, and Jack W. Williams. 2003. *From Conquest to Conservation: Our Public Lands Legacy*. Washington, DC: Island Press.

EDAW Inc., Land and Community Associates, and John Milner Associates. 1993. *Monocacy National Battlefield: Cultural Landscape Evaluation and Archeological Evaluation, Final Report*. Denver, CO: National Park Service, Denver Service Center.

Frederick County Planning and Zoning Commission. 1970. *Analysis of Land Use: A Background Study*. Frederick, MD: Frederick County Planning and Zoning Commission.

Frederick County Planning and Zoning Commission. 1991. *Annual Report*. Frederick, MD: Frederick County Planning and Zoning Commission

Frederick News. 1964. "Civil War Centennial: 100th Anniversary of the Battle of Monocacy will be Observed with two Special Dedicatory Programs." June 1.

Frederick News. 1992. "Monocacy." Editorial, November 14.

Frederick Post. 1951. "New Washington Road Runs through Part of Battlefield." April 4.

Frederick Post. 1978. "Carter Signs Omnibus Parks Bill: Monocacy Battlefield Gets $3.5 Million." November 11.

Frederick Post. 1989. "A 'Gateway' to History." Editorial, November 18.

Frederick Post. 1992. "Monocacy Efforts." Editorial, June 4.

Frederick Post. 2001. "Monocacy Preserved." Editorial, November 19.

Haley, Paul A. 1971. "National Park Service Revising Plans for Monocacy Battlefield Park." *The News* (Frederick, MD), December 13.

Hankin, Sam. 1991. "Monocacy Battlefield Dedicated—At Last." *Frederick News*, July 15.

Heard, Sandra R. 2006. *Presenting Race and Slavery at Historic Sites: Manassas National Battlefield Park*. Washington, DC, National Park Service. Accessed May 12, 2011. http://www.nps.gov/history/crdi/Manassas_Report_Final.pdf.

Historic American Buildings Survey. 2009. *Thomas Farm House, 4632 Araby Church Road, Frederick, Frederick County, MD*. HABS no. MD-1251. Washington, DC. Accessed October 1, 2014. http://www.loc.gov/pictures/item/md1747/.

Jarvis, T. Destry. 2000. "The Responsibility of National Parks in Rural Development." In *National Parks and Rural Development: Practice and Policy in the United States*, edited by Gary E. Machlis and Donald R. Field, 219–229. Washington, DC: Island Press.

Jordan, William R. III, and George M. Lubick. 2011. *Making Nature Whole: A History of Ecological Restoration*. Washington, DC: Island Press.

Lichtenstein, Nelson. 1963. "Monocacy Battlefield Gets Little Care, Yet Battle Fought There One of Most Important of the Civil War. *Frederick News*. July 23.

Linenthal, Edward Tabor. 1991. *Sacred Ground: Americans and Their Battlefields*. Urbana: University of Illinois Press.

Longstreth, Richard, ed. 2008. *Cultural Landscapes: Balancing Nature and Heritage in Preservation Practice*. Minneapolis: University of Minnesota Press.

Lowenthal, David. 1998. *The Heritage Crusade and the Spoils of History.* New York: Cambridge University Press.

Martin Seibert, Erika K. 2011. "The Third Battle of Manassas: Power, Identity, and the Forgotten African American Past." In *Myth, Memory, and the Making of the American Landscape*, edited by Paul A. Shackel, 67–84. Gainesville: University Press of Florida.

Meringolo, Denise D. 2012. *Museums, Monuments, and National Parks: Toward a New Genealogy of Public History.* Amherst: University of Massachusetts Press.

Meyer, Eugene L. 1994. "One County's Growing Pains: Frederick's Ex-suburbanites Fight Their Own Kind." *Washington Post.* November 27.

National Park Service. 2009. *Monocacy National Battlefield: Long Range Interpretive Plan.* Harpers Ferry, WV: National Park Service. Accessed May 28, 2013. http://www.nps.gov/hfc/pdf/ip/2010-02-22-MONO-FinalDocument.pdf.

National Park Service. 2010. "Slave Village Discovered in Maryland." Press release. August 11. Accessed May 13, 2011. http://www.nps.gov/mono/slavevillage2010.htm.

National Park Service. "Battlefield Monuments." Monocacy National Battlefield. Accessed April 17, 2011. http://www.nps.gov/mono/historyculture/battlefield-monuments.htm.

National Park Service. n.d. Interpretive File. Monocacy National Battlefield Library, Frederick, MD.

National Park Service. n.d. "Nature and Science. Monocacy National Battlefield." Accessed September 10, 2013. http://www.nps.gov/mono/naturescience/.

National Park Service. n.d. "Slavery at Monocacy. Monocacy National Battlefield." Accessed October 7, 2014. http://www.nps.gov/mono/historyculture/slavery.htm.

Pitcaithley, Dwight T. 2008. "'A Cosmic Threat': The National Park Service Addresses the Causes of the American Civil War." In *Slavery and Public History: The Tough Stuff of American Memory*, edited by James Oliver Horton and Lois E. Horton, 169–186. Chapel Hill: University of North Carolina Press.

Raver, Martha. 1973. "Researchers Say Frederick County Ill-Equipped to Forestall Growth." *Frederick News*, June 18.

Reed, Paula Stoner. 2004. *Cultural Resources Study: Monocacy National Battlefield*, updated ed. (with Edith B. Wallace). Hagerstown, Maryland: Paula S. Reed and Associates.

Riechmann, Deb. 1989. "Preserving Monocacy's Battlefield." *Frederick Post.* November 17.

Ruane, Michael E. 2010. "Brutal Slave History Unearthed at Frederick County's *L'Hermitage*." *Washington Post*, August 26.

Schackel, Paul A. 2002. "Broadening the Interpretation of the Past at Harpers Ferry National Historical Park." In *Public Benefits of Archaeology*, edited by Barbara J. Little, 157–166. Gainesville: University Press of Florida.

Stern, Laurence. 1956. "Planning Moves Made: Frederick County Girds for Population 'invasion.'" *Washington Post.* September 22.

Stern, Nicholas C. 2010. "'This is Truly Extraordinary': Archeologists Use Radar Device to Uncover Slave Village at Monocacy National Battlefield." *Frederick News-Post*, August 19.

Stone, Charles P., and Lloyd L. Loope. 1996. "Alien Species in Hawaiian National Parks." In *Science and Ecosystem Management in the National Parks*, edited William L. Halvorson and Gary E. Davis, 132–158. Tucson: University of Arizona Press.

Tallman, Douglas. 2001. "Purchase of Farm Completes Battlefield." *Frederick News.* November 15.

Temkin, Martha. 2000. "Guns or Plowshares: Significance and a Civil War Agricultural Landscape." *Maryland Archeology* 36 (March): 25–34.

Thomas J. E., A. Banasik, J. P. Campbell, T. J. B. Carruthers, W. C. Dennison, M. Lehman, and M. Northrup. 2011. "Monocacy National Battlefield Natural Resource Conditional Assessment." National Capital Region. Natural Resource Report NPS/NCRN/NRR-2011/415. Fort Collins, CO: National Park Service.

Thornberry-Ehrlich, T. 2008. *Monocacy National Battlefield Geologic Resource Evaluation Report.* Natural Resource Report NPS/NRPC/GRD/NRR—2008/051. Denver, CO: National Park Service.

Trail, Susan W. 2005. "Remembering Antietam: Commemoration and Preservation of a Civil War Battlefield." PhD diss., University of Maryland.

US Congress. 1976. An Act to Provide for Increases in Appropriation Ceilings and Boundary Changes in Certain Units of the National Park System, and for other Purposes. Public Law 94–578. 94th Cong. 2nd sess., October 21.

US Congress. National Parks and Recreation Act of 1978. Public Law 95–625. 95th Cong. 2nd sess., November 10.

US Congress. 1980. An Act to Provide, with Respect to the National Park System: For the Establishment of New Units; For Adjustments in Boundaries; For Increases in Appropriation Authorizations for Land Acquisition and Development; and For Other Purposes. Public Law 96–607. 96th Cong. 2nd sess., December 28.

US Congress. 1991. An Act to Authorize Additional Appropriations for Land Acquisition at Monocacy National Battlefield, Maryland. Public Law 102–202. 102nd Cong. 1st sess., December 10.

US Department of the Interior. 1992. "The Secretary of the Interior's Standards for the Treatment of Historic Properties. 36 CFR Part 68." August 11. Codified in Federal Register. 1995. 60, no. 133, July 12. Accessed May 24, 2013. http://www.cr.nps.gov/local-law/arch_stnds_8_2.htm.

Watt, Laura Alice. 2001. Managing Cultural Landscapes: Reconciling Local Preservation and Institutional Ideology in the National Park Service. PhD. diss., University of California, Berkeley.

Weeks D., D. Vana-Miller, M. Norris, and A. Banasik. 2007. *Water Resource Stewardship Report, Monocacy National Battlefield.* Natural Resource Technical Report NPS/NRPC/WRD/NRTC-2007-048. Fort Collins, CO: National Park Service.

Whisnant, Anne Mitchell, Marla R. Miller, Gary B. Nash, and David Thelen. 2011. *Imperiled Promise: The State of History in the National Park Service.* Report for the National Park Service by the Organization of American Historians. Bloomington, IN: Organization of American Historians. Accessed March 19, 2012. http://www.oah.org/site/assets/documents/Imperiled_Promise.pdf.

Wiens, John A., Gregory Hayward, Hugh D. Safford, and Catherine M. Giffen, eds., 2012. *Historical Environmental Variation in Conservation and Natural Resource Management.* Hoboken, NJ: Wiley-Blackwell.

CHAPTER 11 | Renaturalization and Industrial
Heritage in America's Largest
Superfund Site

*The Case of the Warm Springs Ponds in
Montana's Clark Fork Superfund Site*

FREDRIC L. QUIVIK

Introduction

Can ecological restoration and cultural landscape preservation be integrated? Advocacy for such integration has occurred in vernacular
landscapes—landscapes shaped by ordinary people using what have
become traditional methods to manipulate the environment for human
purposes. Agricultural landscapes provide one example. This chapter
provides another, using the landscape of the Upper Clark Fork River in
Montana—which has been severely altered by the mining industry for
150 years—as a case study to argue that ecological restoration ought not to
be severed from the preservation of the cultural environment that developed
there. The Upper Clark Fork River landscape embodies a set of historically
significant human interactions with the environment that came to be "traditional" for the communities of Butte and Anaconda. The human interactions embodied in the landscapes of Butte and Anaconda, at the head of the
Clark Fork watershed, are those of industrialized mining, which has been a
significant feature of modern humanity's relationship with the earth.

The landscapes of Butte and Anaconda include layers of conventional
historic architectural resources; of structures associated with all the steps
and processes of industrial mineral extraction; of features embodying
more than a century of social conflict between the mining industry and
other groups whose property and uses of the environment were damaged

by the industrial wastes of mining; and of lands and waters severely contaminated by hazardous materials and eligible for major environmental remediation and ecological restoration. The stewardship of all those layers together is a complex undertaking.

The Clark Fork Superfund site in Montana (figure 11.1) is the largest Superfund site in the United States.[1] Its immensity is often illustrated by the Berkeley Pit, a former open-pit copper mine at the head of the Clark Fork watershed, which is filling with acidic water contaminated with heavy metals such as copper, lead, cadmium, and arsenic. The Clark Fork site is much larger than the Berkeley Pit, however, encompassing environments severely altered by the mining industry in the cities of Butte and Anaconda, much of the Deer Lodge Valley adjacent to Anaconda, and more than one hundred miles of riparian lands along Silver Bow

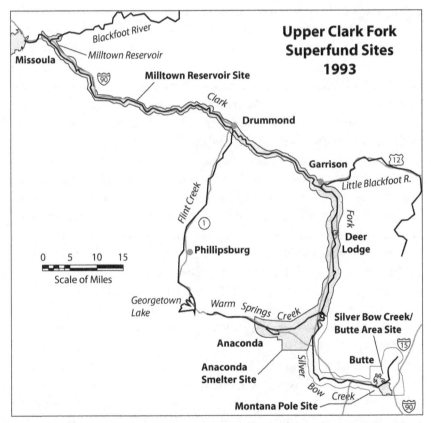

FIGURE 11.1 Map showing the extent of the sites making up the Clark Fork Superfund site. The Warm Springs Ponds are located just upstream (south) of the confluence of Silver Bow Creek and Warm Springs Creek. Map courtesy of the Montana State Library, Geographic Information.

Creek and the Clark Fork River downstream to Missoula. In addition to having sustained the impacts of copper mining, milling, and smelting across nearly 150 years, these environments in the Upper Clark Fork are a rich cultural landscape that embodies developments that shaped the course of Montana history and spawned events that were significant on the national stage as well. In a very real sense, the entire area became a vast mining landscape with several specialized areas, some for mineral extraction, some for mineral processing, and huge areas used as sinks for the waste products of the mining industry (Tarr 1996). Because of the gradual decline of the copper industry, much of the historical fabric of the built environments of Butte and Anaconda survives, giving rise to one of the nation's largest National Historic Landmark districts. At the same time, because of the scale of mining and related activities at Butte and Anaconda, the region presents the nation with pressing demands for environmental cleanup and restoration.

Superfund remediation in the Clark Fork basin has engendered tension among, on the one hand, segments in the community who have long been working to preserve and interpret the landscape layers recognized as cultural resources of the area, and, on the other hand, segments of the community who want to see the hazardous materials removed and natural resources restored. Superfund remediation has also exhibited the complexity that ensues in the overlap of federal programs, each of which is devised to address a specific set of social values. Among the programs that overlap in the Upper Clark Fork are the Comprehensive Environmental Response, Compensation, and Liability Act (CERCLA), the nationwide program enacted by Congress in 1980 and administered by the US Environmental Protection Agency (EPA) to clean up hazardous materials at old industrial sites, and the National Historic Preservation Act, enacted by Congress in 1966 to protect historically significant cultural resources from thoughtless actions by the federal government (Morin 2013; Quivik 2001).

The divide between the two communities of interest in the Clark Fork is similar to the divide, caused by a kind of environmentalist purity, seen in other cases in the United States involving matters of land-use management. For example, Grand Teton National Park is a large, wild area in Wyoming that also has a rich cultural heritage that, in turn, embodies the history that led to the area becoming a national park. The cultural landscape of the park includes historic structures from the early twentieth century, such as White Grass Dude Ranch, which are integral to the park's history and help the National Park Service (NPS) to interpret that history. In recent decades, environmental purists have argued that the NPS should remove the buildings and restore that ground to a wilderness condition. Historic preservationists point to the complex mandate of the NPS, to manage resources for multiple values, including natural, cultural, and recreational. These preservationists, who are used to balancing complex social values in diverse venues, consider the retention of dude-ranch buildings and wilderness values of the park to be compatible. Environmental historian William Cronon has written about a similar set of issues between wilderness and the preservation of cultural landscapes being contested at the Apostle Islands (Bowman 2013, 20–21; Cronon 2003, 36–42; see also Deary, chap. 6, this volume). Cronon (1995) provided an overview of the conflict in his important article, "The Trouble with Wilderness," in which he argues that humans are inseparable from nature and that, while some wild areas may merit being managed by humans to keep human impact to a minimum, finding solutions to the problems arising from Earth's burgeoning human population will not be possible in places defined by the absence of humans. Cronon's ideas can help inform how we integrate cultural preservation and the environmental remediation of hazardous materials.

Since the 1980s, when community groups in Butte and Anaconda set about planning for the comprehensive preservation and interpretation of the communities' historic industrial resources and landscapes, the history of environmental degradation and restoration has been among the important historical themes identified as central to proposed interpretation plans. Once Superfund remediation commenced in earnest in the late 1980s, the potential conflicts between the objectives of cultural-landscape preservation and environmental remediation and restoration became apparent. As a consequence, the EPA in 1993 authorized the preparation of a regional historic preservation plan aimed at integrating and negotiating cultural preservation and environmental objectives (Renewable Technologies, Inc. 1985; RHPP Joint Committee 1993; Heritage Strategies 2012). Since that time, a monumental remediation project has been implemented in several stages, and community groups have continued to try to preserve their cultural resources. Some important cultural resources have been lost to the cleanup, including the historic railroad tracks on the Butte hill that once served to convey ore from the mines to the smelter (Tyer 2013). Superfund remediation has also led to the enhancement of features where culture and nature have intersected, such as the Warm Springs Ponds, enhancements that allow a closer examination of what ecological restoration can mean in a setting so profoundly damaged by industrial activity (Quivik 2007a).

Warm Springs Ponds

Warm Springs Ponds (figure 11.2) are part of an artificial wetland facility built by the Anaconda Copper Mining Company in 1918 to prevent mine waste tailings from migrating further downstream. The facility has been enhanced by recent Superfund remediation and now offers habitat for migratory waterfowl, as well as a number of other ecological functions (Mitsch and Jørgensen 2004, 288). Because the ponds have been so intensively enhanced under the Superfund Program, it is easy to think of them as an artifact of the turn of this century. But they have a long cultural history. I suggest that the Warm Springs Ponds are an example of a project that can serve the objectives of both advocates of ecological restoration and historic preservation, especially if their history is more fully interpreted.

Historically, the Anaconda Company built the Warm Springs Ponds to allow solids to settle out of waters emanating from the tailings deposits located along Silver Bow and Warm Springs creeks at Butte and Anaconda, respectively. Because the waters from Butte were typically acidic and

FIGURE 11.2 View of the Warm Springs Ponds to the southwest showing Pond 2 (*right*), Pond 3 (*left*), and the earthen embankment between them that impounds Pond 3. The Mill-Willow Bypass flows from left to right along the far side of the Warm Springs Ponds. Note the stack of the Washoe smelter at Anaconda in the distance near the center of the photo. Photo by the author.

carried heavy metals in solution, the company also used the ponds as a facility for adding lime, thus neutralizing the acid and causing the metals to precipitate out as sediments collecting on the beds of the ponds. Superfund remediation has now treated most upstream tailings deposits, either in situ or by transporting tailings to designed impoundment areas, thus eliminating most of the acid and metals in solution. The Warm Springs Ponds, however, are still important in the Superfund design scheme as the last point in the remediated area at which monitors can adjust the pH of surface water before it continues on its way down the Clark Fork. This kind of facility also has the potential to serve larger ecological functions, such as providing habitat for migratory waterfowl, and to serve cultural functions, by providing a recreational area for such activities as fishing, hiking, and bird-watching (US Environmental Protection Agency 2000, 17–38; CDM Federal Programs Corporation 2011, sec. 3).

The Upper Clark Fork has been so intensely altered by the mining activity that it is questionable whether it can ever be restored, if that is understood to mean returning it to some pre-mining condition. Many of the ecological functions that once served the area, however, can be restored. Moreover, the impacts of mining have called into being new ecological functions that need to be maintained for purposes of human and environmental health. In the case of the Warm Springs Ponds, those ecological functions are being performed by a cultural feature that has a century-long history in the mining industry.

The Warm Springs Ponds, near Anaconda were an outgrowth of the mining industry at Butte, about twenty-five miles to the east. Butte got its start as a mining town during a brief placer gold rush to Silver Bow Creek and the Butte hill in 1864. After a short boom, the mining camp went into decline, as miners exhausted the scant placer deposits and moved on to other promising prospects in Montana and the American West. A few tenacious miners, called "quartz cranks," stayed in Butte, convinced that the metal-bearing signs they recognized in the rock outcroppings on the Butte hill heralded riches below the surface. By the United States' centennial year in 1876, the camp was beginning to emerge from the doldrums; some of the shallow shafts had opened rich silver ores, and a few entrepreneurs were able to raise the capital to build the stamp mills necessary to treat the silver ore. Meanwhile, a few other miners opened veins of copper ore rich enough to bear the cost of freighting it by wagon overland to Corrine, Utah, where it could be placed on the nation's first transcontinental railroad and shipped east to distant smelters. By the end of the 1870s, Butte was one of the premier silver-mining camps in the West, and copper was beginning to attract significant capital as well (Malone 1981, 3–24).

The capital required to recover silver was relatively modest compared to that required for copper. A company predicated on silver mining needed only a mill equipped with furnaces for roasting the ore; stamps for crushing the ore; and amalgamating equipment for separating the precious metal, with the aid of mercury, from the crushed pulp. Butte's copper-sulfide ores required more elaborate processing, because the copper was chemically bound, in the form of mineral compounds, with other elements, especially sulfur, but also iron and arsenic. The copper minerals were also physically bound in a matrix of host rock. Breaking the chemical bonds to yield pure copper required heat, applied in the costly smelting process. Sometimes, the copper ores from Butte's mines were rich enough to be smelted directly and yield a profit. More typically, however, the ores had first to be subjected to concentration, a physical process, somewhat like that employed at the silver mills, in which the ores were crushed and ground to a suitable particle size so that the bits of copper mineral could be separated from the bits of non-metal-bearing host rock. Concentrators produced two streams: *concentrates*, which could then be smelted at a profit, and *tailings*, a waste product that was typically discharged to a nearby stream. The millions of tons of tailings that had been discharged into the headwaters of the Clark Fork River led to the construction of the Warm Springs Ponds in 1918, and those tailings plus millions of tons more, discharged in the next sixty years, have constituted one of the major challenges in the Clark Fork Superfund remediation.

Smelter Development in Butte and Anaconda

Butte's first copper smelter was the Colorado. Located along Silver Bow Street about a half mile west of Montana Creek, it went into operation in 1879. Over the next five years, several other smelters also went into operation along Silver Bow Creek in Butte. Each had a concentrator, and each discharged its tailings into or next to the stream, so Butte's mining industry began to have profound impacts on downstream riparian areas. By 1884, there were five smelters operating in Butte and discharging metallurgical wastes into Silver Bow Creek. That same year, Marcus Daly opened his Anaconda smelter twenty-six miles west of Butte along the banks of Warm Springs Creek (Quivik 1997, 267–272).

Daly had arrived in Butte in 1876 to supervise development of the Alice mine and mill, which he did until 1880, when he struck out on his own, buying the Anaconda mine and some nearby properties. With the Anaconda mine, he was able to attract investment capital from George Hearst, James Ben Ali Haggin, and Lloyd Tevis, capitalists from San Francisco. They provided the funds to sink the shaft and build the required surface plant. At relatively shallow depths, the Anaconda mine proved rich in silver ore, but at greater depth miners struck rich copper ore. Daly's investors committed to developing the Anaconda as a copper-mining and smelting enterprise. Rather than join the crowded smelting scene at Butte, where timber for fuel and water for concentration were growing scarce, Daly recommended that the Anaconda syndicate build a smelter twenty-six miles to the west, on the north side of Warm Springs Creek, where there was a more abundant supply of water than at Silver Bow Creek. The magnitude of the Anaconda syndicate's undertaking can be seen in the scale of the new works. By then, two of the Butte smelters had the capacity to treat 100 tons of ore daily; the others were smaller. Yet Daly's new smelter opened in 1884 with a capacity to smelt 500 tons of ore per day, and construction was already underway that would double its capacity. To house smelter workers, Daly established the town of Anaconda adjacent to the new works. The Anaconda Company quickly became the largest of Butte's several large copper-mining companies (Quivik 1998, 155–161; Malone 1981, 24–31, 41).

A brief history of the Anaconda Company demonstrates its global importance and why the cultural landscapes of Butte and Anaconda associated with that history are so significant, as well as why the company chose to build the Warm Springs Ponds nearly one hundred years ago. Throughout the 1880s, Butte's output of copper continued to increase, and in 1887 Butte surpassed Michigan's Keweenaw Peninsula as the world's largest supplier of copper. The Butte and Anaconda smelters expanded their capacity, and as their capacities grew, so did their discharge of metallurgical wastes. By 1900, the Anaconda syndicate had reorganized and incorporated as the Anaconda Copper Mining Company (ACM). The company continued to upgrade its technologies and expand smelting capacity so that, by 1900, it had a daily capacity to treat 6,000 tons (Quivik 1998, 170, 195–200).

More corporate changes for the ACM were in the offing as the nineteenth century ended. In 1899, Marcus Daly and interests associated with the Standard Oil Trust formed the Amalgamated Copper Company, a holding company that bought controlling interest in several Butte mining companies, including the ACM. Amalgamated also acquired the companies that operated the Butte smelters (Richter 1916). For about a decade, each of the Amalgamated companies remained a distinct corporate entity that owned and operated its own group of properties. Amalgamated merged all those companies into the ACM in 1910, at which time the last of the Butte smelters closed. By that time, the ACM had built a new smelter at Anaconda, called the Washoe Reduction Works. When it opened in 1902, it was the largest nonferrous metallurgical plant in the world. And the volumes of smoke and tailings it discharged into the environment were similarly monumental (Malone 1981, 141–148; Quivik 1998, 272–280).

Tailings and Streams

Although smoke pollution has attracted more attention by historians of the environmental impacts of the ACM operations in Butte and Anaconda, contamination of streams in the area was another issue that generated considerable controversy, especially in the early twentieth century (Bakken 1991; MacMillan 2000; Quivik 2007b). Perhaps the most noteworthy legal action was the 1903 suit that Hugh Magone brought in federal court against the ACM as well as the companies that operated copper smelters and concentrators in Butte. Magone had a farm in the Deer Lodge Valley, adjacent to Anaconda, and he diverted water from the Clark Fork River onto his land to irrigate his crops. The trial took place in 1905. As with a different suit concerning smoke damage, which Magone's neighbor Fred Bliss filed against the ACM in 1905, the Magone case featured numerous farmers who testified about the damage to their property. In the Magone case, farmers described damage to soils and crops that they believed was caused by water flowing down Warm Springs and Silver Bow creeks, water that was contaminated by the tailings of the Anaconda and Butte concentrators. Magone was awarded damages of $1,700, which was allocated among the various companies, but the judge did not enjoin the companies from continuing to discharge their tailings. The ruling amounted to little more than a minor slap on the companies' wrists (Quivik 1998, 296–305).

In subsequent years, the ACM did expand its efforts to keep tailings from the stream, especially after the company introduced flotation to its concentrator at the Washoe works in 1915. Prior to the conversion to flotation, the tailings discharged by copper concentrators had particle sizes that ranged from fine gravel, through sand, to very fine powder, the latter called *slimes*. The older method of concentration, called *gravity concentration*, was relatively good at recovering copper values from coarser materials, but it was rather ineffective at recovering copper minerals from slimes. The companies knew from assaying their tailings that they were losing valuable copper minerals in the slime tailings that were flowing out the launders from their concentrators, so they continued trying to find improved methods for recovering copper minerals from slimes. Such a method appeared with the development of flotation, a process by which chemical reagents added to the slurry of finely crushed ore cause copper-bearing particles to adhere to bubbles rising through the slurry. The copper can be recovered from the froth that gathers on top of the slurry. The ACM quickly concluded that flotation was so effective that, rather than limiting its use to treating slime tailings before they were discharged, it would be more effective to grind all the ore to a very fine particle size, so that it could all be subjected to flotation (Quivik 1998, 383–392).

Prior to the conversion to flotation, the ACM had stored its tailings in ponds just east of the smelter, so that the tailings would be relatively close in case an improved technology was developed that would allow them to be reprocessed. Once flotation was implemented at the Washoe works, the ACM no longer had reason to save its tailings for possible future retreatment. The company therefore developed a new tailings disposal area several miles northeast of the smelter and west of both Silver Bow Creek and the area where the Warm Springs Ponds would come to be located. Called the Opportunity Ponds, the southern edge of the tailings disposal area was just a mile north of the community of Opportunity. The ACM began developing the Opportunity Ponds in 1914 and expanded the area the ponds encompassed through 1919. The ponds covered an area of several square miles. Such a large impoundment allowed the water carrying the fine tailings to come to rest so that the fine solids would settle out before nearly clear water was discharged from the ponds (Quivik 1998, 449–452).

Prior to construction of the Warm Springs Ponds, the ACM had discharged clarified water from the Opportunity Ponds into Silver Bow Creek directly east of the ponds and just upstream (south) of the confluence of Silver Bow Creek and Warms Springs Creek. The water still contained a very small concentration of fine solids when it entered Silver Bow Creek. By the late-1910s, ACM officials recognized that the company was also liable for damage that might be caused by tailings and contamination in the water of Silver Bow Creek flowing out of Butte, more than twenty miles upstream. Several large tailings deposits there, created by the companies that Amalgamated had consolidated into the ACM, continued to lose tailings and dissolved contaminants to the stream. The company also operated precipitation plants in Butte, which extracted dissolved copper from water flowing through the tailings piles and from water pumped from the Butte mines. The precipitation plants discharged their effluent to Silver Bow Creek. Therefore, to preclude tailings or contaminated water from flowing down Silver Bow Creek and into the Clark Fork River, the ACM built the Warm Springs Ponds along Silver Bow Creek between the outfall from Opportunity Ponds and the confluence with Warm Springs Creek. Built in 1918, the two impoundments of the Warm Springs Ponds provided the ACM with one last chance to purify and clarify water in Silver Bow Creek before it flowed into the Clark Fork (Quivik 1998, 452-456; US Environmental Protection Agency 2000, 4).

The ACM continued to manage the Opportunity Ponds and the Warm Springs Ponds throughout the company's period of operation, even after it moved its concentrator operations back to Butte when a new concentrator was opened there in 1964. Because the Opportunity Ponds were filled with very fine solids, the tailings deposits in the impoundments were prone to a problem called *dusting* whenever an area would become dry. To address the problem, the ACM built a ditch in 1937 to convey water from Silver Bow Creek, near where it exits Silver Bow Canyon, to the Opportunity Ponds. The diversion dam was located on Silver Bow Creek about a halfmile due east of Fairmont Hot Springs, and the ditch ran in a northwesterly direction to the Opportunity Ponds. Water conveyed by the ditch supplemented the water in the tailings from the concentrator. The additional water delivered to the ponds made it easier for the company to keep the entire surface area of the impoundments wet and thereby eliminate or minimize dusting. The ditch came to be called the Yellow Ditch, because of the staining of its channel that was caused by dissolved iron in the waters of Silver Bow Creek (Anaconda Copper Mining Company 1937; Day 1961, 56; Rossillon 2012, 3).

The presence of dissolved metals in Silver Bow Creek points to the other purpose that the ditch served. The water flowing out of the precipitation plants in Butte was quite acidic, having a pH in the range of 3.5 to 4.0, and it carried as much as 2.5 grams of iron per liter, mostly as dissolved ferrous sulfate. The acidic water in Silver Bow Creek had to be neutralized in the Warm Springs Ponds, and this was accomplished by mingling of the outfall of the Opportunity Ponds, with a high pH (alkali), with the waters of Silver Bow Creek. After 1937, diverting much of Silver Bow Creek through a ditch to the Opportunity Ponds, allowed that water to be neutralized as it flowed over the tailings, which were alkaline because of the residual lime added during the flotation process (Day 1961, 56; Rossillon 2012, 3).

The ACM also continued to make improvements to the Warm Springs Ponds. In the late 1950s, the company added a third dam, upstream of the other two, to create pond 3, and in the late 1960s, the company raised the height of the first two dams by five feet each. In 1967, the ACM also began introducing lime to Silver Bow Creek, just before it flowed into pond 3. In about 1970, the ACM, at the request of the Montana Fish & Game Department, built the Mill-Willow Bypass, which made it possible to divert the flow of two tributaries of Silver Bow Creek around the west side of the Warm Springs Ponds. Mill Creek and Willow Creek once flowed into Silver Bow Creek adjacent to the east side of the community of Opportunity, about three miles upstream of the ponds. The two creeks have their head-waters at the south end of the Deer Lodge Valley, do not emanate from the mining district in Butte, and therefore were thought to be relatively pure. The Fish and Game Department believed they could be added to the flow of the Upper Clark Fork without passing through the Warm Springs Ponds. In the 1970s and 1980s, however, the channel of the bypass became choked with tailings from Silver Bow Creek, and several incidents of fish kills in the Upper Clark Fork were attributed to contamination flowing through the bypass (US Environmental Protection Agency 2000, 4–5).

The Anaconda Company continued to operate the Warm Springs Ponds to neutralize water flowing down Silver Bow Creek from Butte and water flowing out of the Opportunity Ponds into the late twentieth century, by which time the company had been acquired in 1977 by Atlantic Richfield (ARCO), the giant oil company. ARCO closed the Anaconda smelter in 1980, closed the Butte mines in 1982, and in 1984 sold its Butte operations to Montana Resources, Inc., owned by Dennis Washington, a Montana contractor. Washington reopened the East Continental Pit and the nearby concentrator almost immediately, and they continue operating today. Meanwhile, because ARCO had shut down its underground pumps beneath the Butte hill in 1982 when it decided to cease mining in Butte, water began to flood the much larger Berkeley Pit, an open-pit operation begun by the Anaconda Company in 1955. The water filling the Berkeley Pit is very acidic and is rich in dissolved heavy metals, leached by the flow of natural ground water through the old underground mine workings that lie beneath the pit. The pit is 1.5 miles long, a mile wide, and about 1800 feet deep. As of 2015, mine water had risen to a depth of over 1,000 feet, and the resulting "lake" is one of the largest toxic bodies of water in existence (Dobb 1996; Berkeley Pit Public Information Committee 2015).

Superfund Remediation

In 1980, the same year that ARCO closed the smelter at Anaconda, the US Congress passed the Comprehensive Environmental Response, Compensation, and Liability Act. The EPA launched a nationwide study to find sites meriting remediation under the Act, and these sites were added to a National Priorities List (NPL). Under the act, the EPA had the authority to order a responsible party to pay for the remediation of an NPL site that the party had created. The EPA would set the standard the remediation had to meet. The agency issued the first NPL in 1983, and the list included Silver Bow Creek from Butte downstream to the outlet of the Warm Springs Ponds, identifying ARCO, as the legal successor to the Anaconda Company's liabilities, as the main responsible party. In 1987, EPA expanded the Superfund site to include the Clark Fork River downstream to the Milltown Dam, just upstream of Missoula. What came to be known as the Clark Fork Superfund site also included the Anaconda smelter site, making the entire Clark Fork Superfund site the largest in the United States (US Environmental Protection Agency 2000, 3–6).

The EPA divided the Clark Fork Superfund site in several operable units, which are defined areas with specific site conditions and a particular set of hazardous materials, which therefore require a distinct remediation design. One such operable unit in the Clark Fork site is the Warm Springs Ponds, preliminary plans for which were issued in 1989. The State of Montana participated with the EPA in developing the plan for the ponds, recognizing that the site was actually part of a much larger, complex system. The ponds are the downstream-most reach of Silver Bow Creek, a contaminated stream extending all the way up to Butte. Several factors had to be considered in treating the ponds: (1) they already contained considerable volumes of settled solids comprised of arsenic, mercury, cadmium, lead, silver, and other heavy metals; (2) they would remain the downstream-most facility for treating the waters of Silver Bow Creek; (3) stream-side tailings and other source contaminants in and tributary to Silver Bow Creek would not be remediated for several years to come; (4) the dams and sediments at the Warm Springs Ponds had to be secured in order to be safe from natural events like earthquake and flood; (5) groundwater beneath the Warm Springs Ponds had to be monitored and protected; and (6) tributaries flowing into Silver Bow Creek in the vicinity of the ponds had to be diverted in such a way that they would not carry tailings or contaminants downstream past the ponds. ARCO would pay for all the remediation at the Warm Springs Ponds, and ARCO hired SHE, Inc, an engineering firm based in St. Paul, Minnesota, to design the remediation and improvement of the ponds (US Environmental Protection Agency 2000, 17–18; Short Elliott Hendrickson, Inc. 2014).

One of the first projects for the Warm Springs Ponds Operable Unit was the improvement of the Mill-Willow Bypass (figure 11.3). Mill Creek and Willow Creek flowed through lands that for decades were subject to the deposition of dust settling from smoke emanating from the Washoe stack, and in their lower reaches to lands that had been inundated from time to time with streamside tailings in Silver Bow Creek. The remediation plan for the Warm Springs Ponds called for the creation of an effective Mill-Willow Bypass, nearly four miles long, that would convey the two streams along the west side of the ponds so that the streams' waters would not add to the throughput of the ponds themselves. The bottomland along the bypass would also serve as a floodway to protect the ponds; in the event of a flood in Silver Bow Creek, a portion of the larger stream could flow through the floodway and not into the ponds, an event that could threaten the ponds' structural integrity and cause catastrophic erosion of the ponds and the sediments behind them. To prepare for construction of the bypass and floodway, all tailings along the alignment had to be removed. Construction of the bypass and floodway included introducing lime rock and new topsoil to create an artificial floodplain, complete with meandering stream and ponds, and the construction of dikes and armored berms for the ponds along the perimeter of the bypass (US Environmental Protection Agency 2000, 19, 26–32).

The Warm Springs Ponds are now largely functioning as planned by the EPA and State of Montana. They continue to remove toxic concentrations of heavy metals from Silver Bow Creek. Because the ponds must be managed by humans, they exist as a part of the landscape that is functioning under long-term institutional controls. Because there is still considerable work that must be completed upstream of the ponds to remove or stabilize hazardous materials, the ponds are an important transition point between a severely impacted part of the larger Upper Clark Fork landscape and the Clark Fork River itself, which now is home to healthy trout, invertebrate, and algal communities. Evaluation of the Clark Fork conducted for the EPA indicates that the river is well on its way to being a restored stream. While there are hopes that some day Silver Bow Creek may also

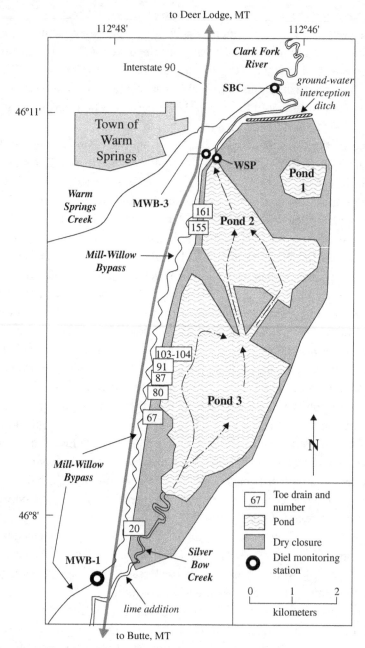

FIGURE 11.3 Site plan of the Warm Springs Ponds. Source: Courtesy of the US Environmental Protection Agency (2000).

be a restored stream, supporting thriving aquatic communities, the task is monumental, involving not only restoration of the stream itself but also addressing a complex array of conditions at its headwaters in Butte, where surface mining is on-going. Conditions at Butte that will continue to threaten downstream reaches include contaminated ground water beneath the upper reaches of Silver Bow Creek and the water filling the Berkeley Pit (CDM Federal Programs Corporation 2011, 5–1 to 5–2).

To reduce the threat of surface contaminants, which are spread across Butte from more than a century of mining, from being eroded to Silver Bow Creek during precipitation events, the Superfund remediation of the Butte hill has resulted the excavation of thousands of cubic yards of material from mineyards, railroad grades, and other cultural features. The excavations have altered the immediate topography and surface conditions of the cultural sites, often rendering them difficult to perceive as former industrial facilities. Certain areas of the Butte hill drain to the Berkeley Pit, so remediation in those areas has been kept to a minimum, in order to preserve part of the cultural landscape and because the water of the Berkeley Pit must be treated in any event, before it is discharged to the head of Silver Bow Creek. Even there, however, cultural values have been lost. Materials from other parts of the Butte hill have been hauled to and dumped on an area east of the Granite Mountain Memorial that drains to the Pit. The memorial is an important historical site in Butte that also used to afford a superb view of the mining landscape. Now the pile of relocated material from elsewhere on the Butte hill has grown so large that it obscures the view from the memorial (Morin 2013; Quivik 2001).

The Superfund remediation of the Upper Clark Fork is a complex mix of reclamation, rehabilitation, and restoration (Mitsch and Jørgensen 2004, 288). Some of the areas along the Upper Clark Fork continue and will continue to be used for agricultural purposes, so reclamation has been a proper transition for these lands impacted by mining. The Clark Fork River itself is being restored to some semblance of the river it once was, although complete restoration will never occur, given the farming, ranching, and urban populations located along its course. Other areas have been rehabilitated, meaning that they have been partially restored to allow improved ecosystem structure and function in surrounding areas, notably, the Clark Fork River. The ponds themselves serve a wetland function, such as habitat for eagles and migratory birds, which once was important to the southern reaches of the Deer Lodge Valley. They treat the waters of Silver Bow Creek, which makes possible the restoration of the Clark Fork River.

And the ponds serve a recreational function for the region, such as fishing (Grant 2009; Munday 2007).

Culture, Nature, and Restoration

Ian Rotherham argues that it is often important in ecological restoration not to sever landscapes from the history and culture of traditional uses of and interactions with natural resources in those landscapes. He is referring to cultural patterns of landscape use and interdependency between humans and nature that developed over centuries and millennia in traditional societies (Rotherham 2011, 277–287). I would argue that the same care should be taken in the restoration of landscapes that are the result of interventions in the industrial era. Such landscapes do not represent a simple, one-dimensional story of thoughtless disregard by industry. Rather, they represent a complex history of industry trying to earn profits by resource extraction while competing with other segments of society who also had designs on occupying and using those same environmental spaces, and by negotiating environmental solutions through mechanisms in the social, political, economic, and legal arenas. The Warm Springs Ponds represent that complexity. They exist because one hundred years ago the Anaconda Copper Mining Company sought to find a way to conduct its vast industrial operations within the environmental, political, economic, and legal realities of the Deer Lodge Valley. The ponds were modified over the decades in response to changing understandings of their role in the Clark Fork ecosystem. And they still exist today as a key feature in one of the largest Superfund remediation projects in the United States. Not only should the ponds be operated to fulfill their ecological role in a complex ecosystem, and their trout and bird populations managed for recreationists; the history of the ponds should also be interpreted to help the public appreciate the depth of time across which they have been part of the human and natural story of the Deer Lodge Valley.

The Warm Springs Ponds and the surrounding wildlife refuge (administered by the Montana Department of Fish, Wildlife and Parks) have numerous trails for public access. The trails feature several interpretive signs that are part of a comprehensive program (paid for by ARCO, called Montana's Copperway) that is intended to serve as a gateway to the cultural heritage of Butte and Anaconda. The signs around the Warm Springs Ponds have the same Copperway design format as the signs in Butte and Anaconda. Although they contain an abundance of interesting information about the ponds and a little about their history, they do little to link the Superfund remediation to the long history of environmental impacts, and responses to environmental impacts, that has enveloped the Clark Fork watershed.

Certain developments are, however, noteworthy. While the Superfund cleanup intended to remove nearly all the tailings along Silver Bow Creek and the Clark Fork River, at least two concentrations of streamside tailings are being preserved, one near a highway rest stop by the intersection of Interstate 94 and Montana Highway 1 (the route from the interstate to the Anaconda), and another on the grounds of the Grant Kohrs Ranch, a historic site on the north edge of Deer Lodge owned an administered by the National Park Service. Grant Kohrs, which interprets the early cattle industry in the western United States, was owned at the beginning of the twentieth century by brothers who were active in the farmers' organization that took legal action in the Magone and Bliss cases to try to curb the Anaconda Company's polluting practices. It is ironically fitting that some of the materials the brothers were fighting to prevent be preserved and interpreted on their ranch as a significant facet of the history of the livestock industry in the American West.

Notes

1. Superfund is the name used to designate the nationwide program to remediate hazardous materials at old industrial sites. The program was created by the Comprehensive Environmental Response, Compensation, and Liability Act, passed by Congress in 1980. The Clark Fork site is now divided into four distinct sites (see figure 11.1), which, when combined, are the largest in the nation.

References

Anaconda Copper Mining Company. 1937. Memorandum dated August 31, 1937, Box 10, Washoe Reduction Works Water Supply Records, Anaconda Copper Mining Company Archival Collection, Copper Village Museum and Arts Center, Anaconda, MT.

Bakken, Gordon. 1991. "Was There Arsenic in the Air? Anaconda versus the Farmers in the Deer Lodge Valley." *Montana: The Magazine of Western History* 41 (Summer): 30–41.

Berkeley Pit Public Information Committee. "Pit Watch." Accessed June 29, 2015. http://www.pitwatch.org/index.html.

Bowman, Leslie Greene. 2013. "Historic Preservation Today: From Save to Sustain." *History News* 68 (Spring): 19–22.

CDM Federal Programs Corporation. 2011. "Third Five-Year Review for the Silver Bow Creek/Butte Area NPL Site. Vol. 4: Warm Springs Ponds Active and Inactive Operable Units." Report prepared for the EPA. June.

Cronon, William. 2003. "The Riddle of the Apostle Islands: How Do You Manage a Wilderness Full of Human Stories?" *Orion Magazine* (May–June): 36–42.

Cronon, William. 1995. "The Trouble with Wilderness: Or, Getting Back to the Wrong Nature." In *Uncommon Ground: Toward Reinventing Nature*, edited by William Cronon, 69–90. New York: W.W. Norton.

Day, Frank H. 1961. "Disposal of Metallurgical Wastes." *Mining Congress Journal* 47 (November): 52–56.

Dobb, Edwin. 1996. "Pennies from Hell: In Montana, the Bill for America's Copper Comes Due." *Harper's* (October): 39–55.

Grant, Carl. 2009. "State-and-Transition Models for Mining Restoration in Australia." In *New Models for Ecosystem Dynamics and Restoration*, edited by Richard J. Hobbs and Katherine Suding. Washington, DC: Island Press.

MacMillan, Donald. 2000. *Smoke Wars: Anaconda Copper, Montana Air, and the Courts, 1890-1920*. Helena: Montana Historical Society Press.

Malone, Michael P. 1981. *Battle for Butte: Mining and Politics on the Northern Frontier, 1864-1906*. Seattle: University of Washington Press.

Mitsch, William J., and Sven Erik Jørgensen. 2004. *Ecological Engineering and Ecological Restoration*. New York: John Wiley & Sons.

Morin, Bode J. 2013. *The Legacy of American Copper Smelting: Industrial Heritage versus Environmental Policy*. Knoxville: University of Tennessee Press.

Munday, Pat. "Commentary." KUFM Radio, May 17, 2007, available at www.cfrtac. org.

Quivik, Fredric L. 1997. "The Historic Industrial Landscape of Butte and Anaconda." In *Images of an American Land: Vernacular Architecture Studies in the Western United States*, edited by Thomas Carter. Albuquerque: University of New Mexico Press.

Quivik, Fredric L. 1998. "Smoke and Tailings: An Environmental History of Copper Smelting Technologies in Montana, 1880-1930." PhD diss., University of Pennsylvania.

Quivik, Fredric L. 2001. "Integrating the Preservation of Cultural Resources with the Remediation of Hazardous Materials: Assessment of Superfund's Record." *Public Historian* 23 (Spring): 47–61.

Quivik, Fredric L. 2007a. "The Historical Significance of Tailings and Slag: Industrial Waste as Cultural Resource." *IA: The Journal of the Society for Industrial Archeology* 33 (2): 35–54.

Quivik, Fredric L. 2007b. "The Tragic Montana Career of Dr. D.E. Salmon." *Montana: The Magazine of Western History* 57 (Spring): 32–47, 92–94.

Renewable Technologies, Inc. 1985. "The Butte Anaconda Historical Park System Master Plan." Butte, MT: Butte Historical Society.

RHPP Joint Committee. 1993. "Regional Historic Preservation Plan." Butte, MT: Report prepared for ARCO.

Richter, R. Ernest. 1916. "The Amalgamated Copper Company: A Closed Chapter in Corporate Finance." *Quarterly Journal of Economics* 30: 387–407.

Rotherham, Ian D. 2001. "Implications of Landscape History and Cultural Severance for Restoration in England." In *Human Dimensions of Ecological Restoration: Integrating Science, Nature, and Culture*, edited by Dave Egan, Evan E. Hjerpe, and Jesse Abrams, 277–287. Washington, DC: Island Press.

Rossillon, Mitzi. 2012. "Yellow Ditch Flume: Its History, Form, and Significance." Report prepared for Anaconda-Deer Lodge County, MT., dated October 3.

Short Elliott Hendrickson Inc. 2014. "Warm Springs Tailings Ponds Remediation, Anaconda, Mont." Accessed November 2, 2014. http://www.sehinc.com/portfolio/warm-springs-tailings-ponds-remediation-anaconda-mont.

Tarr, Joel A. 1996. *The Search for the Ultimate Sink: Urban Pollution in Historical Perspective*. Akron, OH: University of Akron Press.

Tyer, Brad. 2013. *Opportunity, Montana: Big Copper, Bad Water, and the Burial of an American Landscape*. Boston: Beacon Press.

US Environmental Protection Agency. 2000. "Statutory Five-Year Review Report: Silver Bow Creek/Butte Area Superfund Site, Clark Fork Basin, Montana, with Emphasis on the Warm Springs Ponds Operable Units." EPA report. March 23.

CHAPTER 12 | Material Transformations
Urban Art and Environmental Justice

MRILL INGRAM

Introduction

Although we take for granted that people inevitably draw meaning from their surrounding landscapes, restoration practitioners and land managers often fail to consider how restoration projects shape the public's understanding of a place, and how different approaches to interpretation and to intervention into degradation have the potential to provoke productive reflection on layered histories and cultural and ethical as well as ecological significance. On the south side of Chicago, artist Frances Whitehead, professor of sculpture at the School of the Art Institute in Chicago, has undertaken a project, *Slow Cleanup*, that she says explores cultural heritage but that also embraces soil restoration, urban planning, phytoremediation research, and environmental justice. Her intent is to expand our conventional notions of cultural heritage to include the ubiquitous landscapes we create and to contend with their ecological and ethical implications. Her project offers a standpoint from which to reconsider the objectives of all restoration and remediation projects, and to think about how we might expand our purview and foreground questions of audience and meaning.

For several years Whitehead collaborated with a brownfield specialist for the city of Chicago and an academic soil scientist to investigate the challenge of how to sustainably remediate abandoned gas stations. Dotting the city (there are over 400 sites in Chicago), these commonplace abandoned sites pose serious environmental and economic challenges to all cities, especially in areas where redevelopment pressure is low and where abandoned plots can sit for decades: weedy, off-limits, and unsightly. A sustainable remediation of these sites requires that the contaminated soil be cleaned up in place; it cannot be dug up and dumped elsewhere. Whitehead's restoration effort involved expanding the focus of phytoremediation research to include plants suitable for urban sites, ones that might improve the amenities of struggling urban neighborhoods. Whitehead and her colleagues sought to identify plants that could not only clean the polluted soil of hydrocarbons and other contaminants, but would also beautify an urban neighborhood; provide habitat for bees, butterflies, and birds; sequester carbon; improve water quality; combat urban heat islanding; and add opportunities for environmental education. After months of research into Chicago's brownfields and phytoremediation, Whitehead installed a selection of native prairie and horticultural plants into a garden design that also served as a series of test plots of the capability of those plants to remediate. Among her goals was the identification of specific plants that might effectively remediate soil polluted by years of emissions from underground storage tanks, gas pumps, and automobiles. In addition, her installation was designed to create a model for how an expanded idea of remediation work might unfold across gas station sites. The site is meant to entertain: it is laid out in radiating lines so that every plant is viewable from certain vantage points available to neighbors walking by (figure 12.1). Each line also demarcates plots that contain plants that flower consecutively, so that over the seasons the site presents a "phenologic clock" reminding viewers of the passing of seasons and of the pace of "plant time." Whitehead also sought to engage community members by collaborating with urban environmental science students from nearby Chicago State University, many of whom live in the area and helped to perform site assessment and soil testing for the project.

The complexity of these ambitions—to remediate soil and engage with nearby residents as well as scientists, create a landscape of beauty as well as improved ecological function, and increase scientific knowledge as well as urban amenities in inner-city neighborhoods—informs the broad endeavor of ecological restoration in interesting ways, especially because the project attends to issues of environmental justice. This "relational" work seeks to directly engage with the social and material world and to transform it. And while art has often been employed for the purposes of beautification—hiding, distracting from, or making invisible something that people do not want to see—this art project takes a different tack. Although beauty and a sense of pleasure play a strong role in the project design, this effort is even more fundamentally shaped

FIGURE 12.1 *Slow Cleanup*, 2011, with the artist, Frances Whitehead. South Chicago, Illinois. Source: Photo by the author.

by the history and material presence of pollution. It is literally fed by contamination. The process of creating the piece, moreover, has brought attention and resources to the need for the mitigation and redistribution of "green amenities" to neighborhoods like this one. Although the motivations shaping this artist's engagement in environmental restoration may be quite different from that of ecologists, artist-led projects like this achieve many of the same goals, and offer examples of how restoration efforts might engage more directly with the layered histories of each site, and with the social contexts and ethical impacts of every project. Such artist-led restoration projects offer examples of how we might actively "front end" the politics of decision-making in restoration and be wary of simple resolutions. They suggest that we avoid blueprints and respond to each site as a story with its own particular history and sets of relations—some more palatable than others. As anthropologist Tim Ingold writes about understanding the past, events in time are not strung out "like beads on a thread," isolated happenings succeeding one another frame by frame. Instead, any particular event in history must be "seen to encompass a pattern of retentions from the past and protentions for the future" (1993, 157).

Ecological Restoration: Where Is the Environmental Justice?

Ecological restoration is typically oriented by a sense of the benefits from an "accurate" historical landscape reconstruction. Researchers and scholars have for years argued that restoration can weave together the needs of diverse groups of people, flora, and wildlife, creating habitats for humans as well as native plants and animals and an opportunity for people to be more aware of the need to foster other species and ecological health (France 2007; Gobster 2007; Platt 2006; McKinney 2002). The increasing interest in urban ecological restoration, in particular, has been a major driver in the recognition of the need for ecological restoration to embrace issues of history and justice (Ingram 2008).

Writing in Marcus Hall's (2010) edited volume on the role of history and ecological restoration, Barbara Westphal, Paul Gobster, and Matthias Gross describe urban "renaturing" projects in Calumet, Illinois, and Leipzig, Germany, articulating a commonly held and fundamental motivation for such efforts. "We value in some way what was lost and/or what might be gained by increasing the number or viability of the plant and animal communities and the biogeophysical processes upon which they depend. Urban renaturing activities ... are attempting to incorporate the natural and historical legacies of sites into plans for current use" (209). Of course, history is nothing if not contested, and potentially conflicting goals arise from different histories, leading to the question, whose use? More specifically, how does thinking about historical legacy help inform for whom, and by whom, contemporary land uses are determined?

Conflicts over contemporary land use are common, and the past, both environmental and human, is often not well articulated and can be used in an obfuscating way. Laura Watt (2010) writing about restoration in the San Francisco Bay, for example, describes conflicts between people advocating for flood protection, recreational use, wilderness management, and endangered species recovery. The author argues that the concept of restoration has been used as a "way out," allowing participants to replace a needed focus on how to evaluate competing ideas about contemporary management with a false security of an ahistorical ecological goal. She observes that "the concept of restoration masks continuing human involvement in the landscape, and the very human-centered goals and values that the revised landscape will serve" (219).

Restoration efforts don't necessarily mask human involvement, but many have tended to do so. Invasive-species control efforts have been especially criticized for failing to take into account the social and cultural contexts at play both in determining "invasion" and also influencing who suffers from the presence of an invasive species or benefits from its control (Robbins 2004). Comparing three different green spaces in Toronto, Canada, Jennifer Foster and L. Anders Sandbergh (2004) questioned the conventional decision-making processes behind the control of invasive species. They point out that invasive species, especially in urban and postindustrial landscapes, often have broad ecological and social benefits, and that control via the use of chemicals and extensive mechanical removal can be distasteful to people sensitive to environmental disturbance and degradation. In addition, in the sites they compared, invasive species control was an expensive effort that largely benefited the residents of nearby wealthy neighborhoods and was not well considered given continued regular presence of off-leash dogs, which tend to spread invasive plants.

The opportunity to expand ecological restoration to contend with history arises in the framing of project goals, and the question of precisely how history and social justice inform project design and intent. Thus, restoration might involve both the unmasking of the past and reparations for the future. What would happen, for example, if restoration projects aimed to restore a complex of ecological interactions that were prioritized according to the needs of people living in the area? Someone with a conventional notion of restoration might anticipate restoring an interlaced, self-sustaining system. However, the apolitical perspective on restoration is increasingly challenged in this age of the Anthropocene (Hourdequin 2013), especially in urbanized, populated, and postindustrial landscapes. If issues of human justice set a frame of reference and priorities, in other words, then the sciences of restoration, such as plant, soil, and microbial interactions and native species assemblages, must be deployed in the context of this goal.

Anna Whiston Spirn (2006) has been a powerful voice in advocating for urban planning, informed by both ecology and environmental justice. In her work in Philadelphia, she developed the idea of "landscape literacy" to guide her approach that melds urban planning, ecological process, and social justice. She queried ecological degradation in order to understand its history and ethics: how it occurred and who has benefited and suffered. "Why is there so much vacant land?" she asked. "Are there patterns to how and where abandonment occurs? Why are some parts of the neighbourhood so devastated, while others prosper?" (396). The answers to these questions provided key orientation to her subsequent investigations of historical hydrological patterns and plant and animal species associations, as they illuminated how past policies, such as racial segregation and *redlining*, the refusal of banks and realtors to grant loans to people in certain areas, had "produced" the current ecologically problematic landscape. Thus, she shows how urban restoration work needs to begin with a site- and scale-sensitive reading of the layers of landscape. She writes, "People mold landscape with hands, tools and machines, through law, public policy, the investing and withholding of capital, and other actions undertaken hundreds or thousands of miles away. The processes that shape landscape operate at different scales of space and time: from the local to the national, from the ephemeral to the enduring" (397). In response to her reading of this landscape, Spirn dedicated significant energy to teaching not only city planners but also the residents and schoolchildren in these neighborhoods how to read this landscape, so that they, too, are informed about how patterns of flooding and land vacancy are not incidental but a product of past, biased, human decision-making (see also Drenthen chap. 13, this volume).

In a similar vein, Dolores Hadyn's work on urban design and public participation argues that local ethnic and women's history should play a part in a "politics of place construction," specifically, the "making visible of forgotten or ignored parts" (1987, xii). Writing about a grassland restoration project in Melbourne, Australia, Lesley Instone suggests that native plants might be thought of as "witnesses," such that "the Royal Park grasses [would] reference not just the 'natural, native, original' landscape of western Melbourne, but previous human-plant-place relations, many of which are tied up in colonial dispossession, and other problematic connections between humans and nonhumans. The plants as witness may well have a very different tale to tell than the stories of native versus alien that dominate ecological restoration in Australia today" (Instone 2010; see also Spiers's discussion of witness trees, chap. 10, this volume). Seen this way, restoration work informed by environmental justice is tasked with unmasking not only the longed-for landscapes of the past, but also landscapes that people want to forget or that have been buried with the intention of forgetting. Instone's observations suggest that it is not just the "native" or "nonnative" characteristics of plants that become important; it is a more place-specific, historically informed sense of the role those plants have played over time that becomes important. This kind of orientation is necessary to respond to concerns such as those voiced by Elizabeth Spelman (2007), who worries that restoration, though often done with good intentions, can also erase history and the shameful actions tied to it. She wonders, ought some of the damage done to a ruined landscape be left as a reminder?

In contrast to a restoration that would seek to distract from historical trouble (Quinn 1992), the project by Whitehead began with queries into the current and historical, cultural, and political elements of particular polluted urban landscapes. Attracted to the site by the opportunity to remediate ecological damage, the artist was also motivated by an opportunity to do restoration where environmental opportunities are slim and restoration projects are rare. Although an ecological blueprint of current and past native plant and animal associations and environmental process remains relevant to the project, it does not so much undergird its design as inform it on par with other considerations. The potential here is for a thinking through of project objectives that does not take any prearrangement of human and nonhuman species for granted, but approaches each site with a recognition of the creative process of determining history and an expectation that different assemblages or ecologies are immanent (see Keulartz, chap. 3, this volume).

Dangerous Liaisons? Environmental Art and Restoration

The presence of an artist in ecological restoration is no straightforward guarantee that any type of justice will be served, of course. Indeed, the arts have been associated with deception as much as truth telling. Much has been written about the ideological function of landscapes and their representation, especially about how landscapes, both painted and created or "restored," reveal and hide particular histories (Neumann 2011; Olwig and Mitchell 2007; Wylie 2007). Writing about the emergence of European Renaissance art, Denis Cosgrove (1984) notably argued that the composition and structuring of landscape art of that time provided viewers with a sense of mastery over an idealized countryside, one in which much of the material conditions of rural life, and especially the labor required to produce the idyllic countryside, are hidden. For Cosgrove, as Wylie (2007) has described, landscape is "a way of seeing that chimes with elite and aristocratic visions of human society and nature. Such visions are often profoundly distant from the actuality of working and living in landscape, and should be understood as imposing an aesthetic and moral order from afar" (62). Writing similarly about the composition of the eighteenth-century English landscape garden, Grant Kester (2005) notes the Herculean labor required to make "nature appear natural," epitomized by landscape designer Lancelot Brown's gardens, which involved "massive earth-moving projects, the planting and transplanting of vast numbers of trees, and the creation of lakes and ponds" (19). Kester continues, "[T]he natural garden aesthetic provided a screen memory against the actual violence of enclosure and coerced human labour on which landed wealth depended, evoking instead a halcyon illusion of bourgeois power arising organically and autonomously from the surrounding countryside" (27).

Stephen Daniels (1989) argues for a less dogmatic approach to landscape, emphasizing its subversive and redemptive potential, as well as its capability to manipulate and obscure relations of power. He calls attention to this a "tension" in landscape, an inherent quality that cannot be resolved but is a signal to remain vigilant and to continue to inquire into the politics and histories of how landscapes are made and how they function in the present. He writes, "We should beware of attempts to define landscape, to resolve its contradictions; rather we should abide in its duplicity" (218). In other words, we must not be fooled by the possibility of a clear resolution or this tension, but must instead use it in a kind of dialectic exercise that keeps us aware of the ideological and repressive, as well as the emancipatory possibilities presented by landscapes, whether we are looking at paintings or at a restoration site.

It is precisely the false certainty provided by an ecological blueprint that can lure restorationists away from recognizing this important duplicity. However, as noted in the previous section, tensions remain and belie a predictable answer to questions of which historical legacies should guide restoration decision-making and who is to benefit. If landscape can expose relations of productions of class and race differences, then, as Foster and Daniels point out, they can also reproduce them, and reflect and reinscribe divisions. It is with this sensitivity to the power of art that we can reflect on the work of Whitehead. The aesthetics of the project engages with what has been hidden and ignored, a surfacing of environmental injustice. Perhaps more significantly, the project seeks to reverse ecological damage and to benefit people who have historically suffered the brunt of that damage. The created landscape is pleasing but also educational, one designed to further the knowledge in applied environmental science so that it can better serve people living in disadvantaged areas.

To provide some context for this complex of ambitions, it is useful to briefly consider the broader field of environmental art, which since the 1960s has involved people crossing boundaries between science and art and ecology and society. Environmental art is a broad and extremely diverse area,[1] too broad, really, to be able to say anything at all comprehensive. However, several particularly relevant threads shed light on the combination of goals entertained by artists whose projects include environmental restoration. One thread is a sustained interest in participatory, community-oriented, socially engaged art, or "relational aesthetics," as Bourriaud (2002) has described an extensive effort among artists to engage primarily with people and to focus on the social process (Kester 2004). For example, Reiko Goto and Tim Collins's *Nine Mile Run Greenway* project, sought to create an integrated and informed "public conversation" among scientists, city planners, educators, and urban residents about the reclamation of a brownfield in Pittsburgh, Pennsylvania. Polluted for decades by the steel industry, the riverside area was being redeveloped as a mix of housing and public green space (Collins 2000). The restoration of the brownfield, argued the artists, provided an opportunity to entertain new ideas about public and "natural" spaces, about better ways to include more people in a democratic consideration of changing land use, and also to think about different ways of reckoning with the land's industrial legacy—its layered past. "Can we integrate economic benefit with public use and ecosystem function?" the artists ask (Collins 2000, 462). "Will we continue to accept the dichotomy of wilderness or zoo as the primary 'spaces' of natural experience? Or is there something new to consider at the place where the land meets the river and the soot of industry continues to stain the soil?"

This "social turn" is complemented by another, largely feminist thread in the arts promoting attention to the importance of maintenance and ongoing work of caretaking in society (Ingram 2014). In the 1960s, for example, Jo Hanson started a sidewalk-sweeping campaign in San Francisco's Haight-Ashbury district. Hanson organized citywide street sweepings and children's anti-litter art projects and in the late 1980s, convinced the city's waste recycling and disposal agency to develop an artist-in-residency program. Artist Merle Laderman Ukeles coined the term *maintenance art* to describe her aesthetic drive to call attention to the necessary but often denigrated work of cleaning, feeding, repairing, and otherwise maintaining families and environments. While a lot of her work focused on maternal care, she also worked with the New York City sanitation department for years, executing a number of projects that aimed to raise awareness of and appreciation for the efforts of sanitation workers in, as she put it, "keeping New York City alive."[2]

Another important thread can be found in art that pursues active intervention in cases of ecological degradation. Mel Chin's *Revival Field* is one foundational example. In St. Paul, Minnesota, at the Pig's Eye landfill (which is also a Superfund site), Chin collaborated with scientists to create a project to both clean soil and also research the efficacy of *hyperaccumulators*, plants known to be effective at pulling heavy metals from contaminated soil. He enclosed an area of polluted earth with a chain-link fence, and subdivided it with paths that formed an *X*, which he described as a metaphorical reference to the work's pinpoint cleanup that also separated different varieties of plants from each other for study (1992). In 1990, the Citizens' Environmental Coalition Education Fund submitted a proposal to the National Endowment for the Arts (NEA) to fund Mel Chin's work on *Revival Field*. Despite recommendations by committees who reviewed the proposal, the director of the NEA initially accepted the project, but then rescinded funding, citing questions of aesthetic quality (in other words, it was not "art"). Chin argued that the project was a kind of sculpture using the tools of biochemistry and agriculture, and the funding was eventually reinstated. Although the work is unseen, he explained, "an intended invisible aesthetic will exist that can be measured scientifically by the quality of a revitalized earth. Eventually that aesthetic will be revealed in the return of growth to the soil" (Krug 2006).

This brief overview is but a hint of the dynamism and complexity of environmental art, but hopefully it conveys a sense of the ways artists have been at work contending with the duplicity of art by foregrounding the ethical considerations of layered landscapes, as well as aiming to be effective, to have a specific impact in the world, for example, by ridding a place of contaminants and by furthering the science and practice of restoration science.

Slow Cleanup

Strongly driven by a desire to create art that contributes directly to environmental restoration, Whitehead is centrally concerned with art that "works," that effectively intercedes in environmental degradation. She has articulated her feelings about direct engagement: "Although artists have been understood as the stewards of mischief, tricksters, change agents, we're entering a time when this playful application of our expertise seems out of scale with the challenges facing us" (Whitehead and Atha 2010, 10). This self-imposed demand on her work has required that the artist collaborate closely with both environmental scientists and city agencies and other groups that can help put ideas into action. As previously noted, Whitehead worked with a City of Chicago brownfield expert as well as a soil scientist, and pursued intensive research into both phytoremediation technology and the socioeconomic context of brownfield remediation in Chicago. Part of the charge was to investigate what the city might do with the large numbers of abandoned gas station plots in the lower-income areas of the city, where there is little real-estate pressure or investment income to fund redevelopment of the site. In a study of the Chicago Brownfield Initiative, Ekerdt (2009) has observed that despite more ambitious goals, the city's success in brownfield remediation has relied most heavily on collaboration with private investors, skewing the geographic distribution of remediated sites toward areas of the city where real estate values are higher. The question for Whitehead and her colleagues was how to enhance the value of the sites where land values are low. As she put it, "Researchers are making connections between remediation and habitat, or between phytoremediation and social wellbeing. We thought, let's connect all the dots, make a whole systems cleanup and solve more than one problem at a time" (Whitehead, pers. comm.). Whitehead's broader vision for the project is the identification of a whole new set of horticultural remediators, with multiple values to offer neighborhoods plagued by decades-old abandoned gas station plots and little chance of getting redevelopment funds. Along with demonstrating new cleanup technology, the project also aims to create new pollinator and bird habitat, to demonstrate the potential for urban agriculture, enhance the neighborhood aesthetics, improve water quality, and provide opportunities for environmental education and relaxation.

The team's research clarified that while phytoremediation technologies hold great promise, and in fact are being widely used around the world, their deployment in the United States has been hamstrung both by lack of public funding and the constraints of private investment. Phytoremediation takes time. In fact, *Slow Cleanup* is so named to call attention to the pace at which the process takes place and to leverage time as an asset. Private investors do not always have time, and so more often invest in developing faster-working restoration technologies, such as using microbes to clean up oil spills. Whitehead's research into phytoremediation also revealed that the bulk of plants tested for large hydrocarbon remediation, the type of cleanup needed at abandoned gas stations, have been limited to agricultural plants and prairie grasses. Public funding for phytoremediation has been thin, and research has been largely focused on existing known areas of success. Furthermore, Whitehead came to understand that the phytoremediation of large hydrocarbon molecules is actually a rhizospheric process and is carried out by soil microbes working in plant root zones. Thus, in this type of phytoremediation the plants do not "take up" any contaminants; instead, soil microbes in the plant's root zone help facilitate their dismantling. This meant that Whitehead and her team would not have to worry about the plants' transferring contaminants to the soil surface—and nearer to people. By comparing the root types of known remediators with possible new ones, the team evaluated over 400 trees, shrubs, and forbs, (avoiding grasses since so much is already known about their remediating potential). They selected eighty plant species to evaluate for the program, all of which were planted in a field trial at the chosen gas station site and trialed in a greenhouse lab at Purdue University.

The team had good analytic data that had been collected by the city on the types and depths of toxins at the site and also worked with a group of students enrolled in an urban environmental-science program at nearby Chicago State University. The students were able to use the plot as a learning field site, and they helped to assess and prepare the site in the process. The project aimed to work with these students to do ongoing soil monitoring as the project progressed. *Slow Cleanup* also faced the challenge of transforming the substrate of the abandoned gas station so that plants would grow. The first obvious hurdle was the asphalt and cement paving at the site, which rested on top of a thick bed of crushed limestone or sand—not a friendly environment for plant growth. The problem was solved by removing the hard top, and then repurposing a road-building machine. The repurposed machine was capable of mixing compost into the soil to a depth of 21 inches but also of returning the substrate to its original location, which was important to maintaining the accuracy of data on the location of contaminants.

Whitehead's multifunctional design placed the deepest-rooted prairie forbs, such as the silphiums, on top of the deepest contaminants—where the underground storage tanks had been. Because of the field trials, the demonstration site would only occasionally be open to the surrounding neighborhood, so Whitehead laid out the plots so that they would be pleasing to people standing outside the fence, and so that the plants flower consecutively in a gradual wave from one side of the site to the other, with lower growing plants in the front (figure 12.2). She also worked with the neighborhood alderperson to communicate to residents about the purpose of the site and the longer-term goal of discovering new plants that can help enhance the neighborhoods in multiple ways. The tested horticultural potential remediators included trees, such as serviceberry, redbud, edible apple, and cherry, wild plum, and walnut; shrubs, such as black currant, indigobush, and dogwood; and forbs, such as milkweeds, asters, purple coneflower, blazing star, sweet black-eyed Susan, and blue and hoary vervain.

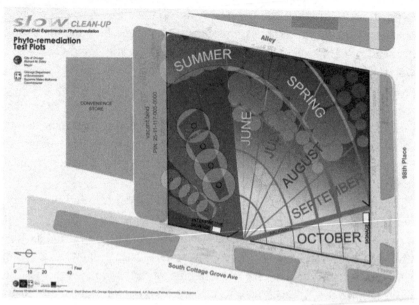

FIGURE 12.2 Layout of *Slow Cleanup*, 2011, by Frances Whitehead, School of the Art Institute of Chicago; Dave Graham, City of Chicago; and A. P. Schwab, Purdue University. The field trials were designed for beauty, function, and environmental education. The site is fenced and only open to the public occasionally, so one design challenge was how to make the site feel available and still maintain enough control for plant study. Designed in a large radial grid, all plants are viewable from a single vantage point, with interpretive signage for the visitors and community. The plants have been grouped to create consecutive flowering drama. Source: Courtesy of Frances Whitehead, used with permission.

The greenhouse trials successfully identified twelve new remediators among the group of tested horticultural plants. These plants enhanced the dissipation of petroleum residues and include blue giant hyssop, yellow coneflower, wild bergamot, yarrow, foxglove beardtongue, and evening primrose. Only one of the plants, purple coneflower, had been tested previously, and in this study it was again found to be an effective remediator. Several other species in the new trials appear to be likely remediators, including black cherry, red-osier dogwood, downy serviceberry, and fragrant sumac, and merit further study. A few forbs were identified as potentially impeding remediation.

Conclusion: Reading Restoration

Remembering Stephen Daniels's warning to be wary of simple resolutions to the duplicity of landscape, we might wonder, do such projects present too pretty a picture? Ought they to have made more explicit the industrial legacies and environmental burdens of these sites? And, how might installing urban gardens on abandoned gas station plots address the longer-term challenges of the barriers to private investment in lower-income neighborhoods or change the funding for accessible, affordable (if slow) phytoremediation technologies? In transforming a neglected rubble-filled plot into a colorful garden, do these projects run the risk of lulling viewers into a sense of a redemptive ecology—that we can arrange ecological process and nonhuman species to clean up after us and look good at the same time, no matter what the history?

In contrast to Elizabeth Spelman's suggestion, there is no intent in Whitehead's project to leave some representation of past damage visible as a reminder. Instead, the artist seems more intent on providing a dramatic—and even perhaps ironic—reprieve from the environmental damage all around, some of which is hidden in water and soil, but much of which remains in evidence. As many urban residents know, polluted streams and rivers and fenced, contaminated, and abandoned plots are not much fun to live with. One of the most dramatic aspects of the project as art is that it directly engages in material transformation, enrolling plants, microbes, and natural processes to tangibly clean soil and water. Furthermore, the process of transformation is arranged to provide possibilities for personal human transformations of a sort: new environmental experiences, a sense of more positive urban ecologies, and specific new knowledge about plants that clean up. But it is not just any type of plant that we have this new knowledge about. An additional layer of the work is that it informs the technologies of restoration, in this case phytoremediation, with the needs and concerns of underserved people. The message may be that "good" restoration work in this case is not only an engagement with ecological process in order to create and maintain a cleaner environment; it is also an active creation that provides an avenue to transcend the inner-city grind: shade, color, perfume, bees, and birdsong and even locally produced food—designed especially for those who are the most deprived of such experiences. In Whitehead's project, ecological process is not hailed as "natural" in a way that covers up the human labor required to create and maintain this restoration. Instead, the juxtaposition of the garden's colorful curving layout and the surrounding gritty urban perpendicularity foreground the labor, of both plants and humans, required to create and to maintain this green space.

Projects like Whitehead's envision collaborative and participatory efforts that reckon with the layers of the past as they engage scientists, students, urban residents, plants, microbes, water, bees, and other urban wildlife. Historical pollution becomes an opportunity for different kinds of contemporary interactions and relationships that work to produce a visually stimulating, informative environment and also a cleaner, healthier one, with more opportunities for an improved quality of life for local residents. On first impressions, such projects might appear to end at a convenient marriage of green technology and beautification. However, *Slow Cleanup* taps into deeper political, economic, and aesthetic issues. Informed by historical and contemporary contexts, the project presents a useful model for ways that ecological restoration projects might become more effective in complex situations where humans are the dominant species, and research into the past is as likely to unearth environmental injustice, as it is a lost and valued ecosystem. The project began with a concern over ecological degradation; solutions were guided by research into sociocultural layers and historical and current social and political circumstances. By offering an example in which the cultural landscape is the starting place, projects like this help expand the reach of environmental restoration into new areas, and also provide guidance into how these kinds of endeavor can embrace issues of social and environmental justice from the very beginning.

Acknowledgments

This material is based upon work supported by the National Science Foundation under Grant No. 0962623. I wish to thank Frances Whitehead and my colleagues for their support during this research.

Notes

1. The term *environmental art* has been used to describe the massive earthworks of people such as Robert Smithson and Christo, as well as the community-oriented and activist artwork described in detail here.

2. http://www.feldmangallery.com/pages/artistsrffa/artuke01.html.

References

Bourriaud, Nicolas. 2002. *Relational Aesthetics*. Dijon: Les Presses du Reel.
Carruthers, Beth. 2006. *Mapping the Terrain of Contemporary Eco-ART Practice and Collaboration*. Report commissioned by the Canadian Commission for UNESCO for Arts in Ecology—A Think-Tank on Arts and Sustainability. http://www.canadacouncil.ca/sitecore%20modules/web/~/media/ PDF/UNESCO/ BethCarruthersArtinEcologyResearchReportEnglish.pdf#search=%22carruthers%22.

Carter, Majora. 2001. "Balancing Development and the Environment in the South Bronx." *Gotham Gazette*, March 19. http://www.gothamgazette.com/commentary/77.carter. shtml.

Chin, Mel. 1992. "Revival Field." In *Allocations: Art for a Natural and Artificial Environment*, edited by Jan Brand, Catelijne De Muynck, and Jouke Kleerebezem. Zoetermeer, 224–227. Netherlands: Foundation World Horticultural Exhibition Floriade.

Collins, Tim. 2000. "Cultural Geographies in Practice: Interventions in the Rust Belt; the Art and Ecology of Postindustrial Public Space." *Cultural Geographies* 7: 461–467.

Cosgrove, Denis E. 1984. *Social Formation and Symbolic Landscape*. London: Croom Helm.

Daniels, Stephen. 1989. "Marxism, Culture and the Duplicity of Landscape." In *New Models in Geography*, vol. 2, edited by Richard Peet and Nigel Thrift, 196–220. London: Routledge.

Foster, Jody, and L. Anders Sandberg. 2004. "Friends or Foe? Invasive Species and Public Green Space in Toronto." *Geographical Review* 94 (2): 178–198.

France, Robert, L. 2007. *Healing Natures, Repairing Relationships: New Perspectives on Restoring Ecological Spaces and Consciousness*. Winnipeg, Manitoba: Green Frigate Books.

Hall, Marcus. 2010. *Restoration and History: The Search for a Usable Environmental Past*. New York: Routledge.

Hayden, Dolores. 1997. *The Power of Place: Urban Landscapes as Public History*. Cambridge, MA: MIT Press.

Hourdequin, Marion. 2013. "Restoration and History in a Changing World: A Case Study in Ethics for the Anthropocene." *Ethics and the Environment* 18 (2): 115–134.

Ingold, Tim. 1993. "The Temporality of Landscape." World Archaeology 25 (2): 152-174.

Ingram, Mrill. 2008. "Editorial: Urban Ecological Restoration." *Ecological Restoration* 26 (3): 175–177.

Ingram, Mrill. 2014. "Washing Urban Water: Diplomacy in Environmental Art in the Bronx, New York City." *Gender, Place & Culture* 21 (1): 105–122.

Instone, Lesley. 2010. "Encountering Native Grasslands: Matters of Concern in an Urban Park." *Australian Humanities Review* 49 (November). http://www.australianhumanitiesreview.org/archive/Issue-November-2010/instone.html.

Kester, Grant. 2004. *Conversation Pieces, Community and Communication in Modern Art*. Berkeley: University of California Press.

Kester, Grant. 2005. "Theories and Methods of Collaborative Art Practice," In *Groundworks: Environmental Collaboration in Contemporary Art*, 18–35. Pittsburgh, PA: Regina Gouger Miller Gallery / Carnegie Mellon University.

Krug, Don. 2006. "Ecological Restoration: Mel Chin, Revival Field." http://greenmuseum.org/c/aen/Issues/chin.php.

Lacy, Suzanne. 2010. *Leaving Art: Writings on Performance, Politics, and Publics, 1974–2007*. Durham, NC: Duke University Press.

Matilsky, Barbara C. 1992. *Fragile Ecologies: Contemporary Artists Interpretations and Solutions*. New York: Rizzoli International.

McKinney, Michael L. 2002. "Urbanization, Biodiversity and Conservation." *BioScience* 52: 883–890.

Neumann, Ron P. 2011. "Political Ecology III: Theorizing Landscape." *Progress in Human Geography* 35 (6): 843–850.

Olwig, Kenneth R., and Don Mitchell. 2007. "Justice, Power and the Political Landscape: From American Space to the European Landscape Convention." *Landscape Research* 32 (5): 525–531.

Platt, Rutherford H. 2006. *The Humane Metropolis: People and Nature in the 21st Century City.* Amherst: University of Massachusetts Press.

Quinn, M. L. 1992. "Should All Degraded Landscapes Be Restored?" *Land Degradation & Development* 3 (2): 115–134.

Robbins, Paul. 2004. "Comparing Invasive Networks: Cultural and Political Biographies of Invasive Species." *Geographical Review* 94 (2): 139–156.

Spelman, Elizabeth. 2007. "Embracing and Resisting the Restorative Impulse." In *Healing Natures, Repairing Relationships: New Perspectives on Restoring Ecological Spaces and Consciousness*, edited by Robert L. France, 127–140. Winnipeg, Manitoba: Green Frigate Books.

Watt, Laura, A. 2010. "Conflicting Restoration Goals in the San Francisco Bay." In *Restoration and History: The Search for a Usable Environmental Past*, edited by Marcus Hall, 218–219. New York: Routledge.

Westphal, Lynn, M., Paul H. Gobster, and Matthias Gross. 2010. "Models for Renaturing Brownfield Areas." In *Restoration and History: The Search for a Usable Environmental Past*, edited by Marcus Hall, 208–217. New York: Routledge.

Whiston Spirn, A. 2005. "Restoring Mill Creek: Landscape Literacy, Environmental Justice and City Planning and Design." *Landscape Research* 30 (3): 395–413.

Whitehead, Frances, and Christine Atha. 2010. "Complexity and Engagement: Art and Design in the Post-Industrial." *MADE* 6: 43–52. http://www.cardiff.ac.uk/archi/made.php.

Wylie, John. 2007. *Landscape (Key Ideas in Geography).* London: Routledge.

CHAPTER 13 | Layered Landscapes, Conflicting
Narratives, and Environmental Art

Dealing with Painful Memories and
Embarrassing Histories of Place

MARTIN DRENTHEN

WHAT SHOULD THE GOAL of ecological restoration of cultural landscapes
be? Many believe we ought to recognize not just the natural history of a
site but the cultural history of the area as well. Finding a fitting answer to
what a landscape means to us requires that we interpret the landscape, *read*
it as a meaningful text. Cultural landscapes are like palimpsests: manu-
scripts that contain different legible layers on top of each other.

But like most texts, landscapes are more than mere information carri-
ers. Understanding the meaning of a novel, for instance, requires that we
allow the text to open up a world, and then imagine ourselves in the place
of the protagonist. This can lead to different readings, all of which can
reveal something about the text and about us as readers involved in that text.
Similarly, understanding the meaning of a landscape requires more than just
reconstructing *its* story, it also requires that we relate it to *us*—find out what
it has to say to us. We need to somehow recognize the storylines inscribed
in the landscape, and decide in what sense those stories are truly ours.

Thus, most landscapes consist of different layers, each of which affords
multiple interpretations. All these interpretations reflect on the question
of who *we* are in these places. An appropriate restoration of a historical
landscape that pretends to be more than just another landscape change
by humans can therefore never simply be the reconstruction of one particular landscape, but should somehow also acknowledge the need to go
beyond any particular interpretation of the story of the land. An appropriate restoration will have to seek a common ground, but it should do

so without suppressing the conflict between different readings of a place. Without such reflective awareness, restoration of the meaning of layered landscapes is doomed to fail.

In this chapter I examine the layered nature of our landscapes and discuss the problem this poses for our understanding their significance. I first introduce a theoretical framework that can help understand how we discover meanings by "reading" landscapes. I distinguish two conceptions of landscape reading: the *semiotic* approach, which is the most common conception of landscape reading, and an alternative *hermeneutic* approach. I will argue that the hermeneutic approach is more suited to understanding how particular *kinds of meanings* shape our moral relations to landscapes. Next I discuss—using the work of Friedrich Nietzsche—how our understanding of the meaning of landscape is complicated, not just by the multi-interpretability of landscapes, but also because of the contemporary problem of postmodern historicism, in which we no longer seem to have any common criterion for deciding between the different interpretations. Finally, I will suggest that—given this postmodern context—the arts have a particular role to play in aiding our readings of a landscape. The power of imagination in art has already been put to work in several restoration projects to highlight meanings in a landscape that are of particular help in understanding the goal of ecological restoration projects, and thus in creating public support. I will illustrate this point by discussing environmental artworks in the Netherlands and Germany that serve as "landscape reading aids." I will suggest, however, that art should also play a more critical role by challenging dominant interpretations of landscape that might suppress painful, embarrassing, or otherwise difficult aspects of (the history of) a place (cf. Ingram, chap. 12, this volume). By bringing forward or even amplifying alternative views and readings, art can help to contest the taken-for-granted meanings of landscape again, and thus bring them back to the heart of the moral debate. I will use a design for an environmental artwork in the Rocky Mountain Arsenal National Wildlife Refuge as an illustration.

Landscapes and Meaning

Authors such as William Jordan (2003), Eric Higgs (2003), and Andrew Light (2003) have argued in recent years that a fruitful approach to the question of the purpose and goal of ecological restoration should not so much start with trying to define what "real," "original" nature is and whether it can be restored, but rather should take a less dualistic, more human-inclusive angle and ask what kinds of meaningful environmental practices are involved in the social process of environmental restoration. From this perspective, ecological restoration is as much about healing the human-nature relationships as it is about healing damaged ecosystems. The question of what the goals of restoration should be revolves around the meaningfulness of the environmental relationship that is implied in these practices. Thus, a prime goal of restoration should be the preservation, restoration, or even enrichment of the *meaning* of places (cf. Holland, chap. 4, this volume).

John O'Neill, Alan Holland, and Andrew Light (2008, 163) argue that "[p]eople make sense of their lives by placing themselves in a larger normative context. For this reason, environments matter to people too: because they embody that larger context." In this meaning-oriented perspective, landscapes and places embody people's history and cultural identity. Places and landscapes are not just valuable to us because of their ecological function, but also because they help us to understand who we are. "Rather, an individual's identity, their sense of who they are, is partly constituted by their sense of belonging to particular places. Particular places, whether "natural" woodlands, streams and ponds, or "urban" city streets, parks and quarries, matter to individuals because they embody the history of their lives and those of the communities to which they belong. Their disappearance involves a sense of loss of something integral to their lives" (O'Neill, Holland, and Light 2008, 39).

Scholars have known for centuries that texts also help us to form our identity and orient ourselves. Therefore, if we want know better how we might understand the meaning of landscapes, it will be helpful to have a closer look to how we understand the meaning of texts.

Landscapes as Texts

Many have compared landscapes with texts before this. The metaphor of the landscape text is popular among geographers and geologists (Watts 1975; Lewis 1979; Yarham 2010), environmental scientists (Wessels 1997), historians and archaeologists (Yamin et al. 1996; Widgren 2004; Cronon 1991), environmental educators (Hendrik and Kloen 2007), and writers (Van Toorn 1998). Popular books and brochures (e.g., Yarham 2010) teach us how we can actually get to know many things about the genesis and geophysical history of a landscape by paying close attention to its details.

Reading the landscape carefully can help to broaden our understanding of a place. Typically, the term is used to point out how landscapes—mostly cultural landscapes—contain signs that can be "read" like meaningful texts that tell a story about ourselves and our history, much in the same way other texts from our cultural heritage do. In the Netherlands the term is used by several conservation groups who believe that landscape legibility is the key to understanding—*and increasing*—people's attachment to particular places and landscapes (cf. Drenthen 2011).

The dominant understanding of landscapes as texts, however, is rather one-sided, as if reading a landscape text would require merely the passive registration or observation of the legible signs in a landscape. We can read texts in many different ways. Informational texts are usually primarily read and understood as a source of factual knowledge, but other types of texts, such as poems and novels, are typically read differently. Their meaning cannot be understood by merely uncovering the signs; they demand explicit interpretation. If we take the possible similarities between texts and landscapes seriously, we should therefore consider the possibility that literature and art can help broaden our understanding of landscapes. Before we turn to the role that art can play in our understanding of a landscape, we will take a closer look at what texts are and what it means to read a text.

What Is a Text?

The work of French philosopher Paul Ricoeur (b. 1913–d.2005) provides a helpful starting point. Ricoeur (1981, 153–164) distinguishes two distinct ways of approaching a text. The first, structural reading (which I call the *semiotic reading*, cf. Drenthen 2011) attempts to explain how a text is structured and how it functions—for instance, by distinguishing the roles and functions of different literary forms and themes within that text. Such a structuralist analysis can and should inform our understanding of a text, because it can give us insight in how the text is structured, and can help explain how the text works, but such a reading remains rather external. A proper (hermeneutic) reading of a text, on the other hand, does not stop there, but aims to understand what the texts means *to us*, what the text says about *our world*. To understand what a text has to say, however, we as readers have to do more than just listen.

According to Ricoeur (1981), there is an important difference between texts and speech: a text is "a discourse fixed by writing" (146). Whereas in speech, a speaker can accompany his signs and explain himself, a *text* assumes a life of its own, becomes independent of its *author*. The meaning of a text is not determined solely by the author, if only because literary texts accommodate much richer readings than the author intended. When it comes to it, the author has no privileged position in determining how the text should be read or what the meaning of the text is. Without an external authoritative source to turn to regarding the meaning of a text, a reader can only revert to the act of reading. It is up to the reader to understand the meaning of the text through an act of *interpretation*.

Ricoeur points out another difference between speech and texts. Whereas a speaker can literally point to the things he is talking about, presenting to an interlocutor a "real" world of which both speaker and interlocutor are part, a text, in contrast, presents an imaginary world that has to be supplemented by the reader, if only because of gaps in the text's references, which ultimately must be filled by the reader's imagination. Moreover, our understanding of the text presupposes the existence of preceding texts that have already determined both the reader and the world of the text as well. "Texts speak of possible worlds and of possible ways of orienting oneself in these worlds" (Ricoeur 1981, 177). But in order to understand the meaning of a text, we not only have to be open to the world as presented by the text, but we should also be willing to "place ourselves"—for the time being—in that world. This does not mean that to understand the meaning of a text means that we should project our own beliefs and prejudices onto it. Rather, we must "let the work and its world enlarge the horizon of the understanding which [we] have of [ourselves]" (Ricoeur 1981, 178).

Thus, text, world, and reader are engaged in a dialectical relationship. According to Ricoeur, good reading requires willingness on the part of the reader to participate in the world opened up by the text and to abstract from the context of one's particular life ("distantiation"), but it also means to be involved, to be "present" in the act of reading. A reader has to bring to life the narrative of the text, bring to bear the meanings of words and concepts that play a role in his own life ("appropriation"). Good reading requires both distantiation and appropriation.

What we can learn from Ricoeur's hermeneutics is that understanding a text requires far more than merely excavating the unseen signs; it also implies active interpretation. To truly understand the meaning of a text, one has to engage oneself in the reading of the text and allow a relation to develop between oneself and it. Understanding a landscape text should therefore not be reduced to scientific approaches that are primarily interested in the "objective" features of a landscape. When attempting to understand the meaning of a landscape text, we should actively include explicitly *human* perspectives.

Legible Landscapes as Food for the Spirit

The term *legible landscape* was first introduced into the Dutch landscape debate exactly with such a broad inclusive view in mind. The Dutch writer, poet, and landscape activist Willem van Toorn (cf. Drenthen 2009) introduced the term to express his ideas on the moral relation between humans and landscapes in a way that is less about the objective features of the land, and much more about what these places reveal about ourselves. The concern for the traditional Dutch river landscape plays an important part in Van Toorn's novels and essays. The term *legible landscape* refers to landscapes that can be "read" as meaningful texts because they "remind us along complicated and sometimes unconscious lines that there is a past, that people who lived in that past had to deal with the world just as we have to, that they had to protect themselves against nature and at the same time use its resources" (Van Toorn 1998, 66). The reason we should value the legibility of the landscape has to do with our own sense of identity. "We have to stay in touch with this past—not because the past is better than the present, but simply because we owe our existence, our identity, our vision of the world to it, and because we can only think about the future by making use of our past experiences" (66). Thus, Van Toorn's legible landscapes embody what O'Neill, Holland, and Light (2008) call the "larger normative contexts" in which we can place our lives.

Landscape Legibility and Environmental Restoration

The legibility of a landscape also plays a role in ecological restoration practices. Ecological restoration does not just aim to restore a landscape to a healthier condition; it usually also entails an attempt to protect the value and meaning of that landscape by restoring the historical continuity of a place. "Historic fidelity" is seen as a key value in ecological restoration next to "ecological integrity" (Higgs 2003). *Ecological integrity* refers to the structure, composition, and function of an ecosystem operating within the bounds of natural or historical range of variation. *Historical fidelity,* on the other hand, is the idea that the practice of restoration should attempt to approximate, within reasonable bounds, some past state of the damaged ecosystem. Typically, however, ecological restoration is aimed at not just *any* historical continuity but a special kind of continuity—to the part of history that is usually referred to as its "predisturbance condition." In other words, ecological restoration is the attempt to restore a narrative continuity as seen from the perspective of the "deep time" horizon of natural history. O'Neill, Holland, and Light (2008) argue that we humans

> make sense of our lives by placing them in a larger narrative context, of what happens before us and what comes after. Environments matter because they embody that larger context. This is clearest in the cultural landscapes that surround us that specifically embody the lives of individuals and communities. However, . . . this is true also . . . with respect to natural processes. Unintentional natural processes provide part of the context in which intentional human activities take place and through which we understand their value. (O'Neill, Holland, and Light 2008, 198)

The narrative meaning of nature is that it stretches way past the confines of human history, and thus provides us with a broader context:

> [N]atural environments have histories that stretch out before humans emerged and they have a future that will continue beyond the disappearance of the human species. Those histories form the larger context for our human lives. However, it is not just this larger historical context that matters in our valuation of the environments in which we live, but also the backdrop of natural processes against which human life is lived. (O'Neill, Holland, and Light 2008, 162–164)

One should add that there is another dimension of the natural landscape in contrast with a cultural landscape, and that is its deeper time horizon (cf. *deep time*) with regard to "what happens before us and what comes after" that puts in perspective the all-too-human view of the world. Seen from this perspective, ecological restoration is a form of making sense of the world.

Willem van Toorn, in contrast, almost exclusively associates landscape legibility with cultural landscapes. To his mind, intentionally reshaping landscape through rewilding is a threat to landscape identity, because it is *not* based on a credible interpretation of landscape. On the contrary, it merely projects and imposes fashionable ideas about nature onto the landscape, out of "a light-hearted kind of post-modern way of thinking in which history is just a grab bag, from which one can carelessly throw away anything that is not fashionable" (Van Toorn 1998, 76). As a result, in these restored nature areas "humans are present only as tourists—and no longer as residents for whom the signs and narratives of the land are food for their spirit" (77).

It is apparent that for both O'Neill and his colleagues and Van Toorn, the history of a landscape is no accidental element of its narrative meaning. Being able to read a historical landscape appropriately is essential for developing a meaningful and good relation to that landscape. But what is an appropriate attitude toward a historically layered landscape?

Palimpsest Landscapes

Landscapes can be conceived of as texts, but as special kinds of texts. All landscapes are layered. This is true for both cultural and natural landscapes. Cultural landscapes consist of different layers reflecting historically different eras that had an influence on how the landscapes evolved. But the same is true for natural landscapes. As time goes by, old things get covered up by new things, and the process of sedimentation goes on and on. Sedimentation is an ongoing process: history piles up in a landscape, one could say. In his essay "Layering: Body, Building, Biography," Bob Mugerauer (2013) shows how sedimentation is a process that can be discerned everywhere in nature, on each level of scale. The most relevant difference between the layeredness of natural and cultural landscapes is the type of narrative that is needed to interpret these layers and attach meaning to them. In one narrative humans are the main agents, in the other case, nonhumans have various forms of agency as well.

The layeredness of a landscape poses a challenge to each attempt to restore the meaning of a place. Archaeologists know this: each archaeological site is like a layered text, where one can peel off different layers that each reveal different stories about the same place in different times, provided one can make sense of the signs and traces. Today, archaeologists often decide not to excavate ancient remains in the soil, because excavation would inevitably lead to the destruction of the other landscape layers. It is for this reason that archaeologists see the landscape as a *palimpsest*. A palimpsest is a multilayered text, consisting of different textual layers written on top of each other. What does this layeredness of the landscape mean for the goals of ecological restoration?

Ecological Restoration and the Problem of Historicism

The question of the goals of ecological restoration in degraded landscapes has been hotly debated for years. Many criteria have been proposed. Some restoration ecologists and many popular accounts of the goal of ecological restoration seem to assume that restoration implies the re-creation of past landscapes using a specific historic reference point. The primer of the Society for Ecological Restoration stresses, however, that ecological restoration is not about re-creating a specific point in the past but, rather, about assisting nature to restore itself and resume its historic trajectory (SER 2004, 1). Yet, both perspectives assume that there exists a point in the past in which the natural landscape was still "intact,"[1] and this situation provides a "baseline" for today's restorations. However, as soon as one has to identify a viable historic reference point for this intact situation, the obvious question is, why this and not another? Many moments in the past have been proposed, ranging from the Pleistocene, or the end of the last Ice Age, to the beginning of the Industrial Revolution and the beginning of the twentieth century.

For debates about restoration of degraded *cultural* landscapes, the problem deepens. For one may think that nature somehow provides a baseline, but how are we to acknowledge landscapes that have been formed partly because of human influences? How are we to decide which of these human influences were degrading or intrusive to the "original" state, and which are valuable modifications? In European conservation debates, the historic reference point of AD 1900 is often mentioned: the moment right before the large-scale landscape changes that took place as a result of the rapid increase of industrialization and intensification of agriculture. The underlying assumption seems to be that at a certain point in time, human changes started to become disturbances, that human influence increased not just quantitatively but also qualitatively. Whereas certain old cultural landscapes are worth restoring, others are merely regarded as degradation of what was there before. But again, as soon as one decides on a specific historical reference point, one will face the obvious question, why this reference point and not another? Should we try to restore landscapes that were the result of former types of land-use, which have often become outdated today? Why? Or should the conclusion be that whatever we decide what the landscape should be like, we are merely creating the landscapes we happen to like?

The reason we seem to have so much difficulty in orienting ourselves within the landscape's long cultural history has to do with a predicament of our time that the nineteenth-century German philosopher Friedrich Nietzsche foresaw. Our time, so he argues, suffers from an "historic disease." According to Nietzsche, we contemporaries spend so much time studying history and other cultures because deep down we are aware (or at least, could be with sufficient reflection) that all our cultural images and interpretations are deeply historically contingent (see also Keulartz, chap. 3, this volume). In *Beyond Good and Evil*, Nietzsche describes modern humans as beings that have at their disposal several moralities, articles of faith, tastes in art and religion handed over to them in history, but are unable to find a form that really suits them.

> The hybrid European—a tolerably ugly plebeian, taken all in all—absolutely requires a costume: he needs history as a storeroom of costumes. To be sure, he notices that none of the costumes fit him properly—he changes and changes. Let us look at the nineteenth century with respect to these hasty preferences and changes in its masquerades of style, and also with respect to its moments of desperation on account of "nothing suiting" us. It is in vain to get ourselves up as romantic, or classical, or Christian, or Florentine, or baroque, or "national," *in moribus et artibus*: it does not "clothe us"! (Nietzsche 1886, sec. 223)

We postmodern pluralists hope to gain a sense of freedom from constantly changing costumes because we are longing for something that fits, and yet we are no longer able to seriously engage ourselves with any particular interpretation of the world for a longer time.

If what Nietzsche is saying indeed connects to the problem of historical landscapes as well, then the problem of finding one historical frame of reference for restoring landscapes will prove to be impossible. The best we can do, then, is to recognize tension between the different historical layers and meanings inscribed within a landscape, to celebrate the very layeredness of the landscape itself! Nietzsche continues:

> But the "spirit," especially the "historical spirit," profits even by this desperation: once and again a new sample of the past or of the foreign is tested, put on, taken off, packed up, and above all studied—we are the first studious age in puncto of "costumes," I mean as concerns morals, articles of belief, artistic tastes, and religions; we are prepared as no other age has ever been for a carnival in the grand style, for the most spiritual festival—laughter and arrogance, for the transcendental height of supreme folly and Aristophanic ridicule of the world. (Nietzsche 1886, sec. 223)

Indeed, many today are interested in studying past times and other cultures. We study our own history in an attempt to know who we are and in the hopes of finding in that history a clue how to proceed. Nietzsche believes, however, that we should not look for models and criteria in the past, for each particular interpretation of the past will only serve as a temporary blinding to the truth that we have these endless possibilities. Instead, we should learn to playfully combine the different images that history hands over to us—we should be the playful artists who use the different historical costumes for a carnival, without the desperation of someone who is still looking for a fully fitting costume:

> Perhaps we are still discovering the domain of our invention just here, the domain where even we can still be original, probably as parodists of the world's history and as God's Merry-Andrews,—perhaps, though nothing else of the present have a future, our laughter itself may have a future! (Nietzsche 1886, sec. 223)

If Nietzsche's diagnosis is accurate, then art has a more-than-trivial role to play in the way we relate to layered landscapes. Art can powerfully evoke landscape meanings and still leave room for playful and creative reinterpretation; it can acknowledge the existence of "deeper" meanings that have a special place in our history of interpretations and yet remain open to other possibilities.

Palimpsest landscapes contain different legible layers on top of each other, and each has a myriad of possible interpretations. Whereas recognizing the top layers of the cultural landscape text can urge us to restore those elements that help us to understand and appreciate the landscape as part of our history and identity (or restore older cultural patterns), the acknowledgment of the deeper and older layers would have us attempt to restore the continuity with natural history that humans have changed in the past. These perspectives on "landscape legibility" can sometimes be combined, but will often contradict. Protectionists of cultural heritage will want to protect the recent layers that reveal people's aspirations in recent history. Rewilding ecologists, on the other hand, will be inclined to stress the special importance of the deep-time horizon of natural systems, because in hindsight, many cultures of place have proven to be very unsustainable and presupposed interpretations of the natural world that have been shown to be problematic. Ecologically restoring a layered landscape will therefore somehow have to give some priority to older layers over younger ones, but it should seek to do so without ignoring or totally wiping out the more recent stories. And it has to recognize that any kind of environmental restoration will never be able to go back in time, but inevitably will add a new layer to the palimpsest. An appropriate restoration of historical landscapes will need to be more than just a projection of fashionable ideas, a intentional reconstruction of a landscape that we happen to prefer. The key idea of ecological restoration is to restore the continuity with the natural history—or to "help nature resume its own historic trajectory." But as soon as we recognize that the meaning of the human interventions cannot be reduced to being merely "disturbances," we can see that this idea is too simple. One can acknowledge that particular human practices have had a devastating effect on the ecology of a place and conclude that the ecological restoration of that site must somehow seek to undo the harm that was done and at the same time acknowledge the ambiguity of the place's history and meanings.

Restoring a layered landscape also urges us to do justice to the complex meanings inscribed in the landscape palimpsest. One way to come to terms with the conflicting meanings is in a form of a narrative of change and reconciliation: we interpret the story of a landscape, its environmental degradation *and* its environmental restoration as part of a story about this landscape and about our involvement with it. Without a form of reflective awareness of the limitations and contingencies of each particular interpretation of the landscape, the restoration of the meaning of layered landscapes is doomed to fail.

Yet, I believe that for certain conflicts of interpretation it will not be easy to reconcile; or rather, reconciliation should not be too easy. Certain conflicts of interpretation about the meaning of a landscape are actually an adequate reflection of what a landscape really means. Some readings of a landscape can be combined, other layers will be difficult to incorporate in a story. Yet, such difficult interpretations help to form a more complete picture and can provide our life with a context that is truly transcendent. Art, as I will show, can play a role in completing and complicating our understanding the full and complex meaning of a landscape. I use the Millingerwaard in the Netherlands, the Landschaftspark Duisburg-Nord in the German Ruhrgebiet, and the Rocky Mountain Arsenal National Wildlife Refuge in the United States as examples.

Environmental Art as a Reading Aid

The Rocky Mountain Arsenal National Wildlife Refuge is a former military site near Denver, Colorado. I visited it on an excursion while attending the conference on which portions of this book are based.[2] The place has a very interesting and controversial history, and therefore can count as a really good example of a layered landscape.

Many historically relevant and—seen from our age—sometimes shocking events took place here. After a long geological history, a short-grass prairie landscape formed and for millennia was inhabited seasonally by native people. In the nineteenth century, the area was inhabited by European settlers, who turned the place into homesteads. The relatively recent history of the area is one of military presence, beginning with the US involvement in World War II and efforts to liberate Europe from the Nazi occupation. But it also has a history of chemical weapons production and environmental degradation, mainly due to chemical pollution caused by the production of chemical weapons in the late 1940s and early 1950s and rocket fuel for the Apollo space program in the 1960s (for additional accounts of the site's history, see chaps. 8 and 9, this volume, by Coates and Havlick, respectively).

Most of these historical events can no longer be seen in the landscape today. The chemical pollutants have been isolated and contained, and much of the area was stripped of its contaminated surface soils. Efforts by restorationists today are aimed at restoring a new, fertile soil that can support the species belonging to the alleged "predisturbance condition": shortgrass and mixed-grass prairie. If these attempts succeed, little will be left to show what happened here. Already, few signs remain of the lives of the 600 families that lived here for many decades; the primary schools that existed here have been demolished, and there is no sign of the chemical plant whose construction displaced the agricultural fields and families. The landscape bears no reminder of what to many must be a painful memory: that the United States produced chemical weapons here.

All restoration attempts in the Rocky Mountain Arsenal National Wildlife Refuge seem to head in the same direction: to attempt to restore the site to a "predisturbance condition," to get rid of all human disturbances, and re-create a situation that must have existed at a point in the past before the Europeans came. At this point, I do not want to go into the well-known debate about the problematic implications of the underlying concept of wilderness[3] at work in this notion of an original predisturbance state. Rather, I want to take a more positive approach and show how environmental art could bring to light the meanings of the land and give voice to the recent layers that cannot be easily combined with the (legitimate) choice to restore the shortgrass prairie. I believe that environmental art can be helpful in complicating our interpretation of the landscape, and can help us incorporate elements of the complex history of a place into its narrative.

One thing that art can do is highlight particular historical remainders of a place that are easily overlooked or ignored in the overall restoration. Art can function as a lens that makes the invisible visible; point to things that are easily overlooked; and thus, reveal less obvious, hidden historic meanings and layers. Some artists can creatively apply historical meanings anew, for example, by explicating hidden layers through translocation and translation, and thus contribute to the active re-appropriation of elements of the place narrative and acknowledge meanings that are otherwise easily ignored. Some fine examples of this kind of recovery artwork can be found along the Limes, the old border of the Roman Empire, in the Netherlands. Different artists have created installations in a public space that remind visitors that the road they are walking on was in fact the northern border of the Roman Empire almost 2,000 years ago.

By highlighting this historical feature, the artists enable visitors to recognize the particular nature of this place. Art can help us see structures and historical remains that may be hard to see, or even invisible, but that we need as the elements in the story of a place if we are to understand what the place is. Although such artworks often merely emphasize historical *facts* about a place, they also hold a narrative meaning, because they confront us with the fact that a place has a much longer history than we realize. By opening up a deeper time horizon, an artwork reveals something about the history of the place, but in such a way that the spectator comes to realize his or her limited understanding of the depth of time. These reading aids can be very subtle and nonintrusive. In the case of Rocky Mountain Arsenal National Wildlife Refuge, they can be easily combined with the overall attempt to restore the prairie. For example, one could hang a wood swing from a tree at the location of a former school, to remind future visitors that the shortgrass prairie they stand on was once a place where people lived, where children grew up.

Sometimes, however, an artwork will have to provoke a new narrative that has an explicit moral dimension in order to stress particular meanings of a place. One of the nicest examples of such a work that I know of is the Woodhenge tree monument in the Dutch river rewilding area Millingerwaard.

The Millingerwaard is one of the first sites in Europe where it was decided that the river forelands, which had been claimed from the river to be used as farmland, had to be given back to the river, to give more "room to the river" with the aim of flood prevention. The dikes were breached, the clay deposits taken out, and beavers introduced, all with the goal of kick-starting the natural processes of erosion and sedimentation that had formed the landscape before humans started to interfere. At the start of the project, in the 1980s, many locals protested against it, claiming that their valued historical landscape would be destroyed.[4] They claimed that the new area would not be nature, but merely a product of and tribute to human ingenuity: *these days we can even make ecosystems* (cf. Drenthen 2009).

In 1995, a few years after the project started, several 8,500-year-old half-fossilized hardwood trees were dredged out of the nearby Rhine River—a tangible reminder of the fact that a landscape similar to the one that was currently being formed had existed here many years before. The site managers decided to erect these trees into a Stonehenge-like configuration and place them on top of a newly formed river dune in the area (figure 13.1).

The Woodhenge tree monument at Millingerwaard makes a statement: the meaning of this area cannot be reduced to human efforts to fight floods and design nature but is also a tribute to the natural forces that are creating the place now as they have done for centuries. This form of *rewilding art* evokes an experience of deep time that widens the

FIGURE 13.1 Woodhenge tree monument at Millingerwaard. Source: Photo by Martin Drenthen.

context from which we tend to look at our world and ourselves. These half-fossilized trees belonged to one of the first generations of oaks that recolonized Western Europe after the last Ice Age. By putting our everyday time-horizon in perspective, the tree monument points to the value of the longer natural history of the place, and reminds us that the presence of humans in this landscape is not to be taken for granted. We are relative newcomers—this place has had a long history of which we were not a part. As such, the monument pays tribute to natural forces, and suggests a deeper, explicitly normative interpretation of the meaning of rewilding in this area. Rewilding art like this can invite reinterpretation of the landscape, not by ignoring the recent additions, but by recognizing that we inevitably inscribe (not impose) new layers on the land, while enabling us to pay tribute to what already exists.

The Art of Inviting Nature to Comment: Reconciliation and Critique

But sometimes ecological restoration needs art that does more than that. William Jordan has argued that ecological restoration should not aim to restore ecosystems as such, but disrupted human-nature relationships. In his book *The Sunflower Forest,* he discusses some interesting examples in which the process of restoration can be seen as a process of reconciliation with nature.

The restoration of Germany's Landscape Park Duisburg Nord is generally considered to be a good example of how the care for cultural identity can be combined with efforts to find a more ecologically sound culture of place. In this former heavy industrial site, a park was designed that is open to the public for recreation but also harbors many nonhuman life forms (figure 13.2).

The site is heavily used by humans, and yet has the highest biodiversity in North Rhine-Westphalia. Moreover, nature here is actively invited to take over old industrial installations: old steel machines are grown over with weeds, creating a sometimes lush environment that humans and nonhumans like. The project was applauded because it succeeded in getting the local inhabitants of a highly urbanized region to care about the restoration of the site, without denying their attachment to the long history that led to the ecological degradation of the landscape. As a result, the community today is consciously and collectively engaged in leaving behind the historical era in which it was believed that humans could master nature through fossil-energy-fueled heavy industry. By allowing nature

FIGURE 13.2 Landschaftspark Duisburg-Nord. Source: Photo by Martin Drenthen.

to take over, to overgrow the former industry sites, the project celebrates the return of nature, and at the same time supports a cultural transition in which locals are actively engaged in a collective effort to find a more ecological culture of place. As a result, the landscape park is a breathable, livable place for humans and nonhumans alike, where one can really feel the vibrant ecologically minded transition going on. And yet, the people of Duisburg also have an ambivalent feeling toward their history: although they are pleased that they no longer have to live in heavy pollution, it was *their* way of life. There exists a strange ambivalent pride in their collective memory of the "ugliness" of the Ruhrgebiet: *Ruhrgebiet, Woanders is' auch scheiße* (Ruhr district, it also sucks elsewhere!), a local saying goes. It is this ambivalence toward an unsustainable history that has found a new expression in the Landscape Park: the collective history is acknowledged, and yet the decision was made to leave the past behind and move forward. The transition is achieved not by denying the downside of history but, rather, by confronting it. Restoration can lead to a reconciliation, but only if the collective is prepared to deal with the past.

But sometimes, the idea of reconciliation is itself problematic and the idea that one can come to a closure is itself troubling. The Dutch artist and writer Armando uses the terms *guilty landscapes* to express a particular ambivalence in certain natural sites that witnessed dark histories.[5] Armando lived in the Dutch city of Amersfoort before, during, and after the Second World War, close to a concentration camp located in the woods. Armando knew that the innocent forest of his youth had witnessed the horrors of war and the Holocaust. The disturbing thing, however, was that, somehow, the beauty of the site was not diminished; on the contrary it was intensified by the knowledge of what had happened. Armando shows that it can be deeply disturbing, or even wrong, that certain places are beautiful. The experience of such a painful place is highly complex: nature still is a place of beauty and peace, but the aesthetic experience is highly ambivalent: "one shouldn't allow oneself to be aesthetically moved by such scenes, it doesn't seem right."[6]

Indeed, in some places, events took place that require us to resist easy interpretation, to confront uneasy questions and troubling interpretations of place. Guilty landscapes witnessed troubling events that *should not* be reconciled easily, comfortably. In these cases art can play a role as nothing else can: to remind us about what we would rather forget, bring up uncomfortable interpretations, address embarrassing histories, and force us to come to terms with the darker side of our history.

Ecological restoration can in itself be interpreted as a reinterpretation of the landscape, because it emphasizes a new and critical place narrative that puts humans and their history in perspective, opens up to deep time and to the perspective of other species. Environmental art can help this reinterpretation by focusing our attention to things easily overlooked. Rewilding art, such as the Woodhenge tree monument in Millingerwaard, can pay tribute to that which came before and will remain after we're gone. But there is also a need for other, more radical art in restoration projects, which actively invites nature to talk back but not in a reconciliatory tone per se.[7]

Art in general can challenge us to change our common perspective by turning the mirror against us. The kind of art that I am proposing, "Nature Mocking Art," takes on this idea by imagining what the nonhuman others would think of us humans, given the ecological wrong that we have done.

Restoring certain ecosystems and places requires that we first acknowledge our own role in its damage, and see the darker sides of our own past before moving on. We restore landscapes because we made mistakes in the past, and know we did. Restoring an injured landscape can quickly turn into a way of pretending that nothing happened, if we are not prepared to confront ourselves seriously with our past deeds. We first need to recognize the full gravity of the wrong we did. Moreover, if we want to move on, we need some form of reconciliation with that past, and for that we need pardon. However, one cannot forgive oneself for wrongs in the past, one has to be pardoned by the other. That is why we need Nature Mocking Art. Nature Mocking Art does not attempt to repair our wrongs, it does not directly strive for reconciliation; rather it gives nature a chance to mock us for our wrongs—and, possibly, forgive us.

Of course art cannot directly speak on behalf of nature or the landscape. Landscapes do not care. Nature Mocking Art gives voice to our own bad conscience in a playful manner, by making visible the other nonhuman world—a world that does not participate in our all-too-human projects and ambitions but does suffer from our mistakes and obsessions—and lending it a voice. Would that nonhuman world—if it could have an opinion—not find our paranoia ridiculous, wouldn't it want to mock us, make a fool of us? And shouldn't it be allowed to do so? Such a form of Nature Mocking Art does not have to be a deceitful attempt in which we merely use nature like a ventriloquist, because it can explicitly give a role to nonhuman agents, nature's others need to become part of the evocative work.

Art can be a reading aid that helps us to understand the meaning of a landscape, but it can only do so if it does not shy away from difficult stories when these, too, are part of the meaning of a place. One might even say that it is precisely *in* the controversy about its meaning that a landscape gets noticed; only when we stop taking for granted the easy, conciliatory interpretations of a place can it start conveying meanings. Provocative artworks have a role to play here, if only because they force us to look again, reconsider our initial view and judgment, pay attention to what beckons to be noticed.

The kind of artwork that I propose emphasizes a particular meaning of nature that is often at work in our conservation and restoration efforts: nature as a transcendent, meaningful order that we use for moral orientation. The concept of wildness often seems to have a similar moral meaning: it serves as a critical border concept, a "view from the outside" that we use as a criterion with which we can put ourselves in perspective (cf. Drenthen 2005, 2007). It plays with this notion by introducing an "outside stance" that can serve as a critical mirror that shows the all-too-human foolishness of much of what went on in our relation to particular landscapes.

When visiting the ecological restoration at the Rocky Mountain Arsenal National Wildlife Refuge, I was surprised to see how little acknowledgment there was of the problematic nature of the past human activities, such as the production of chemical weapons. Having grown up in a landscape whose the historical layers are evident everywhere, I was shocked at how this site was being restored. Even though I agree that restoring the site to shortgrass prairie can be a legitimate endeavor, I do believe that the current management ignores, suppresses, and destroys the landscape layers that have a story to tell about the meaning and history of this place. I believe art can be helpful in supporting a more complete understanding of the landscape palimpsest in Rocky Mountain Arsenal National Wildlife Refuge, even if the general direction does not change.

For Rocky Mountain Arsenal, I envision a Nature Mocking Art work that consists of a series of statues of big, brightly colored, plastic toy soldiers that are watching each other, just as the military personnel watched one another in the twentieth century (figure 13.3). Looking back on it now,

FIGURE 13.3 Nature Mocking Art—proposed artwork at Rocky Mountain Arsenal National Wildlife Refuge. © Martin Drenthen (for the color version of this picture, see http://www.docenten.science.ru.nl/drenthen/soldiers-color.jpg).

much of the Cold War rhetoric and war preparations can seem foolish, as if the obsessive fixation on the Danger of the Evil Enemy Empire made the care of our own living landscapes seem insignificant. The proposed work invites the prairie dogs on the site to "comment" on the embarrassing history of the site. They will be seen standing next to the toy soldiers, also on the lookout, but seeing them standing next to the soldiers will somehow put in perspective the human militaristic project of the mid-twentieth century, which polluted the site with poisonous chemicals and the minds of people with paranoia: militaristic states distrusted other military states on the other side of the world and prepared for chemical warfare, meanwhile, poisoning the natural world. Nature Mocking art invites nature to speak back; it allows nature not just to correct our ecological wrongs, as in Duisburg, but also to set the record straight, to correct the narrative and show that humans have been foolish. Only then, can we move on to seek reconciliation.

Of course such an artwork will be provocative, and many will feel angry about this particular interpretation of the meaning of what happened here. That's okay. There are many stories to tell, stories as well that stress the hopes and ambitions of the people living here, the big and small narratives of life on a military site near Denver—stories about patriotism, about love for the land, about loss, and more.

Conclusion

In this chapter, I have argued that the way we interpret the landscape is always already entangled with how we look at ourselves. Conversely, our identities are at stake as soon as the meaning of landscape stops being self-evident. I argued that the conventional "objective" or semiotic approaches to landscape interpretation are not really suited to understanding this relation but that a hermeneutic perspective on reading landscapes can help us understand the interconnectedness of landscape and moral identity. I discussed how our understanding of the meaning of landscapes is further complicated in contemporary culture, because most traditional frames of interpretation have stopped being self-evident. It may be true that there are several images and interpretations of landscape and self, but we no longer seem to have a criterion with which to determine the value of these different interpretations. Each proposed criterion itself is already just another voice in the history of competing voices and identities. That is why ecological restoration cannot simply choose, according to a value judgment, from among different historical reference images the particular reference that will be used for restoration (cf. Haak 2007). If we agree that the goal of ecological restoration is not just the repair of damaged ecosystems but also about correcting our disturbed relationship with nature and finding our place in the natural world (Jordan 2003), then we already implicitly recognize that there is a nonhuman world that should serve as a reference point, a frame of orientation, a framework in which we critically reflect on ourselves. I believe that art can be useful to restoration projects because of its evocative ability to highlight this moral dimension of ecological restoration. However, this also means that art should not just be used as an ornament but as a lens. Moreover, if art is to play a role in highlighting the moral dimension of ecological restoration, it should not only be used to "sell the idea of ecological restoration," but to seriously question ourselves. Even if that means that its message will be uneasy and disconcerting.

Notes

1. In philosophical debates about ecological restoration a similar idea is seen: "original" nature is seen as the moral measure with which one should estimate the value of restored landscapes. Cf. Robert Elliot (1997).

2. Needless to say, what I say about the meaning of the site will never be more than my attempt to reconstruct some of the meanings connected to the place. As a foreigner and stranger to the site, its history, and the Colorado culture, I will not be able to do justice to all or even most of the cultural meanings connected to the site. I do believe, however, that my readings of the landscape—from the perspective of a Western European environmental philosopher—reveal some of the relevant meanings of this place.

3. E.g., this idea of wilderness seems to presuppose that the original inhabitants are somehow less "human" and that their influence on the landscape is somehow seen as part of nature. For a discussion of this and other criticisms, see Callicott and Nelson (1998); Nelson and Callicott (2008).

4. By now a vast majority of the local inhabitants consider the project to be a success.

5. I make use of the special issue of *Volume* magazine devoted to the concept of a "guilty landscape" (Oosterman 2012), especially the editorial by Arjan Oosterman.

6. Armando, cited in Oosterman (2012).

7. See the work of Shiloh Krupar and Sarah Kanouse for some strong examples of art that aims to complicate rather than reconcile our relation to landscapes.

References

Callicott, J. Baird, and Michael P. Nelson, eds. 1998. *The Great New Wilderness Debate.* Athens: University of Georgia Press.

Cronon, William. 1991. "Landscape and Home; Environmental Traditions in Wisconsin." *Wisconsin Magazine of History* 74: 83–105.

Drenthen, Martin. 2005. "Wildness as Critical Border Concept; Nietzsche and the Debate on Wilderness Restoration." *Environmental Values* 14 (3): 317–337.

Drenthen, Martin. 2007. "New Wilderness Landscapes as Moral Criticism; A Nietzschean Perspective on our Fascination with Wildness." *Ethical Perspectives* 14 (4): 371–403.

Drenthen, Martin. 2009. "Ecological Restoration and Place Attachment; Emplacing Nonplace?" *Environmental Values* 18 (3): 285–312.

Drenthen, Martin. 2011. "Reading Ourselves through the Land: Landscape Hermeneutics and Ethics of Place." In *Placing Nature on the Borders of Religion, Philosophy, and Ethics*, edited by F. Clingerman and M. Dixon, 123–138. Farnham: Ashgate.

Elliot, Robert. 1997. *Faking Nature: The Ethics of Environmental Restoration*. London and New York: Routledge.

Haak, Christian. 2007. "History, Ecosystems, and Human Agency in Restoration Ecology." *Global Environmental Research* 11: 113–117.

Hendriks, Karina, and Henk Kloen. 2007. *IVN: Handleiding Leesbaar Landschap*. Culemborg: CLM.

Higgs, Eric. 2003. *Nature by Design: People, Natural Process, and Ecological Restoration*. Cambridge, MA: MIT Press.

Jordan, William III. 2003. *The Sunflower Forest: Ecological Restoration and the New Communion with Nature*. Berkeley: University of California Press.

Lewis, Pierce. 1979. "Axioms for Reading the Landscape: Some Guides to the American Scene." In *The Interpretation of Ordinary Landscape: Geographical Essays*, edited by D. Meinig, 11–13. New York: Oxford University Press.

Light, Andrew. 2003. "Ecological Restoration and the Culture of Nature: A Pragmatic Perspective." In *Environmental Ethics*, edited by Andrew Light and Holmes Rolston III, 398–411. London: Blackwell.

Mugerauer, Robert. 2013. "Layering: Body, Building, Biography." In *Interpreting Nature: The Emerging Field of Environmental Hermeneutics*, edited by Forrest Clingerman, Martin Drenthen, Brian Treanor, and David Utsler, 65–81. New York: Fordham University Press.

Nelson, Michael P., and J. Baird Callicott, eds. 2008. *The Wilderness Debate Rages On*. Athens: University of Georgia Press.

Nietzsche, Friedrich. 1886. *Beyond Good and Evil: Prelude to a Philosophy of the Future*. Translated by Helen Zimmern. New York: MacMillan.

O'Neill, John, Alan Holland, and Andrew Light. 2008. *Environmental Values*. New York: Routledge.

Oosterman, Arjen. 2012. Editorial in *Volume #31: Guilty Landscapes,* edited by Arjen Oosterman et al., 2–4. Amsterdam: Stichting Archis.

Ricoeur, Paul. 1981. *Hermeneutics and the Human Sciences. Essays on Language, Action and Interpretation*. Edited and translated by John B. Thompson. Cambridge: Cambridge University Press.

Ricoeur, Paul. 1992. *Oneself as Another*. Translated by Kathleen Blamey. Chicago: University of Chicago Press.

SER (Society for Ecological Restoration International Science and Policy Working Group). 2004. *The SER International Primer on Ecological Restoration* (version 2). www.ser.org and Tucson: Society for Ecological Restoration International.

Van Toorn, Willem. 1988. *Leesbaar Landschap*. Amsterdam: Querido.

Watts, May Theilgaard. 1975. *Reading the Landscape of America*. New York: MacMillan. Originally published in 1957.

Wessels, Tom, Brian Cohen, and Ann Zwinger. 1997. *Reading the Forested Landscape: A Natural History of New England*. Woodstock, VT: Countryman Press.

Widgren, Mats. 2004. "Can Landscapes Be Read?" In *European Rural Landscapes: Persistence and Change in a Globalising Environment*, edited by H. Palang, H. Sooväli, M. Antrop, and G. Setten, 455–465. Boston: Kluwer Academic Publishers.

Yamin, Rebecca, and Karen Bescherer Metheny, eds. 1996. *Landscape Archaeology: Reading Interpreting American Historical Landscape*. Knoxville: University of Tennessee Press.

Yarham, Robert. 2010. *How to Read the Landscape*. London: A & C Black Publishers.

CHAPTER 14 | Conclusion

Layered Landscapes as Models for Restoration and Conservation

DAVID G. HAVLICK AND MARION HOURDEQUIN

AS THE CHAPTERS IN this volume illustrate, layered landscapes come in a wide array of forms, phases, and locations. In many respects, layered landscapes are everywhere. This is ever more apparent as human activity increasingly shapes and impacts the world in which we live. Yet the pervasive local, regional, and global changes wrought by humanity can also serve as a reminder of the deep connection between nature and society. As many of the cases in this book suggest, the boundaries between these two domains often blur. With a growing recognition of human agency in effecting environmental change and modifying landscapes, we may also find ourselves turning with increasing frequency to ecological restoration as a means to peel back the damage and reconnect ecosystems and the populations that depend on them. These represent key lines of intersection for this volume: in the face of efforts to erase *certain kinds* of human history—typically environmental degradation and damaged ecosystems—how might we also ensure that *other kinds* of meaningful histories are not eradicated?

Few, if any, places on the planet exist as a single historical point where human activity, influence, and meaning can be adequately registered in isolation. The layered landscapes highlighted in this book stand out for their cultural or ecological significance, but the examples shared here should also spur us to think carefully about the (possibly) more mundane spaces of our daily lives. We do not need to commemorate every detail of all geographic space, but surely there are many landscapes we take for granted that warrant a richer mix of reflection, appreciation, and understanding.

One point we wish to make, then, is that layered landscapes ought to be noticed in order to foster a deeper understanding of the history, nature, and culture that surround us. As Drenthen emphasizes in his closing chapter, ecological restoration focused on such landscapes should "do justice to the complex meanings" of these layers. As his example from the Rocky Mountain Arsenal National Wildlife Refuge illustrates, this type of reconciliation may not be—in fact, should not always be—easy. The point of representing and interpreting layered landscapes, after all, is not necessarily to make us comfortable in a given landscape, but rather to push us to come to terms with the diverse mix of features found in many settings.

This enhanced understanding can, in turn, inform environmental policy and practice. To interpret and manage Rocky Flats only for wildlife habitat and open space, for example, would reflect limited conceptual engagement with the site's nuclear past. As Hourdequin emphasizes in chapter 2, however, for many activists and local residents who are unwilling to relinquish their concerns about the nuclear history of Rocky Flats's plutonium production and accidents, the site necessarily also remains a political space. Whatever the lasting ecological conditions here, there are cultural terms that must be met to satisfy the complex and often conflicting legacies of Rocky Flats's layered histories.

A second point we wish to emphasize is that broadening the scope of ecological restoration efforts to account for cultural goals will in many cases prove beneficial on both ecological and cultural grounds. Ecological restoration has long been characterized as a set of practices that aims to redress environmental damage, but coming to terms with layered landscapes will mean also bringing cultural concerns more into focus as part of the conversation that ecological restoration can so fruitfully prompt. There are many ways to embrace a broader scope for ecological restoration, a number of which have been described in these chapters: by developing deeper and more unifying socioecological narratives, integrating scientific and economic contexts, through richer historical renderings, as sites of experimentation, or by artistic engagement. Not all of these ways fit every context and some, as several chapters reveal, can move toward different trajectories, but what they hold in common is attentiveness to meaning, to a depth of understanding that can be found in landscapes, and to an effort to make visible rather than obscure diverse perspectives. This often means going beyond ecological measures to contend with cultural significance and, in some cases, vice versa.

We see both directions of this conversation, for example, in the chapters by Spiers and Quivik. At Monocacy Battlefield, the emerging challenge is not simply to represent the specific history of a Civil War battle, but to reveal and interpret other histories and to appreciate and support the dynamic ecology of this site. Somewhat conversely, Quivik points out how the ecological changes rendered by more than a century of mining along Montana's upper Clark Fork River should not be considered in isolation from the cultural contexts of this activity. The same is largely true in the Scotland presented by Deary, though the time line spans multiple centuries and the cultural imprints on the land have been almost entirely naturalized. The jarring realization brought into view by ecological restoration efforts here is that natural and cultural landscapes can no longer be easily disaggregated. Ecological pursuits need to take into account cultural changes in order to meet traditional standards of authenticity, but these same goals run in the face of today's notions of how the "natural" Scottish landscape ought to exist.

These examples, along with others in this volume, press us to consider—or more carefully reconsider—the lingering tension that exists for ecological restoration: how to negotiate devotion to historic fidelity against historically unmoored approaches that act with little or no regard to history. Our hope is that this book may help point a way forward by encouraging us to view and interpret landscapes more fully in their social and ecological complexity. This approach allows for restoration that is meaningfully grounded in but not rigidly tethered to the past.

By now it should also be clear that context matters—that particular social and ecological characteristics of a given landscape ought to influence restoration activities and goals. This remains a key point in terms of how the perspectives brought forward in this book can influence or inform restoration theory and practice. Ultimately, we aspire to no single grand recipe here, but rather encourage thoughtful, place-based approaches that may include one or several of the ideas found in these pages. Whether the inspiration comes from a philosophical structure suggested by Nietzsche; an embrace of experimentation; an approach integrating art, ecology, and community engagement; or some other mix, we anticipate that the social and the ecological will increasingly need to be wedded in restoration efforts. This will surely only become more forcefully apparent in the epoch that many label the Anthropocene, where nature itself is characterized by its human influence and modification.

In recent years, the field of restoration ecology has resounded with calls of alarm—or awakening—about the Anthropocene. Prominent among these is the idea that the past no longer matters, that we are now confronted by novel ecosystems that, in effect, encompass the entire planet. At least on the former count, we are inclined to think otherwise. The chapters provided here demonstrate that layered histories and complex landscapes offer ways forward that honor and represent the past, but creatively and dynamically. Even in novel ecosystems, perhaps especially in these domains of "new nature," understanding and acknowledging cultural layers will prove to be of utmost importance if restoration is to remain salient and sensitive to context. As Drenthen provocatively notes, restoration itself adds layers and meanings to landscapes. It remains our collective challenge to recognize, interpret, and embrace these layers in various forms so that we may restore without undue erasure and commemorate without abiding degradation.

INDEX

Aberfan, Wales 59

Acadia Centre for Estuarine Studies 126

Acadia(ns) 114, 116–118, 125

adversarial society 87, 88

Allard, Wayne 27, 135, 141, 142, 154n7

Anaconda Copper Mining Company (Anaconda Company, or ACM) 206, 209–213, 218. *See also* Atlantic Richfield Corporation (ARCO)

Anaconda, Montana 205–210, 214, 218–219

Annapolis River (Canada) 7, 113–119, 123–129

Annapolis Royal, Canada 116, 118, 125, 126, 130

Annapolis Valley Affiliated Boards of Trade 114–116, 118

Anthropocene 87, 105, 226, 265

antiquarian history 5, 37–40, 50–51

Aplet, Gregory 108

architecture, modern 45–46

Armando 255–256

Aroostook National Wildlife Refuge (Maine) 26–27

art
  environmental 229–231, 251–260
  landscape 3, 228
  and meanings 249
  restoration and 8, 9, 222–236, 240, 256–260

Assabet River National Wildlife Refuge (Massachusetts) 7, 19, 27, 160–162, 164–166, 168–174, 176–178

Atlantic Richfield Corporation (ARCO) 213–215, 218

Atomic Energy Commission (AEC) 20, 133

authenticity
  and heritage 120
  in restoration 3, 6–7, 95–96, 98–109, 184, 197, 265

Bacon, Francis 77

balance of nature 14–15, 30n1, 144. *See also* equilibrium theory (in ecology)

baseline(s), historical 14, 22, 100–101, 106, 108, 122, 144, 247

Benjamin, Walter 46, 47

Berkeley Pit (Montana) 203, 213, 217

Big Oaks National Wildlife Refuge (Indiana) 25, 163, 177

biodiversity 61, 115–116, 127, 129, 130, 137, 141, 143, 150–152

brownfields 34, 83, 85, 134, 143, 222–223, 230–232

bunker tours 19, 165, 171, 172

Butte, Montana 202–214, 217–218

Caledonian Pine forest 98

Campbell, Claire 121

Canadian Heritage Rivers System (CHRS)
113–118, 123–125, 127–128, 131n1
capercaillie (*Tetrao urogallus*) 102, 106
chemical weapons 135, 251
Chin, Mel 230–231
Civil War (US)
battlefields 184, 193, 195, 198n1
heritage 183, 185, 186, 197
interpretation 8, 184, 186, 189, 194,
195–196
Clare, John 62
Clark Fork River (Montana) 8, 202–204,
207–208, 210, 212–217
Clean Annapolis River Project
(CARP) 126–129
climate change 2, 15, 63
climax ecology 15, 106
Cold War 26, 259
Colorado Department of Public Health
and Environment 139
Commerce City Historical Society 175
Comprehensive Environmental Response,
Compensation, and Liability Act
(CERCLA) 204, 214, 219n1.
See also Superfund
Cosgrove, Denis 228
Cospuden Mine (Germany) 81
critical history 5, 44–51
Cronon, William 21, 22, 98, 205
cultural heritage 7, 99, 101–104, 222
cultural landscape(s) 102, 106, 178–179,
192, 205, 209, 239, 245–247
cultural preservation 205

Daly, Marcus 208–209
Daniels, Stephen 229, 234
Davis, Jeffrey Sasha 145, 151
deep time 152, 245, 249, 252, 253, 256
Department of Defense (DOD) 134, 141,
161, 174
Department of Energy (DOE) 133,
138–139, 140, 142
Duchamp, Marcel 46
dynamic ecology 15, 144. *See also*
balance of nature; equilibrium theory
(in ecology); new ecology

ecological/environmental integrity 116,
118, 122–125, 127, 244
ecosystem services 113, 126, 129
eminent domain, use of 174
Emscher Park (Germany) 48
environmental change
global 13
rapid 14, 18–19, 30, 105
environmental justice 9, 222, 223,
225–228, 236
environmental stewardship 7, 113, 114,
129–130
EPA. *See* US Environmental
Protection Agency
Epitectus 55–56
equilibrium theory (in ecology) 14, 35, 106
erasure, historical 4, 7–8, 145–147,
175–176, 228, 263
ERDA. *See* US Energy Research and
Development Administration (ERDA)
environmental ethics 30, 69
European Route of Industrial Heritage
(ERIH) 50–51
experimental landscapes 6, 73–88
exurban sprawl 190, 196

Ferropolis (Germany) 43–44
fire management 28
fire suppression 145
Fort Devens Sudbury Training
Annex 165. *See* Assabet River
National Wildlife Refuge
(Massachusetts)
future generations 63–64, 113
futuristic restoration 19

Garcia-Zamor, Jean-Claude 82
gas stations, abandoned 9, 222–223, 232–234
Geevor Tin Mine Heritage Centre
(England) 38–39
Great Bay National Wildlife Refuge
(New Hampshire) 25, 27, 177
guilty landscapes 255–256

heritage. *See also* cultural heritage
and environmental values 119–125

human 115–116, 118, 123, 127
natural 17, 102–103, 112, 122–124, 129
stewardship 112–113, 129–130
hermeneutic approach (to reading
landscapes) 240, 242–243
hibernacula (for bats) 27, 177
Higgs, Eric 13
Highland Clearances (Scotland) 97, 99,
101, 104
historical continuity 67–69, 244
historical fidelity 3, 13–15, 17–19,
29–30, 98–101, 105–106, 108,
244. *See also* authenticity, in
restoration
historical reference point. *See* baseline(s),
historical
Holland, Alan 22, 24, 241, 245
hybrid landscapes 14, 18, 22, 30n2, 34,
36, 95, 100–101, 103, 105–106, 108,
176–177

identity
community 113, 119
and landscape 145, 241, 244–245,
249, 259
and narratives 23, 26
national 7, 40, 96, 120–121, 123
ignorance 76–77, 88
industrial sites, former. *See*
postindustrial sites
Industrienatur 49
Institute for Energy and Environmental
Research (IEER) 139
Instone, Lesley 227
invasive species 145, 151, 191–192,
225–226
Iron Curtain borderlands 178
Iversen, Kristen 20–21, 137

Jordan III, William 254

Kaiser-Hill 139
Kant, Immanuel 40–41
Krupar, Shiloh 151

Lake Cospuden, Germany 80–81

Landscape Park Duisburg Nord
(Germany) 48–51, 134, 250,
254–255
Landscape Park Duisburg North. *See*
Landscape Park Duisburg Nord
(Germany)
landscape reading 240, 259. *See also*
reading, hermeneutic approach;
reading, semiotic approach
landscapes
as texts 241–242
guilty (*see* guilty landscapes)
legibility of 242, 249
Landschaftspark Duisburg-Nord. *See*
Landscape Park Duisburg Nord
(Germany)
Latz, Peter 49, 50
legible landscape(s) 244–246. *See also*
landscapes, legibility of
L'Hermitage. *See* Vincendiere plantation
(L'Hermitage)
Light, Andrew 22, 24, 106, 241, 245
London Consolidated School (Texas) 59
Longfellow, Henry Wadsworth 117
loss
sense of 54–71
subjectivity of 65–66
vulnerability to 57
Lowenthal, David 119

Malevich, Kasimir 46
Marinetti, Filippo Tommaso 46
McKibben, Bill 64
McKinley, Wes 142, 150, 154n14
meaning(s)
environmental art and 251–252, 257–259
heritage and 119
of landscapes 1–10, 19–21, 54–71,
106, 107, 109, 154n9, 179, 222, 239,
240–241, 242, 249–250, 257, 260n2,
263–264
loss of 99–100
narrative and 22, 24, 25–29, 245–246
in nature 57, 257
of place 103
of texts 243

meaningful relations 58, 65
military bunkers 30, 160, 161, 165, 172, 177. *See also* bunker tours
military igloos. *See* military bunkers
military-to-wildlife (M2W) 24, 161–163, 174, 176–179. *See also* weapons-to-wildlife conversions (W2W)
Mill-Willow Bypass (remediation measure) 206, 215–216
Millingerwaard (Netherlands) 252–254
mining 38–40, 43–44, 80–83, 202–219
Monocacy National Battlefield (Virginia) 8, 183–198
monumental history 5, 40–44, 50, 51
Moore, LeRoy 140, 141, 147

Naess, Arne 29
narrative(s) 5, 21–30, 98, 106, 119, 121–123, 128, 145, 146, 148, 184, 197, 245–246, 250, 252
Nash, Roderick 35–36
National Wildlife Refuge System (US), mission 167
natural equilibrium (in ecology) 14
natural heritage
  stewardship 112, 129
  value(s) 7, 108, 115–116, 118, 122, 123–124, 129
natural range of variability 15
natural state 1, 13, 15, 22
naturalness 18, 75, 95, 100–101, 108, 170
Nature Mocking Art 9, 257–259
nature/culture binary. *See* nature/culture distinction
nature/culture dichotomy. *See* nature/culture distinction
nature/culture distinction 16, 18, 30n2, 35, 108, 176–177
new ecology 15. *See also* dynamic ecology
New Lake District (Germany) 80
Newman Flower, Sir Walter 66–69
Nietzsche, Fredrich 5, 36–38, 40–41, 44–45, 248–249

Nine Mile Run Greenway (Pittsburgh) 230
nonequilibrium theory (ecology) 35
nonknowledge 6, 73, 75, 77, 83, 84–88
novel ecosystems 2, 15, 265–266
Nozick, Robert 60
nuclear weapons 5, 20, 27, 133, 142, 152

O'Neill, John 22, 24, 241, 245
Operation Desert Glow 138
Opportunity Ponds (Montana) 211–213

palimpsests 9, 98, 239, 246, 249–250, 258
Parks Canada 7, 113, 118, 121–125
phytoremediation 223, 232–234, 235
plutonium (Pu-239) 20, 21, 27, 133, 137, 139–140, 142, 146, 148, 150
Port-Royal, Canada 116, 117
postindustrial sites 2, 5, 6, 8, 34, 38–40, 42–44, 46–51, 80–86, 134, 138–152, 202–219, 254–255
postmodernism 105, 240, 248
Preble's meadow jumping mouse 137, 141
precautionary principle 79
predisturbance condition(s) 1, 14, 18, 35, 144, 172, 245, 251
presettlement conditions 98, 104, 107–108, 143, 144, 145
pristine
  condition 124
  ideal 87
  nature 14–15, 100, 105
  wilderness 14–15, 35, 106–107

Rackham, Oliver 61
Railton, Peter 63, 64
reading. *See also* landscape reading
  hermeneutic approach 240, 242
    (*see also* hermeneutic approach (to reading landscapes))
  semiotic approach 240, 242
receptivity 16, 19, 29–30
reconciliation 250, 254, 255–257, 264
recreational value 115–116, 123

remediation, environmental 6, 8, 9, 26,
    83–86, 89n4, 138–140, 145, 164, 170,
    178, 202–219, 222–223, 232–234
remembrance 66–69
restoration
    art (*see* art, restoration and)
    collaborative 9, 197–198, 235–236
    goals 1–3, 4, 13, 14, 87, 105, 172, 177,
        226, 247, 264
    urban (*see* urban restoration)
Revival Field (Minnesota) 230–231
rewilding 95, 98–99, 100, 104, 105–108,
    144, 245, 249, 252–254
Ricouer, Paul 36, 242–243
risk assessment(s) 6, 76, 86, 87, 88n1
River Task Force (Annapolis River) 124,
    126, 127
Rockwell International 138, 142, 153n3
Rocky Flats (Colorado)
    Citizens Advisory Board 140, 141, 142
    Cold War Museum (*see* Rocky Flats
        Institute and Museum)
    Comprehensive Conservation Plan 27,
        143–145, 147–148, 150
    controversy over refuge signs 27–28,
        147–148
    Institute and Museum 147
    National Wildlife Refuge 27, 134, 138,
        141–151
    nuclear plant 20–21, 133–134,
        136–140
    protests 136, 145–146
Rocky Mountain Arsenal (Colorado)
    chemical manufacturing
        plant 135, 164
    Comprehensive Conservation
        Plan 173–174, 179n3
    contamination 164, 166, 168–169,
        176, 178
    earthquakes 164
    National Wildlife Refuge 9, 19, 26,
        135, 149–150, 154n10, 161–164,
        166–178
    visitor center 154n10, 168–170, 173, 175
Rocky Mountain Peace and Justice
    Center 139–140

Roosevelt, Theodore 138
ruination 46

Schroedinger, Erwin 61–62
Scottish Natural Heritage 97
Seneca 55–56
Shell Oil Corporation 164
Silver Bow Creek (Montana) 203, 207,
    208–217, 219
Simmel, Georg 49
slavery 185, 189, 191, 193–197
Sloss Furnaces (Alabama) 40
Slote, Michael 16
Slow Cleanup (Chicago) 222, 224,
    231–234, 236
Spirn, Anna Whiston 226–227
Stoics (philosophy) 55–57, 61, 66, 68, 69
Superfund 138, 143, 153n4, 166, 178,
    203–207, 214–218, 219n1. *See also*
    remediation, environmental

Thomas, Edward 64
Thomas, R.S. 60–61, 63
tidal power station 115, 125, 128, 129

Udall, Mark 26, 27, 135, 141, 142
uncertainty
    acting in the face of 81–82
    in science 75, 78–79
undisturbed nature, as a restoration
    ideal 5, 13–19. *See also*
    predisturbance condition(s)
urban restoration 9, 227
US Army 24, 160–161, 163,
    164–165, 168
US Civil War. *See* Civil War (US)
US Energy Research and Development
    Administration (ERDA) 133,
    137, 140
US Environmental Protection
    Agency 138, 139, 143, 153n4, 166,
    204–205, 214–215
US Fish and Wildlife Service (US
    FWS) 27–29, 134–135, 141–145,
    148, 160–161, 164–165,
    167–175, 177

US Fish and Wildlife Service
    mission 172
US National Park Service 183–184,
    186, 188–189, 191, 193–197,
    204–205

value(s)
    conservation 102–103
    ecological 135, 137, 142, 152
    heritage 113–125, 129–130, 148
    intrinsic 43, 55, 69
    loss of 70, 99
    preserving or restoring 19–21, 69–70,
        107, 176–179, 244
    restoration 100, 105, 108
    social 204–205
    wilderness 95, 109, 205
van Toorn, Willem 244, 245–246
Vincendiere plantation
    (L'Hermitage) 189, 193–195, 197
von Ranke, Leopold 36
voyageurs 121, 122, 124, 125, 127

Warm Springs Ponds (Montana) 8,
    202–219
weapons-to-wildlife conversions
    (W2W) 24, 26, 134, 141, 145,
    147, 149
Weisman, Alan 135
Western Apache 21, 23
Western Gas Factory
    (Netherlands) 42–43, 50
Whitehead, Frances 9, 222–224, 229,
    231–235
wilderness 7, 35, 96–100, 103–108, 121,
    205. *See also* value(s), wilderness;
    wildness
wildness 97–99, 105–109
Williams, Bernard 56–57, 69–70
Wilson, E.O. 70
witness plants/witness trees 190, 227
Woodhenge (Netherlands) 252–254
Wynne, Brian 75

Yosemite Valley (California) 35